Performing Robert Burns

Performing Robert Burns

Enactments and Representations of the 'National Bard'

Edited by Ian Brown and
Gerard Carruthers

EDINBURGH
University Press

Edinburgh University Press is one of the leading university presses in the UK. We publish academic books and journals in our selected subject areas across the humanities and social sciences, combining cutting-edge scholarship with high editorial and production values to produce academic works of lasting importance. For more information visit our website: edinburghuniversitypress.com

Edinburgh University Press Ltd
The Tun – Holyrood Road, 12(2f) Jackson's Entry, Edinburgh EH8 8PJ

First published in hardback by Edinburgh University Press 2021

Typeset in 10.5/13 Bembo by
IDSUK (DataConnection) Ltd, and
printed and bound by CPI Group (UK) Ltd, Croydon, CR0 4YY

A CIP record for this book is available from the British Library

ISBN 978 1 4744 5714 9 (hardback)
ISBN 978 1 4744 5715 6 (paperback)
ISBN 978 1 4744 5716 3 (webready PDF)
ISBN 978 1 4744 5717 0 (epub)

Contents

1

The Performance of Burns

Ian Brown and Gerard Carruthers

This collection of critical essays considers the idea of 'performing' Robert Burns (1759–1796). In his lifetime Scotland's national poet wrote or edited more songs than poems, and yet we seldom ever hear him called Scotland's 'national song-writer'. Given the pervasive international presence of 'Auld Lang Syne', 'A Red Rose', 'Ae Fond Kiss' or 'Green Grow the Rashes' to name but four of his 'greatest hits', Burns perhaps deserves such an epithet. 'Green Grow the Rashes', for example, provides supposed derivations for 'Gringo', the Hispanic term for white Americans, after Mexicans had supposedly heard Burns's song sung either on American cattle trails by expatriate drovers, who in the early days of US cattle drives were predominantly Scots because of their long experience driving cattle south for English markets,[1] or by invading United States troops during the war between the two nations of 1846–8.[2] Whether or not either version is exactly true, they are testimony to the pervasiveness of Burns's song in North American culture. We see this again in the case of 'Auld Lang Syne' which was banned by the Union side during the American Civil War over fears it would invoke home-sickness in their troops. The tune was struck up again on the Union side on 9 April 1865 as General Ulysses Grant rode from camp to accept the surrender of the confederates.[3] 'Auld Lang Syne', reckoned to be the second-most sung song perennially after 'Happy Birthday' has a culturally-rich performative history, becoming a Hogmanay anthem after the Canadian dance band of Guy Lombardo performed it at New York hotels from the 1920s. Here is the origin of it becoming the signature song, bringing in the new year in Times Square, New York, down to the present day, with the Lombardo version also propelled through the wider twentieth-century world by the age of radio. The song has particular purchase in Asia too where in Japan it is heard in some stores to signal that they are soon to close, and it was the tune originally to the words of the national anthem of a united Korea. At his funeral in 2015, the body of the founding father of modern Singapore, Lee Kuan Yew, was transported on a gun carriage while 'Auld Lang Syne' was played by a lone piper.[4] In this last case, we see the legacy of British imperialism, particularly of British Gurkha troops who had served in the region, combining with a technologically-transmitted general popularity that Burns's songs have enjoyed.

Of course, in the case of 'Auld Lang Syne' we need to be a little careful about attributing to it Burns's 'genius' solely, since the best-known tune is that selected for the lyric by Burns's editor, George Thomson (1757–1851) rather than that preferred by Burns.[5] Burns worked with two music editors in his lifetime, James Johnson (*c*.1750–1811) with whom he produced the volumes of *The Scots Musical Museum* (1787–1803, and so going on beyond Burns's death) and Thomson. The poet's work with these two editors represented large-scale antiquarian labours in the history of Scottish song (in the case of the work with Johnson culminating, veritably, in a curated 'museum') collecting, editing and creating songs.[6] Burns, then, as a writer and a scholar was in lifetime as much about song as about poetry. His popularity across the continents and through time also involved classical composers' settings, and sometimes also drawing-room arrangements of his lyrics, of his chosen tunes and of tunes chosen for his choice of lyrics. Thomson had Beethoven, for instance, set Burns's 'Highland Harry' to music, and Haydn handled the poet's 'My Love She's but a Lassie Yet'.[7] In his lifetime, Burns worked in complex ways with Thomson, Haydn's pupil, Ignaz Joseph Pleyel (1757–1831) and with Johnson and the Edinburgh musician and arranger, Stephen Clarke (d.1797). These relationships are explored at length in the recent Oxford University Press edition of the Works of Robert Burns by Murray Pittock and Kirsteen McCue, revisiting anew, implicitly and *inter alia*, a long tussle over Burns's musical authenticity between 'classical' and 'folk' renditions. Both of these are notoriously slippery terms with 'traditional' meaning something like the latter, in terms of a word that would have been actually recognisable to the poet. In this volume in the 'classical' context, Kirsteen McCue in 'Burns on the Concert Platform, 1879–1959' discusses the richness of the Burns engagement with, especially, Alexander Campbell Mackenzie (1847–1935) and Malcolm Arnold (1921–2006) and their fruitful ongoing orchestral settings of Burns's work. In even more recent times (2008), James Macmillan (b. 1959) has magnificently set Burns's 'Lament of Mary Queen of Scots on the Approach of Spring' to music and Arvo Part (b. 1935) with his typical minimalist brilliance has produced a breath-taking, 'My Heart's in the Highlands' (2000).[8]

As well as a resistance in some quarters over the past fifty or so years to classical, or 'operatic' renditions of Burns, the wrong kind of 'popular' has been seen by some to mark Burns performance. In the present volume, no doubt damningly in the eyes of some, Paul Maloney shows that classically-trained singers such as John Wilson (1800–1849) and John Templeton (1802–1886) stood at the centre of a popular Burns music-hall culture that extended to comedy and a whole sub-culture of song and other material that referred and paid tribute to Scotland's national poet. This wide performative Burns space has had too little attention paid to it until now. Little known today, and covered by Paul Maloney and Adrienne Scullion is the vibrant late nineteenth-century, west-of-Scotland adaptation of 'Tam o' Shanter' in theatrical pantomime, where even here amid lavish choreography and burlesque, the performance of Burns was made to speak to regional and national identities, especially in this context celebrating the importance of the poet himself. Of wider appeal and endurance, incorporated within and across many sub-forms and performances, a post-1960s 'folk' tradition of Burnsian music has perhaps 'won out' over classical, drawing-room and music-hall renditions. The last would include also late derivatives of music-hall, such as television 'Variety' shows instanced in *The White Heather Club* (BBC TV, 1958–68) and *The Andy Stewart Show* (Scottish Television 1975–6). The BBC Hogmanay television shows over a number of decades from the 1960s show a marked movement away from Burns renditions by the likes of Stewart (1933–1993), Bill McCue (1934–1999) and Moira Anderson (b. 1938), all highly accomplished performers emerging from classical and music-hall traditions towards a raft of performers thought to be somehow more 'traditional', even 'authentic' in the Burns context. This latter group would include artists such as singer-guitarist, Dick Gaughan (b. 1948), fiddler Aly Bain (b. 1946), accordionist Phil Cunningham (b. 1960), Karine Polwart (b. 1970), Emily Smith (b. 1981) and many others. It would even extend to Eddi Reader (b. 1959) and Paolo Nutini (b. 1987), more centrally pop or rock performers, demonstrating the fusion increasingly seen – since the 1960s – of rock and folk music. The cadences of both these musical genres can be heard in the series of recordings directed by Fred Freeman, *Robert Burns: The Complete Songs* (12 CDs, 1995–2002) from Linn Records as well as in renditions by Reader, Nutini and others.[9] In all kinds of instances we ought to see Burns continuing to provide contemporary musical inspiration, often in surprising outcomes, such as, for instance, the remarkable fusion collaboration between James Yorkston, Jon Thorne and Suhail Yusuf Khan on 'Westlin' Winds' released in 2020.[10]

Bob Dylan (b. 1941) has claimed Burns as a huge inspiration after being exposed to the Scot's compositions in New York as a room-mate to Jean Redpath (1937–2014) and in the performances also of the Irish group, The Clancys and Tommy Makem. In the present volume, Moira Hansen reflects on the Burnsian career and archive of Redpath and one of Scotland's greatest traditional singers, Sheena Wellington (b. 1944) offers a short memoir of her own fascinating career as a performer of Burns's songs. Kath Campbell provides insight into Burns in a historical 'folk context' doing so in relation to the Greig-Duncan Folk Song Collection, an early twentieth-century project marshalled by Gavin Greig

(1856–1914) and James Bruce Duncan (1848–1917) and other collectors before, during and after Burns's lifetime to whom his work is related. Here, then, we find proof, if it were needed, that the web of Burns song-creation is endlessly complex not only as one might attempt to describe it in its own terms, but also in its fluid, living, organic art- (and folk-) performance. Matters of taste may come into it, but nothing in Burns musical-performance is fixed in absolute truth or, indeed, 'authenticity'. Indeed, the continuing accessibility and popular versionising of Burns and his work and its recreation in musical forms can be seen in such phenomena as the performance with 'Full Cast, Corps de Ballet, Choir and Orchestra'[11] of T. C. Fairbairn's 'Folk Song Opera' *Robert Burns* during the 1947 summer season at Butlin's Holiday Camp, Ayr, or Scottish Opera's *The Tale o' Tam o' Shanter* which toured primary schools in various part of Scotland in 2017, involving large numbers of Primary 5–7 children in participation. Experimental operatic work of this broad nature also includes events like the performance at the Robert Burns Birthplace Museum in 2014 of Charpentier's *Actéon* in Scots which sought to highlight the similarities with Burns's Tam o' Shanter.

As John Burnett and Gerard Carruthers discuss in their chapter on eighteenth- and nineteenth-century editing of Burns, there is a certain amount of editor-performance beginning with Burns himself. The poet casts a regional and then a national role and stage for himself in the 'Kilmarnock' (1786) and 'Edinburgh' (1787) editions of his book, *Poems, Chiefly in the Scottish Dialect.* From the beginning of his career in print, Burns employs for himself the idea of being a 'bard', which by the time he is writing is suitably Celtic-Scottish, following particularly the Celtic fashion for James Macpherson's 'Ossian' phenomenon. The term also potentially references William Shakespeare, 'the bard of Avon', simultaneously regional and (later) national poet.[12] Burns's authorial performance across his first two publications, then, might be seen as slyly inhabiting a similar expanding ambition. As Burnett and Carruthers show, his editors might be seen to have a range of motives in presenting Burns on the page. These include (as well as clever editorial performance by Burns himself) several sets of national, Romantic and monumental performance by the poet's nineteenth-century editors. Recent developments in book-history should make us aware of a vast range of peritextual performance (illustrations, glosses, notes and other presentational features that accompany the 'primary' text) surrounding Burns in print as with other writers. In the preface to the 'Kilmarnock' edition, Burns accents his role as a 'rustic [. . .] obscure, nameless Bard', or a provincial storyteller largely untouched by metropolitan culture, a pose aided and abetted by Henry Mackenzie's brand-defining epithet for Burns of 'heaven-taught ploughman'.[13] Yet another aspect of Burns's performance as poet is his deliberate reprise-modelling of himself on his great Scots-poetry predecessor, Robert Fergusson (1750–1774). In Edinburgh during his period of lionisation in 1786, Burns in homage visits places associated with Fergusson, is involved in a scheme to raise funds for a proper headstone at the poet's grave in the Canongate kirkyard, and famously hymns Fergusson, no doubt sincerely but also seeing in the Edinburgh poet a lyricised mould for his own life-performance so far: 'O thou, my elder brother in Misfortune,/By far my elder Brother in the muse'.[14] Burns's poetic personae, both in his texts and his life-settings for these, represent a variety that might generate a critical monograph in themselves, which belie attempts to fix Burns the poet too precisely or one-dimensionally.

Seen in Burns Suppers and public commemorations of the poet through the nineteenth century and down to the present day, Burns clearly helps Scotland perform its populist, primitivist self-image. And before this and feeding into such posthumous performance, the poet's work took cues from the 'Kilmarnock' preface, so that his poem 'To A Haggis' (1787) established the idea, much more than previously had been the case, of this cuisine as Scotland's national dish. Likewise his poem, 'The Author's Earnest Cry and Prayer' (1786), featuring the line, 'Whisky and freedom gang thegither' and another text, 'Scotch Drink' (1786) hymning 'John Barleycorn/Thou king o' grain' inscribe the idea of Scotland's no-nonsense national drink in a way that had not previously been so strong.[15] This performative function, where Burns's 'fiction' becomes fact, is seen again in the case of his poem, 'The Holy Fair' (1787), the title of which Burns had appropriated from a theological pamphlet of 1759. Burns uses this title to mount a critique of Presbyterian communion gatherings, implicitly usurping the label and arguing that the secular activities of this gathering are actually more important than the religious pretext. Real life imitates art when the summer secular carnival of the 'Mauchline Holy Fair' comes into being during the twentieth century, an event still going strong today.[16]

One might assume that if Burns were to return today, he would be astonished at the performative width through which he is rendered. He might expect to hear his songs performed but he would likely find novel the hugely popular set-piece renditions of 'Holy Willie's Prayer' (1785), 'Tam o' Shanter' (1790) and other poems at Burns Suppers, lent theatrical context by being acted out often with props and, in the case of these two texts, also through comical interaction with the audience. This is something rather different from a general eighteenth-century culture of poetry recital with which the poet would have been familiar. The Freemasonic context in which the Burns Supper develops during the nineteenth century under the guiding hand of the Reverend Hamilton Paul (1773–1854) sets up a ritualistic performing format comprising supper, speeches, poems and songs. Clark McGinn has recently written a wide-ranging history of the Burns Supper performed throughout the world and for over 200 years.[17] In the present volume, Ronnie Young takes us through the elements of the Burns Supper showing how ritualistic consumption provides performances of identity relating to nation, class and other factors.[18] Christopher Whatley's chapter here too describes the identity issues at stake from Burns's death in 1796 down to 1914 amid large-scale civic performance of commemorating the poet. Intriguingly, Whatley reads in such publicly active commemoration the way in which Burns's memory, for good or ill, formed a strongly cohesive element binding together Scottish society.[19] As well as, annually, 25 January itself, the Burns Festival at Ayr in 1844, the centenary celebrations of 1859 and the 150th anniversary of 1896 and other commemorative points represented culturally cohesive occasions amid the potential often for great political turmoil. It is this pattern, in general, that has seen the Burns 'movement' often disparaged as conservative and old-fashioned. Potential fatigue in the longevity of the Burns Supper, although the actual mass of evidence suggests that this is not the case, has led in recent years to the increasing rhetorical phenomenon of the 'alternative Burns Supper'.[20] A striking example of another form of 'alternative Burns' is found in the work of the late drag king Diane Torr (1948–2017), who worked in New York from the late 1970s. Stephen Bottoms reports:

> Diane always retained a strong sense of Scottishness, hosting riotous Burns Night suppers in New York, and in her performance Ready, Aye Ready (a standing cock has nae conscience), based on Robert Burns's bawdy poems, at the East Village theatres La Mama and PS 122 (1992).[21]

Bottoms notes she 'moved home to Glasgow in 2002 'from where she was able to further capitalise on interest in her work in Europe'.[22]

The Burns movement which has embraced the anniversaries and the suppers set in Burns season from some time before and through Burns's birthday, 25 January, and often for some weeks beyond, has also been keen on performance elsewhere, particularly via schools competitions which the World Burns Federation has assiduously and skilfully cultivated. The performative nature of the meetings and suppers of the Burns clubs that make up the Worldwide Burns Federation are re-enactments of the fraternal associations, including the Tarbolton Bachelors' Club (a performing debating society), freemasonry and the Crochallan Fencibles, the drinking, dining and singing club that spawned the notorious material of *The Merry Muses of Caledonia* (1799) in which Burns himself performatively operated. The federation and its clubs also embody an ongoing part of that commemorative culture in general identified by Whatley. As well as children's competitions, there are numerous adult competitions including 'The Whistle', where Burns's ballad of this name is recited, a contest that was first held in Burns's presence at Friar's Carse (the Dumfriesshire home of the poet's friends the Riddells) in 1793.[23] There is also a high-quality annual competition in Muirkirk, Ayrshire, the 'World John Lapraik Masters Speaking Competition', where Burns's poem, 'Epistle to J. Lapraik', a poetic friend of Burns from the town, is recited from memory by competitors.[24] In Dunedin,

New Zealand, in recent years there have been original poetry and song competitions in honour of Burns.[25] There is also, more widely, a 'Robert Burns Guild of Speakers', interested in Burns but also in the culture of debating in general.[26] This capacity for Burns to stand in an international context for more than his cultural roots has been reported by Ian Brown: on a 2002 visit to the English department of the State University in Yerevan, Armenia, department members were actually surprised to learn that the proletarian poet they so admired was also Scottish.[27]

Burns wrote prologues for the stage, as Jim Davis and Tracy Cattell remind us, the first of these 'Prologue [Spoken by Mr. Woods on his Benefit-Night, Monday 16th April, 1787]' showing the poet enjoying an expanded cultural society in his first period in Edinburgh. William Woods (1751–1802) was an English actor settled in Edinburgh, apparently a friend of Burns's predecessor, Robert Fergusson. In Woods's mouth we find a patriotic Scottish performance directed by Burns: 'Hail, Caledonia, name for ever dear!/Before whose sons I'm honour'd to appear!'[28] And as Burns has Woods praise his nation, the poet cannot help a sly, confident, self-reflexive note as, ostensibly, he praises the Scottish Enlightenment: 'Philosophy, no idle pedant dream,/Here [i.e. in Scotland] holds her search by heaven-taught Reason's beam'.[29] Praising Scottish historians and writers, the prologue ends with an 'all the world's a stage' metaphor as the nation's indefatigability is celebrated:

> Still self-dependent in her native shore,
> Bold may she brave grim Danger's loudest roar,
> Till Fate the curtain drop on worlds to be no more.[30]

Here, in line with the preface to the 'Edinburgh' edition of his poems in 1787 (see the chapter by Burnett and Carruthers), we find Burns using the stage to amplify his aspirations to speak to a national agenda. In the first of several prologues for the theatre in Dumfries, 'Prologue ["No song nor dance I bring from yon great city"]' (1789), sent to George Sutherland, the actor-manager of a theatre company, Burns makes a heartfelt plea for public support for the theatre as a new year beckons. In Shakespearean tone, the text in the voice of Father Time enjoins the young folk of the town to demonstrate a best-foot-forward attitude both to life and the theatre-project:

> Ye sprightly youths, quite flush with hope and spirit,
> Who think to storm the world by dint of merit,
> To you the dotard has a deal to say,
> In his sly, dry, sententious, proverb way!
> He bids you mind, amid your thoughtless rattle
> That the first blow is ever half the battle.[31]

In his 'Scots Prologue for Mrs Sutherland's Benefit Night' (1790) we see Burns writing enthusiastically yet again for a fund-raising event for the fledgling theatre in his now home-town of Dumfries. Soliciting money from potential patrons, the text says that there is no shortage of Scottish themes that might find their way to the stage, including Wallace, Bruce, the great martial Borders family of Douglas, and Mary, Queen of Scots. Burns's passionate theatrical prologues where he appeals for national dramatic writing have led many to wish that Burns might have written *in extenso* for theatre. The truth is that during the 1790s especially, Burns's creative energies were largely taken up by song-writing and -editing, that performative art for which he had most inclination and perhaps talent. The strong association of Burns with national culture that expanded through the nineteenth and into the twentieth century, however, saw some chatter in 1947 involving one of Scotland's greatest dramatists, James Bridie (1888–1951) and the Burns Federation about establishing the 'Burns Memorial Theatre' at Ayr as the National Scottish Theatre.[32]

Of theatre about Burns's life in the twentieth century there has been a considerable amount.[33] Joe Corrie (1894–1968) produced a one-act and a four-act drama, respectively, in *The Rake o' Mauchline* (1938) and *Robert Burns* (1943). Both of these see Burns as a political visionary but with a weakness for the opposite sex. The poet's real Achilles heel in the latter play, however, is his principled stand against kirk hypocrisy which is largely portrayed as a fight too big for one man alone in late eighteenth-century Scotland. Intricately argued, Corrie's drama lacks deep historical nuance, primed as it is by his radical, secular, socialist outlook. Like most things, Burns is often seen by modern playwrights through an amenable lens of contemporary identity politics. Lara Jane Bunting (b. 1969) authored *Love But Her*, expanded from a twenty-minute long piece of drama written originally for the Scottish Youth Theatre and staged by Brunton Theatre in Musselburgh in 1993.[34] It looked at Burns's life from the point of view of his long-suffering wife, Jean Armour and, well-crafted play that it was, it was successfully revived for the Edinburgh Fringe in 2009. Also standing in this tradition is the musical theatre of *Armour: A Herstory of the Scottish Bard* performed by graduates from the Royal Conservatoire in Glasgow in 2018. The author and musical director was Shonagh Murray (b. 1991), who wrote a follow-up, *Burns: A Lost Legacy* (2019), again focusing on the females in Burns's life and looking especially at the experiences of Sarah Burns, the poet's granddaughter. Both these plays enjoyed a popular run at the Fringe in 2019.[35] Perhaps the strangest seeming stage-offering associated with Burns has been *Robert Burns: The Musical* (2015) premiered in Aberdeen and based, apparently, on ideas by David Gest (1953–2016) and pop-music superstar, Michael Jackson (1958–2009), touched on by Alistair Braidwood in his chapter on Burns and film. It is full of glitz, is not very profound and its main trick is to transpose Burns's life to the twenty-first century. Rhona Brown in her essay for this volume sees H. Fletcher Lee's *Robert Burns: A Play in Three Acts* (1926), Robert Kemp's *The Other Dear Charmer* (1951) and Tom Wright's *There Was a Man* (1965) as the most interesting dramas about the poet as they are driven by the poems and songs (and to a lesser extent by the letters) more than the biographies that had appeared by the time they were written. This begs the question whether there might be scope for a new theatrical production of Burns's life based rather more minutely on the most up-to-date biographical facts rather than Burnsian 'fictions'. What the Burns text-led drama would seem to show, however, is just how deeply performative, indeed recitative, these productions have been. This is certainly the case for *There Was a Man* which became a hugely successful vehicle for the actor John Cairney (b. 1930) who toured world-wide with the production and whose stand-alone Burns recital for shorter television spots made him a Scottish A-list celebrity.[36] Cairney also spent much time and effort attempting to interest film producers in a 'bio-pic' of Burns, some of the material from Cairney's efforts here finding its way into *Burnscripts : Dramatic Interpretations of the Life and Art of Robert Burns* (2011).[37]

In 1968 Cairney was also involved in a six-part television dramatisation of Burns's life, the most substantial television offering surrounding the poet, leaving aside the cumulative effect of occasional (Hogmanay) and more incidental television performances and sketches. As Cairney found, the big screen has not been a particularly fruitful context for the portrayal of Burns. A silent film, *Tam o' Shanter*, was made in Hollywood in 1915, directed by and starring Murdock MacQuarrie. Two other short American films are *The Romance of Robert Burns* (1937), directed by Crane Wilbur, which has Burns, fed up with life in Edinburgh, rushing back to Ayrshire on a suspiciously Western-style stage-coach to marry Jean Armour who jilts another suitor for the poet at the altar; and *Robbie and his Mary* (1959), directed by Herschel Daugherty, which was likewise superficial in delving into and sentimentalising one singular episode in Burns's biography. *Comin' Thro' the Rye* (1947), a longer affair with a running time of fifty-five minutes directed by Walter C. Mycroft, was another American production larded by an over-reliance on Burns's songs and heavy-handed third-person narration. The film centres itself on Burns's relationships with his first inspiration, Handsome Nell, Jean Armour, 'Highland Mary' and the poet's 'Clarinda', Agnes Maclehose. As Alistair Braidwood has remarked there is then a curious gap of many decades until a Scottish offering, *Red Rose* (2004) directed by Robbie Moffat.[38] Refreshingly, this is less focused on Burns's love life. Ridiculously, it sets out a plot by the government to murder the poet. Burns's real-life physician, William Maxwell, a Catholic seen kneeling at a statue of Mary, Mother of Christ (by which we are to know he is a bad one) is co-opted by the government to murder, under pretence of ministering to, Burns by slowly poisoning his friend.

The film, in short, is a crudely executed, historically awful piece of conspiracy theory which flopped in the cinemas and was given away free with the tabloid newspaper, *The Sun*. In the present collection, Alistair Braidwood looks at five films in particular, reflecting on some familiar and changing Burnsian filmic emphases through the decades about the writer. Perhaps Burns's most successful big-screen presence has been in the ubiquity with which his 'Auld Lang Syne' has been deployed. This has appeared in Charlie Chaplin's *The Gold Rush* (1925), the Shirley Temple vehicle, *Wee Willie Winkie* (1937), the Christmas-classic *It's A Wonderful Life* (1947) and many others down to a more modern age that shows no signs of the song's utility diminishing. 'Auld Lang Syne' appears as part of the common cultural background, for instance, in *When Harry Met Sally* (1989), *Forrest Gump* (1993) and *Sex and the City* (2008).

The promiscuous, performing limbs of Robert Burns stretch widely in performance of his own life and work and in the inspiration that he provides more generally for other performers. This volume pays attention to performative contexts and genres, often opening fresh perspectives on the performance of 'Robert Burns'. The chapters of this volume offer a rich but, in the nature of things, merely introductory opening contribution to the investigation of the growing critical study and analysis of performance and performativity in relation to Robert Burns, his work and his mediated reception.

Notes

1. Ian Brown, 'Tartan, Tartanry and Hybridity', in Ian Brown (ed.), *From Tartan to Tartanry* (Edinburgh: Edinburgh University Press, 2010), p. 11.
2. See Nigel Leask, 'Robert Burns and Latin America', in S. Alker, L. Davis and H. F. Nelson (eds), *Robert Burns and Transatlantic Culture* (Farnham: Ashgate, 2012), p. 134.
3. See https://historicaldigression.com/2011/01/02/auld-lang-syne-banned/
4. https://www.bbc.co.uk/news/world-asia-32082134
5. See Kirsteen McCue, 'Burns's Songs and Poetic Craft', in Gerard Carruthers (ed.), *The Edinburgh Companion to Robert Burns* (Edinburgh: Edinburgh University Press, 2009), pp. 84–5; see also the forthcoming Volume 4 of the Oxford University Press Edition of the Works of Robert Burns, Kirsteen McCue (ed.), *Songs for George Thomson* (2020).
6. See Murray Pittock (ed.), *The Scots Musical Museum*, 2 vols (Oxford: Oxford University Press, 2018) (Volumes 2 and 3 in the Oxford University Press Edition of the Works of Robert Burns).
7. https://www.independent.co.uk/news/uk/this-britain/ludwig-and-rabbie-a-partnership-that-ended-in-tears-517806.html

8. https://boosey.com/cr/music/James-MacMillan-Lament-of-Mary-Queen-of-Scots/52152; https://www.arvopart.ee/en/arvo-part/work/487/.
9. Burns recording remains a somewhat under-researched area of 'performance'; a good starting point, in general, for exploration here is Thomas Keith, 'A Discography of Robert Burns, 1948–2002', *Studies in Scottish Literature* 33–4 (2004), pp. 387–412.
10. https://www.youtube.com/watch?v=GbogSD4DQPw
11. https://www.britishnewspaperarchive.co.uk/search/results/1947-01-01/1947–12–31?basicsearch=%22robert%20burns%22&phrasesearch=robert%20burns&retrievecountrycounts=false&place=dundee%2C%20angus%2C%20scotland&page=2 [accessed 20 July 2020].
12. Ian Brown considers in detail the contrasting treatment over the centuries of Shakespeare and Burns as versions of national bards in his chapter, 'Bards, Britishness, Buildings, and Cultural Memory', in his *Performing Scottishness* (London: Palgrave Macmillan, 2020), pp. 57–91.
13. James Kinsley (ed.), *The Poems and Songs of Robert Burns*, Volume 3 (Oxford: Clarendon, 1968), p. 971; see Henry Mackenzie's unsigned essay in *The Lounger* (9 December 1786), reprinted in Donald Low (ed.), *Robert Burns: The Critical Heritage* (London and Boston: Routledge & Kegan Paul, 1974), pp. 67–71.
14. Kinsley (ed.), *The Poems and Songs of Robert Burns*, Volume 1, p. 323 (ll.3–4).
15. Kinsley (ed.), *The Poems and Songs of Robert Burns*, Volume 1, 'The Author's Earnest Cry and Prayer', p. 191 (l.185); 'Scotch Drink', p. 173 (ll.17–18).
16. http://www.mauchlineholyfair.com/
17. Clark McGinn, *The Burns Supper: A Comprehensive History* (Edinburgh: Luath, 2018).
18. It is interesting to note the composer James MacMillan's claim concerning the deep performative identity of the Burns Supper, a 'parody of the Mass'; see *Scottish Christian.com* (18 October 2009). This is a stance that chimes with the claim made by the poet Edwin Muir (1887–1959) that Burns operates for some Scots as a substitute Christ-figure.
19. See also Christopher A. Whatley, *Immortal Memory: Burns and the Scottish People* (Edinburgh: John Donald, 2016).
20. https://www.thenational.scot/news/18186005.nine-alternative-burns-night-events-try-weekend/; but see also the report commissioned by the Scottish government, Murray Pittock, *Robert Burns and the Scottish Economy* (2020), https://www.gla.ac.uk/media/Media_705140_smxx.pdf. Both highlight in differing ways the supper's enduring popularity, citing for 2009 3,673 supper events worldwide with participants amounting to nine million people.

21. Stephen Bottoms, 'Diane Torr: Obituary', *The Guardian*, 29 June 2017.
22. Ibid.
23. https://www.berwickshirenews.co.uk/news/ian-can-whistle-tune-success-world-champion-2365300
24. https://en-gb.facebook.com/events/293675641060560/
25. https://www.dunedinlibraries.govt.nz/whats-on/competitions/robert-burns-poetry-competition-the-far-foreign-land
26. http://www.rbwf.org.uk/tag/robert-burns-guild-of-speakers/
27. Ian Brown, *Performing Scottishness* (London: Palgrave Macmillan, 2020), pp. 77–8.
28. Kinsley (ed.), *The Poems and Songs of Robert Burns*, Volume 1, p. 331 (ll.11–12).
29. Ibid. (ll.17–18).
30. Ibid.
31. Kinsley (ed.), *The Poems and Songs of Robert Burns*, Volume 1, p. 499 (ll.15–20).
32. See University of Glasgow Special Collections, GB 247 STA Bridie 527h.
33. There is also a plethora of fiction and poetry about or inspired by Burns. If the work of the poet is primary and the criticism, biography and translation secondary source, then we might perhaps say that there is a tertiary set of sources in the artistic (including painting and illustration), literary (with one subset of this being drama) and the overlapping media dramatisation of Burns in film, on television and also on radio. One of the best radio pieces, in an area even less researched than Burns in film and TV, is the Liz Lochhead adaptation of the Helen Simpson short story, 'Burns and the Bankers' for BBC Radio Four (2012).
34. https://archive.list.co.uk/the-list/1993-01–15/49/
35. https://edinburghfestival.list.co.uk/article/103329-armour-a-herstory-of-the-scottish-bard/
36. For more here, see http://johncairney.com/robert-burns
37. *Burnscripts: Dramatic Interpretations of the Life and Art of Robert Burns* (Edinburgh: Luath, 2011). Cairney has also published a collection of his offerings for Burns Suppers, *Immortal Memories* (Edinburgh: Luath 2002).
38. For more on this and other films, see Alistair Braidwood, 'Missing Reels', in Johnny Rodger and Gerard Carruthers, *Fickle Man: Robert Burns in the 21st Century* (Dingwall: Sandstone Press, 2009), pp. 80–7.

2

Performance and Print in Editions of Robert Burns in the Eighteenth and Nineteenth Centuries[1]

John Burnett and Gerard Carruthers

If one, very standard definition of 'performance' is 'an act of presenting a play, concert, or other form of entertainment', then at the root of such acts is the performative potential embedded in the ordering of the script or score to be enacted for audience reception. The act of editing a book, especially of creative 'fiction' (broadly defined and including poetry) can be understood as a version of such ordering, shaping the work for reception by listener or reader, a performed act in itself or, at the very least, preparing a 'script' for the performativity embedded in the work.[2] The 'presenting' in the definition just quoted will generally be taken to refer to the action by an actor, musician or similar performer rather than a stage-producer/director, playwright, composer or musical conductor, but theatre studies and musicology recognise these roles as important in the shaping of performance. The 'performer' in the case of an edition of Robert Burns can be defined as the poet himself, but, although we are used to poets as performers reading their own work aloud, this role, when applied to the printed page, the 'script' to be read, remains ordinarily a metaphor. Meanwhile. the print 'edition' provides an output often thought to be in the past tense, rather than in the vital performative-present in the way the script of any play of any period retains its performative potential. We are used to such potential in, for example, Shakespeare's *Romeo and Juliet* being reprised, say, in a modern-city, gang-culture setting. Re-presentation of literature on the page, as opposed to its theatrical rendition however, in a new edition, a translated or an illustrated version, or a comic-book version, is not usually reckoned to come within the ambit of performance, even though the process of editing can modify the 'script' into something that *performs* in a different fashion.

There is an advanced theoretical body of critical thought around ideas of active aesthetic-creating consumption. The 'performance of reading' is by now a fairly mainstream idea surrounding the notion of the reader as performer-interpreter (and as opposed to the simple idea of reading competence).[3] Aesthetics has long been interested in reader- or viewer-response as a vital part of the function of art. In the case of works of art, or even museum exhibits, recent years have seen a new theoretical emphasis upon the 'curator' as a vital, guiding presenter, as an interlocutor or even an interpreter providing access to the art-object or exhibition. By analogy, the editor, especially the full-fig academic editor, is in practice a highly active performative-reader-interpreter, like a director, conductor or a curator. In the case of the last function, especially, there is something that goes beyond mere analogy when considering the editor: there is an active presentational-interpretive role in the editorial process long recognised but under-described. This can certainly be seen in the case of editing Robert Burns. Not only recent, re-emphasised ideas about curatorial function, but twenty-first-century developments in book history open up the possibility of seeing the editor (and other individuals, including publishers) and processes involved in book production in a more performative light. The emphasis of this chapter is on the role of the editor, but the publisher was part of the performance too. Here we will mention only one aspect of this. Burns stands out as the most heavily-illustrated poet in nineteenth-century Britain – indeed the only writer who was published with more illustrations was Shakespeare as a playwright – and the choice of the artist and the selection of subjects were matters for the publisher.

Let us begin with a fairly obvious example of the conjunction of print and performance: Burns's long and large popularity in chapbooks, cheaply produced and sold pamphlets often hawked by pedlars and on the streets. Iain Beavan has shown that there is a strong emphasis upon contemporary performance in the production of chapbook material of Burns and other song-writers during the nineteenth century, including even printing the details of performers of material and audience venues. Beavan writes, 'The chapbook printers churned out many versions of Burns's songs, under a variety of titles, incorporating such qualifying terms as "choice", "celebrated" and "favourite".'[4] The extent to which such epithets were responses to observation of audience/readership at real performances (probably they were to some extent) or to which they were marketing conceits (probably also a factor) is difficult to determine. However, such conventions usefully point to a notional extra-textual sphere (before and after publication) where the readership or audience is actively considered and engaged. As Beavan has also observed, the promiscuous use of Burns's name for texts dubiously or not at all his, or alternatively the absence of the poet's name sometimes in chapbook publication of actual Burns composition attests to John Blackie's assertion that 'The Scottish songs are not the songs of Ramsay, or Burns [. . .] but the songs of the Scottish people, of whom Ramsay and Burns, and a host of others, were merely spokesmen for the nonce.'[5] Authorship and publication of Burns during the nineteenth century, then, become in chapbook culture appropriated from the author and represent a kind of meta-cultural phenomenon in their print-rendition cum the way in which they are consumed/performed by their readership and, also, as these texts are admitted within an abstract sphere of (performative) community. In the humble chapbook, then, something transitional and performative is going on, beyond even the relatively straightforward or direct relation to the temporality of Burns song-performance which the chapbook often claims. In the chapbook, performance is commemorative as the original performance is reimagined to some extent in the private reading experience of those who buy it. It also acts presumably *pour encourager* additional performance either in the private domestic or in the public sphere. And in a third level of performance, assuming the John Blackie idea to carry some weight, where *national*-ity, whatever that exactly means, is enacted in abstract but also ultimately concrete manner through contributing to a 'community of feeling'. We might point here as well to an important micro-canon, of the most enjoyable songs and poems in the context of chapbook market-performance, that enabled poorer people to consume and perform Burns.

The publication of the best-selling *The National Burns* (1879–80) tends to support the idea seen in the chapbook genre and voiced in the theory of Blackie of some kind of national, perhaps people's or 'folk' rendition/performance of Burns. The Rev. George Gilfillan (1813–1878) was the editor of *The National Burns* published in fifteen parts at two shillings each and so designed to be affordable to those of modest means. It was also sold by travelling salesmen.[6] Gilfillan, scholar of the Covenanters and proselytiser for working-class poets was part of an antiquarian impetus in the nineteenth century advancing, to some extent, a populist, Presbyterian definition of Scotland. Produced posthumously, the final execution of *The National Burns* by publisher William Mackenzie included also 'a series of full-page engravings from designs from some of our first Scottish artists'.[7] In addition, *The National Burns* contained 'a novel and important feature [. . .] those fine old Scottish Airs, the preservation of which from oblivion was one of the great objects of Burns in writing for them his immortal songs'.[8] In other words, the National Edition, most unusually, was a major edition of Burns which included printed music. Mackenzie continued in his 'Prospectus':

> The work will be published in Fifteen Parts, at Two Shillings each, each part containing forty-eight pages Letterpress, printed in the best style on fine toned paper, and Two Plates. It may also be had in Thirty Parts, price One Shilling each; and on its completion every subscriber will receive a copy of a magnificent life-size Portrait of Burns on returning the tickets which appear on the covers of the last eight parts, for packing and delivery of which the nominal charge of Sixpence is made.[9]

This multi-media edition of Burns (to apply a modern, often performative analogy) was about words, music and images presented specifically to a popular nation where the readership was explicitly engaged as part of that grouping and reached through contemporary marketing (the redeemable tickets) as well as in an appeal to aesthetic plenitude. We might notice also the monumentality of *The National Burns*, in precisely the period for the making of large-scale civic monuments in the Scott Monument (1844), the Wallace Monument (1869) and, of course, the Burns Monument (Alloway, 1823). The Gilfillan-Mackenzie publication likewise attempts monumental performance in print and illustrative form as part of this same zeitgeist.

Standing influentially behind Gilfillan-Mackenzie also, is an earlier publication, *The Land of Burns* (1840) edited by John Wilson (1758–1854), part of the Tory grouping around *Blackwood's Edinburgh Magazine* and Robert Chambers (1802–1871), a man of more radical political sympathies. The volumes were produced by Blackie in Glasgow with eighty-two steel engravings by David Octavius Hill (1802–1870).[10] The publisher Blackie conceived the book as a text on places associated with Burns in parallel with Hill's plates, and John Wilson was engaged to write the commentary. Events, however, showed the difficulties which a publisher might have with a wilful editor. Wilson produced a long introductory essay on Burns which had little to do with the locations of Burns's life and work, with the consequence that Blackie went to the living person who had done most research on the life of Burns, Robert Chambers, to provide more exact topographical commentary. *The Land of Burns* was 'the best of its kind that has ever issued from the Scottish press'.[11] It was said to be the most expensive book (i.e. in total cost to the publisher) printed in Scotland up to that date.[12] The publication was a great success and was discussed in *The Scotsman*; its reviewer opined,

> Where our youthful steps wandered – whether with joyous playmates or loving companions – there is the earth greenest, and the sun brightest. Poetry, in like manner, leaves a spell where it is first breathed. The ground on which the poet treads is classic. He lives in an atmosphere of light, and all with whom his name is associated, become, to some extent, sharers of his glory.[13]

He goes on, 'What would not Englishmen give for similar memorabilia of the life and genius of Shakespeare? We have here brought vividly before us every thing that can throw light on the character and writings of her own hearty Burns; and as a national work we regard it as of permanent value.'[14] *The Land of Burns*, then, was seen not primarily as a rendition of selected (often extracted) songs, poems and letters by Burns, but, more importantly, as a kind of performance of Scottish national geography and culture (in which Burns was an important, loquacious tour-guide). Often Hill's illustrations are partly primed by, but are not necessarily particular to, Burns's texts. Human figures in the landscapes are not necessarily relatable to Burns's works but are a generally humanising, harmonic element. That Hill's paintings were admired for their combination of nature, the human, the biographical and the creative was recognised by Alexander Maclagan in 1850, in 'Stanzas written after seeing "The Valley of the Nith" a picture in the Scottish Academy's Exhibition of this year, by D. O. Hill, R.S.A', probably a version of the title-page vignette for the second volume of *The Land of Burns*.[15]

> Lo! here we look upon laughing earth,
> And deem we hear the reapers' shouts of glee, -
> In fancy listen to the genial mirth
> Bursting from Nature's minstrels, bird and bee!
> Here Tam o' Shanter's glorious dream had birth,
> Immortal vision, hail![16]

Hill's landscapes are often panoramic, and the reader might take each one and make her or his own connections with one or several of Burns's texts. There is an assumption of the informed, active reader tasked with making performative connection. The view of Ayr from the south, for example, looks over the Doon Valley and the line of Tam o' Shanter's ride to Alloway is more or less straight down the middle of the picture for those who already know Burns's texts, without this poetic route being explicitly pointed out.[17] We might also observe a pattern of artistic and cultural performative circulation demonstrated as Hill and Blackie had a plan to give the original oil paintings for *The Land of Burns* to 'a Burns gallery near the poet's birthplace; but [this] was not carried out, on account of funds for the necessary building not being forthcoming'.[18] Clearly we have then, too, a performance of Romantic regionality-cum-nationality of people and place in Burns's works and in circulation beyond these texts. This is the case both in the proposed art gallery and as *The Land of Burns* itself makes circuits between the avatar Burns, his work and a real landscape, which is actual but at the same time romantically inflated by the national poet and by Hill the artist. *The Land of Burns* ultimately is a kind of echo chamber where Burns and Scottish landscape reflect one another in a symbiotic fashion that it is assumed will resonate strongly in the reader's ears (and eyes).

Burns in his lifetime, of course, played a major part in explicitly setting up his poetic agency, in a way that was simultaneously self-identifying (perhaps even self-aggrandising) and self-effacing as he assumed the mantle of rustic bard. *Poems, Chiefly in the Scottish Dialect* (1786), Burns's first book, published at

Kilmarnock, gestures towards primitivist performance, as he talks of himself in the third person in his preface:

> Unacquainted with the necessary requisites for commencing Poet by rule, he sings the sentiments and manners, he felt and saw in himself and his rustic compeers around him, in his and their native language.[19]

Here, Burns sets up his 'bardic' performance where the implication of such an identification involves a relation to oral and local tradition. In fact, relationship to orality is not much in evidence in the 'Kilmarnock' edition and rootedness in local history is also not as much a keynote feature of the production as is sometimes assumed. Burns's use of the stanza forms, the 'standard Habbie' and the 'Christ's Kirk' stanzas is something he has learned from his predecessors in Scots poetry, Allan Ramsay and Robert Fergusson, neither of whom existed in very close proximity to Ayrshire. The remarkable thing not often enough noticed is the way in which Burns is bringing to bear within his native Ayrshire a mode of writing from outside: these stanza-forms and Scots poetry in general (as opposed to song, which has a more continuous history in his native county down to his own time). These elements reperformed with largely contemporary Ayrshire subject-matter were more to be associated with Edinburgh and the north-east of Scotland, encompassing Episcopalian, Catholic and Jacobite undertones. Broadly too, the Scots poetry mode down to the 1780s is more linked in eighteenth-century party and cultural terms with the Tory party interest. This as opposed to the Whig political and cultural interest, where 'Whig' in its particular Scottish nuance is associated with Presbyterianism and loyalty to the 1688–9 British dynastic settlement which had deposed the Stuarts from the throne (to which the Jacobites wished to restore them). Burns as Scots poet in Ayrshire, then, is a new-minted performance for the later eighteenth century with a number of other poets from the Presbyterian west of Scotland *becoming* Scots poets as they follow his example.[20]

As the poet hints also in the preface to the 'Kilmarnock' edition, there is another force at work. Burns writes, 'it was not till very lately, that the applause, perhaps the partiality, of Friendship, wakened his vanity so far as to make him think any thing of his was worth showing; and none of the following were ever composed with a view to the press'.[21] Famously, the 'Kilmarnock' edition is enabled by the collection of 612 subscriptions, and to a large extent these subscribers represent a network of Ayrshire Enlightenment individuals, who are associated with Moderate (liberal) as opposed to Popular Party (conservative) Calvinist Presbyterianism. Strong among these Moderate subscribers was the desire to reward Burns for his service to their cause. Burns's 'Holy Willie's Prayer' was written in 1785 and circulated in manuscript form lambasting those Popular Party 'Holy Willies' who had attempted to prosecute (in a case where the extant details remain somewhat obscure) the lawyer Gavin Hamilton who was defended by another lawyer, Robert Aiken. Both men were friends of Burns and subsequently Hamilton distributed many proposals for Burns's volume and Aiken collected 145 out of 612 subscriptions to make the Kilmarnock edition happen.[22] In other words, the 'Kilmarnock' edition is also widely performative of the Ayrshire Moderate interest, firstly as reward for party-poet Burns who enjoys this 'partiality of friends', secondly in carrying – *inter alia* – a distinct flavour of moderate theology and finally as literary utterance in itself where the puritanical outlook of the extreme conservatives frowned upon such profane and secular literature (most especially in the case of ideologically-suspect Scots poetry).

Following the success of the 'Kilmarnock' edition a second (Edinburgh) edition of *Poems, Chiefly in the Scottish Dialect* (1787) was prepared by Burns. Again by subscription and located now in the Scottish capital, Burns's new preface sees him move from regional, pseudo-bardic performance to that of 'bard' on a more national stage. The preface to the 'Edinburgh' edition is addressed 'To the Noblemen and Gentlemen of the Caledonian Hunt' and begins with an expression of a more extensive aspiration, where Burns identifies himself as 'A Scottish Bard, proud of the name, and whose highest ambition is to sing in his Country's service.'[23] And we see why the poet performs specifically for the Caledonian Hunt as he rhetorically asks it, 'where shall he so properly look for patronage as to the illustrious Names of his native Land; those who bear the honours and inherit the virtues of their Ancestors?'[24] From Ayrshire poet, patronised and performing for an enlightened Moderate circle, Burns has now transformed himself into national poet performing, on the face of it, for the aristocratic elite of Scotland whose forebears had played such a prominent part in constructing a distinctive national history. However, as Burns performs this part it is not the whole story: he is also producing for and is aided and abetted in the 'Edinburgh' edition by the concerted subscription-collection and readership of bourgeois Enlightenment intellectuals and freemasons in the capital (including, for instance, Dugald Stewart, Professor of Mathematics at the University of Edinburgh who was a proselytiser from within both these groupings). The peritextual prefaces of Burns's first and second edition of *Poems, Chiefly in the Scottish Dialect* ought to remind us as much as later iterations of his work such as *The National Burns*, that Burns's work is often mediated (especially before about 1850), indeed designed for particular audiences rather than, simply, a generalised readership.

The foregoing is not necessarily to imply that Burns's national poetic aspiration was insincere. Indeed, in the 'Edinburgh' edition and elsewhere, the poet has a trenchant sense of national mission: celebrating topography, history and the culture of Scotland in general. This is why *The Land of Burns*, product of a post-Romantic sensibility as we have seen, stands in a line largely established by Burns the Romantic artist. One part of Burns's National Romantic project is his work with James Johnson in compiling the six volumes of *The Scots Musical Museum* (1787–1803, and so continuing after Burns's death in 1796). These are historic songs collected, improved and sometimes written by the poet. As Murray Pittock claims, 'Burns' editorial role and his authorial role are inseparable,' and this perhaps accounts for the generic transmutation where his (and Johnson's) edition becomes a 'museum'.[25] Here, in a performative shift of gear, their work is explicitly set in a context of curation and exhibition as opposed to 'mere' antiquarian editing. Pittock describes the very active concept at work where Burns and Johnson 'not only work within what Stanley Fish terms an "interpretative community", but [it is] also in the very terms in which the edition is framed, [that it] seek[s] to create a new community which bears a tangential – though umbilical – relationship to the old one'.[26] Such iteration of audiences past and present is of an order with, say, the updating of Shakespeare plays for the present and yet again highlights a wide set of paratextual performative functions including publisher (James Johnson was also publisher for *The Scots Musical Museum*), editor, author and readership, this last extending to present 'community', and a past community which cannot of course read the present text but whose role as past audience to national cultural history is presumed as a factor.

This is not the place for a more extensive essay that might be written on Burns's use of voice, mode, genre and so on in his creative work, all of which involve, as with our commentary above on the two prefaces to *Poems, Chiefly in the Scottish Dialect*, strong elements of performance. However, we might just allude to several other examples of artistic print-performativity surrounding Burns's creative output when he was alive that go 'beyond the page'. 'Holy Willie's Prayer' was thought never to have been officially published in Burns's lifetime until recent excellent book-history detective work by Patrick Scott. Scott demonstrates that the supposedly 'pirated' chapbook version of the text printed in 1789 was published by John Wilson, the publisher of the 'Kilmarnock' edition and, so, strongly suggests that Burns himself stands behind this issuing of the text.[27] Why would Burns wish to publish 'Holy Willie's Prayer' at this time? The best answer is that this is the point when the attempted Popular Party prosecution for heresy of Burns's friend the liberal clergyman Rev. William McGill is approaching its high point.[28] Burns, then, 'restages' 'Holy Willie's Prayer', so effective in the dispute of 1785–6 surrounding his chums Hamilton and Aiken. The chapbook appearance is in itself performative or an act, where Burns is downplaying his own connection with the text and mustering, via its mimicry of cheap chapbook form, implied popular support for his/McGill's side of the debate against the powerful conservatives in 1789. A second example of textual performativity is to be found in 'Tam o' Shanter'

(1790) which is produced to accompany an illustration of the ruined Alloway Kirk in the work of a friend of Burns, Francis Grose (1731–1791), who edits a series, *Antiquities of Scotland* (1789–91). In this publication, the poem is set as a long, rather ludicrous footnote (or paratext) to the illustration of the ruin of Alloway Kirk, supposedly the main subject here.[29] However, Alloway Kirk ruin was a not particularly distinguished Scottish landmark, especially when compared to the likes of Linlithgow Palace or Edinburgh Castle, and operates essentially as a pretext for Burns to write his poem. The joke cooked up by Burns and Grose is, however, consonant with Burns's mock-epic text of 'Tam' which describes the plight of a man 'heroically' battling supernatural elements which might all be in his mind. The bathos of seeing Alloway kirk as a worthy 'antiquity' of Scotland mirrors the bathos of Tam's own overblown scenario fired up by something that is not actually there. Here, then, is an important original setting for a Burns text – *Antiquities of Scotland* – where the paratextual performance is important but is lost in subsequent reprintings without the illustration of the kirk. A final example of Burns's own editorial performance, this time, however, intratextual rather than extratextual occurs in Burns's poem, 'Halloween' (1786). This features a highly manipulative use of paratext where Burns's enlightened, antiquarian notes to his own poetic text create with the text an indeterminate liminal space: are we to take these customs seriously as the narrator seems to at certain points, or are we to read 'Halloween' as a bundle of superstition which we – the enlightened reader – might look down upon, or at least hold at anthropological arm's length? That indeterminacy of interpretation, a potentially disturbing, open-ended reading experience is ultimately what Burns establishes from competing cultural contexts of which he is cleverly aware. There has been little work done on Burns's fictive editorial characterisation, an important element in his creative and print performativity of which much more might be made across his oeuvre.

Alongside Burns's *Scots Musical Museum* and *Select Collection of Original Scots Airs* in six volumes (1791–1841), the other big, ongoing song project in which Burns is involved with another musical-editor, George Thomson, the Burns song-collection that is most famous, is the posthumously-published, *The Merry Muses of Caledonia* (1799). The material in this volume is collected or written by Burns for private use (or performance) within the male, Edinburgh convivial club, 'The Crochallan Fencibles'. Never intended for publication, then, *The Merry Muses* becomes a notorious publication-label down to the 1950s where it is reiterated in many new 'editions' with numerous songs licentiously added in to make it a more expansive collection of pornographic texts. Amid such undoubted accretion a response is mounted in 1911 by 'Vindex' (Duncan McNaught, the editor of the *Burns Chronicle*) who reprints (rather than 'republishes') an edition of *The Merry Muses* with the subtitle of 'A Vindication of Robert Burns in connection with the above publication and the spurious editions which succeeded it'. Under the aegis of the Burns Federation, this was not for sale and for 'subscribers only'. McNaught's aim was not only to dissociate Burns from later accretions to the original corpus of *The Merry Muses* but also from most of the texts that are to be found in the original 1799 issue of the tome. Using clever, but ultimately over-stretched circumstantial analysis of the material, Vindex comes to the conclusion:

> We are, therefore, left no choice but to utilise the material at our disposal as best we may, for the purpose of demonstrating that the association of Burns's name, either as author or editor, with the ribald volumes entitled 'The Merry Muses,' is not only an unwarranted mendacity, but one of the grossest outrages ever perpetrated on the memory of a man of genius.[30]

This edition, reserved for purchase by men vetted within the Burns Federation is a very curious case of having one's cake and eating it. Down to the prosecution of *Lady Chatterley's Lover* in 1960, *The Merry Muses* could not be officially or legally published. It would have been deemed pornographic until that time, and other strange iterations or performances of its material occur earlier than 1911. For instance, as can be worked out from the later nineteenth-century type-facing and the paper, the '1827' printing of *The Merry Muses* is, in fact, produced in '1872', a ploy clearly designed to wrong-foot the contemporary censor.[31] The performative, paratextual acrobatics around *The Merry Muses* will require even more extensive examination in future Burns scholarship.

Burns's posthumous reputation is shaped through the nineteenth century by editors who publish his work and who are in the prominent situation of shaping an emerging canon (a large percentage of which comprised texts never printed in the poet's lifetime and not known to the majority of Burns's contemporaries at the time). The first edition that makes some claim to be an extensive 'collected' edition is *The Works of Robert Burns; with an account of his life, and a criticism on his writings. To which are prefixed, some observations on the character and condition of the Scottish peasantry*. This four-volume set was edited in 1800 by James Currie (1756–1805). As an editor of Burns's work, Currie has not been universally popular with 'Burnsians' largely because of his over-emphasis on Burns's consumption of alcohol. However, Currie worked with great diligence and sensitivity gathering material, assuring, for instance, some correspondents of Burns of his discretion in his use of their material, and he was intent on producing a fine edition of the works, the proceeds for which would accrue to Burns's widow and young family.[32] Currie also starts the trend in Burns editing of life-and-work-all-bound-up-together. He brings Burns alive, as a person the reader could have known, could have spoken to. The printing of the letters is essential here, where Burns talks honestly about himself, rather than having the reader deal with the multiple (fictional) personae of the poetry solely. Currie's edition was larger and on better paper than most other compilations of Burns produced in the first few decades of the nineteenth century. It was aimed at a more well-heeled market than the chapbook one and employed Thomas Bewick (1753–1828), a celebrated publisher and engraver of natural history, to do the title-page vignettes. Alongside Currie's 'Scottish Peasantry' essay in the prefatory material, these environmental aspects helped Burns – in a continuation of Henry Mackenzie's epithet as a 'heaven-taught ploughman' – into the nineteenth-century Romantic canon.[33] Currie as editor too, bringing to light many new texts and providing the first extensive biography in his edition, conducted a performance of Burns largely in symbiotic relationship with his country in a way that reverberates through the later iterations by Gilfillan and in *The Land of Burns*. Currie waxes lyrical about Burns in his prefatory remarks:

> With a deep insight into the human heart, his poetry exhibits high powers of imagination – it displays, and as it were embalms, the peculiar manners of his country; and it may be considered as a monument, not to his own name only, but to the expiring genius of an ancient and once independent nation.[34]

As well as identifying features of 'natural-ness' that would soon be embraced within the mainstream Romantic movement, Currie also sounds an elegiac pronouncement (which is also Romantic in itself): that Burns and his culture were entities that were passing. To some extent, this is predicated on the likes of Burns's own editing with *The Scots Musical Museum*, and helps inscribe the idea of cultural conservation around Burns and his work as well as around many other aspects of Scottish culture in the nineteenth century. This becomes an abundant, elegiac, antiquarian note, where texts and books (especially by Scotland's 'national poet') are bound up with the Scottish people, landscape and monuments. That Romantic performance of the nation inscribes Scotland in the worldwide imagination, but is seen by some in the twentieth century as central to Scotland's supposed denial of modernity.

On a more prosaic level of editorial performance, however, Currie is occasionally open to the charge of misdemeanour. One cardinal editorial sin was adding material in the instance of a letter by Burns to John McMurdo, which Currie dates December 1793, where the poet talks about *The Merry Muses*. Currie has the letter read as follows:

> I think I once mentioned something of a Collection of Scots Songs I have some years been making: I send you a perusal of what I have got together. I could not conveniently spare them above five or six days, and five or six glances of them will probably more than suffice you. *A very few of them are my own* [our italics]. When you are tired of them, please leave them with Mr Clint of the King's Arms.[35]

When G. Ross Roy obtained access to the original manuscript for the first time since Currie for his edition of Burns's letters published in the 1980s, he found that the phrase in italics was not in the original. This non-authorised phrase was to form a large part of the underlying case mounted by McNaught for Burns's more distant relationship with *The Merry Muses* in 1911, disreputably pornographic in Currie's time as certainly as in McNaught's. Here, then, we find editorial performance producing high distortion.

Currie's Burns goes through many editions and indeed (re-)iterations.[36] With the seventh edition of Currie (1813), Burns illustration moves in a new direction through the employment of one of the leading London artists of the day, Thomas Stothard (1755–1834), and a first-rate London engraver, Robert Cromek (1770–1812), the man who had collected *The Reliques of Robert Burns* (1808) which had been published by Cadell & Davies and advertised as an additional volume to the four-volume Currie set.[37] Cromek's *Reliques* borrowed its title from Thomas Percy's *Reliques of Ancient English Poetry* (1765), a collection of ballads and songs, or what – generally – we might today call 'folk culture', further adding to Burns's populist mystique. As well as publishing new letters and information about Burns, Cromek's *Reliques* published many songs for the first time, garnering material and its context from a self-confessed pilgrimage (which in its religious undertone also helps connote the gathering of 'relics'). Cromek is explicit in his preface about his particular performative peregrinations as editor-cum-field-worker:

> I have followed the steps of the poet, from the humble Cottage in Ayrshire in which he was born, to the House in which he died at Dumfries. – I have visited the farm of Mossgiel where he resided at the period of his first publication; I have traversed the scenes by the Ayr, the Lugar, and the Doon. Sacred haunts![38]

This pilgrimage, it is implied, allows Cromek added empathy as well as content. Cromek more than any other sought his expanded authorised version, as he consulted the family of Burns and others such as the Campbells (the family of Burns's 'Highland Mary'). Following Currie's death, Cromek continued the former's project through the same close association with the Burns family and the publisher Cadell and Davies. The Cadell-Currie-Cromek axis was in competition, indeed, fought a veritable texts race with the publisher Thomas Stewart who was intent on supplying the hungry cheaper end of the market, that was similar to that for chapbooks. Within the partnership of Stewart and Meikle in Glasgow and printed by the hugely efficient printers Chapman and Lang, *The Poetical Miscellany containing posthumous Poems, Songs, Epitaphs and Epigrams by Robert Burns* (1800) gathered up a number of pamphlet-printings, including 'The Jolly Beggars', 'Holy Willie's Prayer' and 'The Kirk's Alarm' all of which were eschewed by Currie and Cromek due to explicit sexual and ecclesiastical political content they felt to be too controversial. Stewart also published for the first time in extenso another marked Burns 'performance', where that word is used quite precisely: the correspondence between Burns and Agnes Maclehose (1758–1841) under the pastoral pseudonyms of 'Sylvander' and 'Clarinda'.[39] This led to a lawsuit from Cadell and Davies in partnership with Burns's original Edinburgh publisher, William Creech and on behalf too of Burns's family which this grouping won.[40]

The popular Currie and Cromek editions kept the Burns canon on the conservative side for several decades, although by the 1830s editors were beginning to perform with more freedom. In some ways, superseding Currie and Cromek was the edition by 'Honest' Allan Cunningham (1784–1842), whose *The Works of Robert Burns* (1834) was published in eight volumes, aided by the fact that the material in Currie and Cromek had just come out of copyright. This added a handful of never-before-published songs and poems and several dozen new letters. Part of its selling-point, which fed into the sensibility behind *The Land of Burns* was that it produced a fuller version of Burns's prose 'Border Tour' than Currie had provided and Burns's *Journal of a Tour to the Highlands*. Cunningham's edition, however, from the start and in subsequent issues proceeded to produce several pieces of dubious authenticity, the most notorious, perhaps, being the lyrically-awful song, 'Happy Friendship'. This appears in Cunningham's 1840 edition of *The Works of Robert Burns*, with the claim that the editor had seen a manuscript owned by a Captain Hendries whose uncle, allegedly a friend of the poet's, had asked Burns to write his text for a party, which Cunningham 'now for the first time communicate[s] to the public'. Given his activity elsewhere across his version of the Burns canon, including producing a large amount of 'new' biographical information that is suspiciously unreliable, we might see Cunningham, indeed, as a 'performer'.

At the same time as Cunningham's edition also appeared *The Works of Robert Burns* (1834–6) in six volumes edited by James Hogg (1770–1835) and William Motherwell (1797–1835).[41] It contained fewer than a dozen new poems and songs and even fewer letters. Its book performance like all the major Burns editions for the rest of the century has to be seen in the context of books no longer being issued generally in paper covers or light-blue boards for subsequent bespoke binding by the purchaser but in elaborate bindings. Robert Chambers edited *The Poetical Works of Robert Burns* (1838), incorporating largely the work (including biography) of Currie, but adding a few new poems and letters to the canon.[42] Chambers's complex bibliographical trail of editions and issues of Burns includes his 'People's Edition' of 1840, and his work for *The Land of*

Burns. It can be seen in retrospect as the developing of ideas and collecting of biographical material which emerged in 1851 in a four-volume life of Burns which included all the poems, songs and prose in their correct chronological places. While his competitors were developing a new form of performance, the 'publisher's binding', often highly decorated, Chambers used new technologies to produce bindings which were very cheap and handsome, if not robust. The larger-scale edition of Burns in the tradition of Currie was to be found, indeed perhaps reached its peak, in *The Works of Robert Burns* (1877–9) in six volumes edited by William Scott Douglas (1815–1883) which expended a lot of good, scholarly effort publishing new letters and making sure these were properly dated.[43] Where Chambers had silently edited Burns's text to reflect his own views of propriety and fear of criticising the Kirk, Scott Douglas tried to be as true as he could to Burns's own words. Publishing of Burns in the nineteenth century also performed to the commemorative anniversaries of the centenary of the poet's birth in 1859 and death in 1896. In the case of the former we see the variegated market as remarked upon throughout this chapter, and as reported in *The Bookseller* for February 1859. This commented that Scotland was 'almost to a man, doing its hero-worship with a zeal and energy hitherto unexampled. There has been a great run on the poet's works throughout Scotland; and while high-priced editions have been in very considerable demand, the different low-priced editions have been largely purchased.'[44] In 1896 amid a plethora of new editions, William Wallace (1843–1921) revised Chambers's edition in *The Life and Works of Robert Burns* in four volumes with several dozen new letters published for the first time, and attempted to follow in the footsteps of Scott Douglas in particular in applying the most responsible standards of scholarship. A parallel interesting performative-commemorative element to 1896 was the *Tourist-Guide to the Land of Burns*, published by Glasgow & South Western Railway for use via their rail network.

Performing for the market, to ideas of the Scottish nation and people and towards the abstract notion of objective scholarship are all important factors in the performance of Burns in print during the nineteenth century. Much more might be said in future about the book-history and print performativity of editors and other producers of Burns editions as well as about Burns himself as an editor both scholarly and in his performative creativity.

Notes

1. Some of the research in this chapter is underpinned by the investigations of the Arts and Humanities Research Council project, 'Editing Robert Burns for the 21st Century: Correspondence and Poetry' (PI: Gerard Carruthers; award no: AH/P004946/1).

2. Lexico Online Dictionary: https://www.lexico.com/en/definition/performance
3. See, for instance, Peter Kivy, *The Performance of Reading: An Essay in the Philosophy of Literature* (Oxford: Blackwell, 2006).
4. Iain Beavan, 'Chapbooks, Cheap Print, Burns and Tannahill in the Nineteenth Century', *Scottish Literary Review* 11:2 (Autumn/Winter 2019), p. 70.
5. Ibid., p. 69.
6. Patrick Scott and Robert L. Betteridge, 'The Part Issue of Hately Waddell's *Life and Works of Robert Burns*', *Journal of the Edinburgh Bibliographical Society* 12 (2017), pp. 67–84, p. x.
7. George Gilfillan (ed.), *The National Burns* (London, Glasgow and Edinburgh: William Mackenzie, 1879–80), prefatory 'Prospectus' [n.p.]; for an illuminating discussion on the publication of Burns in parts through the nineteenth century, see Patrick Scott, 'Reading Burns in Instalments: The Hidden History of Part-Publication', *Robert Burns Lives!* Iss. 256 (2017): https://www.electricscotland.com/familytree/frank/burns_lives256.htm. Scott's essay also highlights the part-publication – and so market-versatility – of the big Burns editions from the 1830s, which adds nuance to but is not a central concern of the present essay.
8. Gilfillan, *National Burns.*
9. Ibid.
10. J. W. Egerer, *A Bibliography of Robert Burns* (Edinburgh: Oliver & Boyd, 1964), #425.
11. *The Scotsman*, 4 July 1838, p. 1g.
12. For instance, William Miller engraved seven plates for *The Land of Burns* in 1835–8, mostly at £35 or £42 a piece but 'Ayr' from Brown Carrick cost £50 (see *Memorials of Hope Park, Comprising some Particulars in the Life of William Miller* (London: privately printed, 1886), p. xxiv.
13. *The Scotsman*, 4 July 1838, p. 1g.
14. *The Scotsman*, 4 July 1838, p. 1g.
15. Described in *Land of Burns*, Volume 2, pp. 73–3.
16. *The Scotsman*, 20 March 1850, p. 3g.
17. *The Land of Burns*, 2 vols (Glasgow: Blackie & Son, 1840), Volume 1, facing p. 3.
18. Robert Brydall, *Art in Scotland; its Origin and Progress* (William Blackwood: Edinburgh, 1889), p. 419.
19. James Kinsley (ed.), *The Poems and Songs of Robert Burns*, Volume 3 (Oxford: Clarendon, 1968), p. 971.
20. An interesting, intensely performative reiteration (or reperformative iteration, perhaps) around Burns's first publication is the recycling of the title among over a dozen later poets, for instance, David Morison, *Poems,*

Chiefly in the Scottish Dialect (Montrose: David Buchan, 1790) and John Lauderdale, *A Collection of Poems Chiefly in the Scottish Dialect* (Edinburgh: J. Robertson, 1796) and including even the re-presentation of a much earlier poet under this badging, David Crauford [1665–1726], *Poems, Chiefly in the Scottish Dialect on Various Subjects* (Edinburgh: J. Pillans, 1798).

21. Kinsley (ed.), *The Poems and Songs of Robert Burns*, Volume 3, p. 971.
22. For further discussion, see Gerard Carruthers, *Robert Burns* (Tavistock: Northcote Press, 2006), pp. 7–10.
23. Kinsley (ed.), *The Poems and Songs of Robert Burns*, Volume 3, p. 977.
24. Ibid.
25. Murray Pittock (ed.), *The Scots Musical Museum I* (Volume 2 of the Oxford Edition of the Works of Robert Burns; Oxford: Oxford University Press, 2018), p. 11. Pittock's *SMM* comprises Volumes 2 and 3 of the OERB.
26. Ibid.
27. Patrick Scott, 'The First Publication of "Holy Willie's Prayer"', *Scottish Literary Review* 7:1 (Spring/Summer 2015), pp. 1–18.
28. See Gerard Carruthers, 'Thomas Muir and Kirk Politics', in G. Carruthers and D. Martin (eds), *Thomas Muir of Huntershill: Essays for the Twenty-First Century* (London: Humming Earth, 2016), pp. 142–8.
29. Francis Grose, *The Antiquities of Scotland II* (London: S. Hooper, 1791), pp. 31–2.
30. *The Merry Muses of Caledonia: A Vindication of Robert Burns in connection with the above publication and the spurious editions which succeeded it* (Privately printed for the Burns Federation, 1911), p. x.
31. *The Merry Muses: A Choice Collection of Favourite Scots Songs Gathered from many Sources* (Privately printed, 'not for sale', '1827').
32. See here the excellent revisionist work of R. D. Thornton, *James Currie: The Entire Stranger and Robert Burns* (Edinburgh: Oliver & Boyd, 1963).
33. See Henry Mackenzie's unsigned essay in *The Lounger* (9 December 1786), reprinted in Donald Low (ed.), *Robert Burns: The Critical Heritage* (London and Boston: Routledge & Kegan Paul, 1974), p. 70.
34. James Currie (ed.), *The Works of Robert Burns with an account of his life and a criticism of his writings*, 7th edn (London: Cadell and Davies, 1813), Vol. 1, p. 31.
35. Currie, *Works of Robert Burns*, Vol. 2, p. 425.
36. For instance, in a rather unlicensed publishing environment we find appearing *The Life and Works of Robert Burns, as originally edited by James Currie. To which is prefixed, a review of the life of Burns, and of various criticisms on his character and writings* edited by Alexander Peterkin (Edinburgh: Macredie, Skelly, and Muckersy, 1815). Peterkin was one of several 'editors' who believed that Currie's editorial model was basically sound, but that he could supersede or be re-performative of Currie in biographical and critical commentary.

37. Egerer, *Bibliography*, #151.
38. Robert Cromek, *Reliques of Robert Burns*, 2nd edn (London: Cadell and Davies, 1813), p. v.
39. *Letters Addressed to Clarinda by Robert Burns* (Glasgow: T. Stewart & A. Macgoun, 1802).
40. See Pauline Gray, 'Prudes, Pirates and Bills of Suspension: The Correspondence of Burns and "Clarinda"', *Burns Chronicle* (Autumn 2007), pp. 9–13.
41. James Hogg and William Motherwell (eds), *The Works of Robert Burns*, 6 vols (Glasgow: Archibald Fullarton, 1834–6).
42. Robert Chambers (ed.), *The Poetical Works of Robert Burns* (Edinburgh and London: W. & R. Chambers and W. S. Orr, 1838).
43. William Scott Douglas (ed.), *The Works of Robert Burns*, 6 vols (Edinburgh: William Paterson, 1877–9).
44. *The Bookseller* (February 1859). The best-selling cheaper editions were those by Routledge (Egerer, *Bibliography*, #633); Gall & Inglis (Egerer, *Bibliography*, #671) and William P. Nimmo (Egerer, *Bibliography*, #624).

3

Robert Burns and Theatre

Jim Davis with Tracy Cattell

During the eighteenth century, theatrical activity in Scotland increased exponentially, reflecting similar increases in other parts of Britain. Setting apart the various strands of non-professional activity, often celebrating specifically Scottish culture and language, the professional theatre in Scotland drew heavily on the English repertoire and could be seen, as Ian Brown puts it, as 'part of a conscious process of post-Union anglicisation'.[1] Initially, Scottish professional theatre developed in Edinburgh, although it faced early opposition from the Kirk, while other background factors such as 'the cost of theatre-going, class bias and, perhaps, cultural and linguistic resistance to anglicisation'.[2] also held it back. Nevertheless, by 1767, when the Canongate Theatre was awarded a patent (becoming entitled Theatre Royal Edinburgh until the new building with that title opened at the east end of Princes Street in 1769), regular attendance at the theatre seems to have been normal practice for the Edinburgh elite. John Jackson managed the theatre from 1781 to 1791, also taking on the management of the Theatre Royal, Dunlop Street, in Glasgow in 1782: members of Jackson's company played at both theatres. In 1791 Stephen Kemble acquired a one-year lease on both theatres; despite some difficulties in 1792–3, Kemble remained active in theatre management in Scotland through to the end of the eighteenth century. Professional touring circuits extended to other parts of the country beyond Edinburgh and Glasgow: by the 1780s Aberdeen was part of the circuit and by 1800 there were nine permanent theatres in Scotland, located at Edinburgh (2), Aberdeen, Glasgow, Dundee, Dumfries, Paisley, Ayr, Greenock, as well as facilities sufficient to house professional performances at Montrose, Inverness, Perth and Arbroath. In the latter years of the eighteenth century there was also increasing interaction with London theatres and actors, which inevitably impacted on the Scottish theatrical repertoire, despite the existence of an increasing number of home-based dramas.[3]

When Robert Burns, by now a celebrated poet, visited Edinburgh in 1786, he mixed in the highest social, cultural and artistic circles, even meeting John Home, the author of *Douglas*, while he was there. It is likely that Burns visited the Edinburgh theatre regularly, but there are only occasional references to theatre attendance in his letters. In February 1787 he talks of his plans to visit the theatre with the Reverend Archibald Lawrie and possibly Lawrie's sister, writing that 'As tonight the Grand Master and the Lodge of Masons appear at the Theatre in form, I am determined to go to the play.'[4] On 16 April, on the benefit night of William Woods, a leading actor at the Theatre Royal, Edinburgh, Woods spoke a prologue that Burns, a friend and masonic acquaintance, had written for him. The English-born Woods had joined the Edinburgh company in 1771 and remained in both city and company for thirty-one years, playing in both tragedy and sentimental comedy. Among the plays performed on his benefit evening was *The Merry Wives of Windsor*. The prologue flatters the Edinburgh audience:

> But here an ancient nation fam'd afar,
> For genius, learning high, as great in war.
> Hail, CALEDONIA, name for ever dear!
> Before whose sons I'm honour'd to appear!

Edinburgh is lauded not only as a centre of science, philosophy and history but also as the place where

> Douglas forms wild Shakespeare into plan,
> And Harley rouses all the God in man.[5]

And the prologue also refers to the freedom and taste of the Caledonian audience in anticipation of their judgment of Woods's performance.

In June 1788, Burns moved to Ellisland, close to Dumfries, combining farming with his work as an excise man. Eventually he gave up farming and settled in the town of Dumfries itself, remaining there until his death at the age of thirty-seven in July 1796. Although known as the 'Bard of Ayrshire' owing to his birth in Alloway, his commitment to the town in which he finally settled is reflected in his membership of the Royal Dumfries Volunteers which he joined in 1795 and the ongoing support which he demonstrated for the town's theatrical activities. Performances were given at the Assembly Rooms in the George Hotel, Dumfries, from 1789 to 1790 by an itinerant company under the management of George Stephen Sutherland. Sutherland was an actor, a member of the Edinburgh Theatre Royal company, apparently also having a role in leading companies presenting work outside the Central Belt: he and his company were active, for example, in the Dundee area where he recruited the actor-playwright Archibald Maclaren in 1783.[6]

Burns wrote Sutherland a New Year prologue, flattering the sense and good taste of the Dumfries audience and expressing gratitude for their support,[7] which, said Burns in a letter to his brother Gilbert, Sutherland subsequently 'had spouted to his Audience with great applause'.[8] Burns had written to Sutherland offering him the prologue on New Year's Eve:

> Jogging home yesternight it occurred to me that as your next night [is] the first night of the New Year, a few lines allusive to the Season, by way of Prologue, Interlude or what you please, might take pretty well. – The inclosed verses are very incorrect because they are almost the first crude suggestions of my Muse, by way of bearing me company in my darkling journey. – I am sensible it is too late to send you them; but if they can any way serve you, use, alter, or, if you please, neglect them. – I shall not be in the least mortified though they are never heard of; but if they can be of any service to Mr Sutherland and h[is] friends, I shall kiss my hand to my lady Muse, an[d] own myself much her debtor.[9]

In March 1790, Burns wrote *A Scots Prologue* for Sutherland's wife to deliver on her benefit night. Burns's commitment to the importance of preserving and championing Scotland's folk and cultural heritage is reflected in *A Scots Prologue,* which opens dramatically with what might be described as a culturally jingoistic promotion of Scotland's literary wealth and is underscored by strongly patriotic and nationalistic sentiments:

> What needs this din about the town of Lon'on,
> How this new Play an' that new Song is comin?
> Why is outlandish stuff sae meikle courted?
> Does nonsense mend, like Brandy, when imported?
> Is there nae Poet, burning keen for fame,
> Will baudily trie to gie us plays at hame?
> [. . .]
> There's themes enow in Caledonian story,
> Would shew the Tragic Muse in a' her glory.

Why use London as a source of the drama, says Burns, when, if only dramatists were available, there are so many Scottish subjects on which to draw. The prologue is polemical, a manifesto for a national drama:

> Is there no daring Bard will rise and tell
> How glorious Wallace stood, how hapless fell?

> Where are the Muses fled that could produce
> A *drama* worthy o' the name o' Bruce?
> [...]
> O for a Shakespeare, or an Otway scene,
> To paint the lovely, hapless Scottish Queen!
> [...]
> One Douglas lives in Home's immortal page,
> But Douglases were heroes every age.[10]

Although the prologue moves on to the players' dependency on the patronage of their audience, the need to support and foster a national drama and new writers is the prologue's central premise.

As Bruce Peter has noted, Dumfries was a prosperous town and a fashionable retreat in wintertime for families from southern Scotland who were 'avid patrons of the theatre'.[11] The generally positive response to Sutherland's company in Dumfries led to Sutherland approaching a number of influential local dignitaries, including Burns's amateur musician friend Robert Riddell, with a view to the erection of a permanent theatre in the town, a move strongly supported by Burns. He had a high opinion of Sutherland, claiming he had rarely met with 'a worthier or cleverer fellow'.[12] Writing to Frances Anna Wallace (Mrs Dunlop of Dunlop) around March 1790, to whom he sent a copy of Mrs Sutherland's benefit prologue, he stated:

> I have made a very considerable acquisition in the acquaintance of a Mr Sutherland, Manager of a co of Comedians at present in Dumfries. – The following is a prologue I made for his wife, Mrs Sutherland's benefit-night. – You are to understand that he is getting a new Theatre built here, by subscription; and among his Subscribers are all the first Names in the country.[13]

A month earlier Burns had been equally enthusiastic in a letter to his friend William Nichol, classics master at the Royal High School, Edinburgh:

> Our theatrical company, of which you have heard, leave us in a week. Their merit and character are indeed very great, both on the stage and in private life; not a worthless character among them, and their encouragement has been accordingly. Their usual run is from eighteen to twenty-five pounds a night; seldom less than one, and the house will hold no more than the other. There have been repeated instances of sending away six, and eight, and ten pounds in a night for want of room. A new theatre is to be built by subscription; the first stone is to be laid on Friday first to come. Three hundred guineas have been raised by thirty subscribers, and thirty more have been got if wanted.[14]

Plans for the new theatre were drawn up during 1790, its design to be based on the Theatre Royal, Bristol, and Thomas Boyd, who had previously superintended the building of a farmhouse for Burns, was appointed architect. The foundation stone was laid later in 1790 and the theatre, which could accommodate up to 600 people, opened on 29 September 1792. The overall cost had been £800, and the theatre's records indicate that many of the patrons who had filled the auditorium on the opening night were admitted by subscribers' tokens, granting entry to the bearers in thanks for a contribution made towards the funding of the theatre's construction.[15] The theatre continued to attract distinguished patrons to its performances, and gained its letters patent in 1811 following a visit by Queen Charlotte the previous season.

On the evidence of a sketch in the National Gallery of Scotland, referenced as a 'Design for a scene for the Dumfries Theatre, done at the desire of Robert Burns, by Alexander Nasmyth', it appears that Burns may have been instrumental in securing the artist Alexander Nasmyth to paint scenery for the theatre. At this time, Nasmyth was dependent for his livelihood on landscape painting and on painting theatrical scenery, having alienated many potential upper-class clients for portrait painting in Edinburgh on account of his liberal political views. Nasmyth was paid a fee of 100 guineas and may have designed the theatre's interior décor as well. Nasmyth had painted a portrait of Burns, with whom he became friendly, in 1787 for the publisher William Creech, who wished to use it as the basis of an engraving for a new edition of Burns's poetry.

At its opening, under the management of James Brown Williamson from the Theatre Royal, Haymarket, London, with Sutherland serving as assistant manager, the Dumfries theatre was considered 'the handsomest provincial theatre in Scotland' by the *Dumfries Weekly Journal*, which also claimed that

> The united elegance and accommodation of the house reflected equal honour on the liberality and taste of the proprietors, and design and execution of the artists, and conspired with the abilities of the performers in giving universal satisfaction to a crowded and polite audience.[16]

Although Burns had not contributed as a shareholder, he was on the theatre's free list thanks to the offices of Robert Riddell.

Within a month of the theatre's opening, Burns was implicated in a political disturbance that took place in the auditorium. In a period when the theatre auditorium provided a secular space for exhibitions of political dissent on the one hand and patriotism on the other, one's behaviour was inevitably under public scrutiny. On 28 October 1792, Burns allegedly remained seated with his hat on his head while the national anthem was played and supported the call for the French republican song 'Ça ira'. This placed his position as an Excise man in jeopardy (an anonymous report was sent to the Excise Board complaining of Burns's political disaffection) and he subsequently wrote in his own defence to his patron Robert Graham of Fintry, Commissioner of the Scottish Board of Excise, on 5 January 1793, denying any involvement in such subversion:

> It has been said, it seems, that I not only belong to, but head a disaffected party in this place [. . .] I was in the playhouse one night, when Ça ira was called for. I was in the middle of the pit, and from the pit the clamour arose. – One or two individuals with whom I occasionally associate were of the party, but I neither knew of the Plot, or joined in the Plot; nor ever opened my lips to hiss or huzza that or any other Political tune whatever – I looked on myself as far too obscure a man to have any weight in quelling a Riot; at the same time, as a character of higher respectability, than to yell in the howlings of a rabble – This was the conduct of all the first Characters in this place, & these Characters know, & will avow that such was my conduct. – I never uttered any invectives against the King –[17]

A month earlier he had described the occasion to Frances Anna Dunlop in slightly different terms:

> Indeed, we are a good deal in commotion ourselves, & in our Theatre here, "God Save the king" has met with some groans and hisses, while Ça ira has been repeatedly called for. – For me, I am a *Placeman*, you know; a very humble one indeed, Heaven knows, but still so much so as to gag me from joining in the cry. – What my private sentiments are, you will find out without an Interpreter. – In the mean time, I have taken up the subject in another view, and the other day, for a pretty Actress's benefit night, I wrote an Address [. . .] called *THE RIGHTS OF WOMAN.*[18]

Clearly Burns sympathised with the disaffected members of the audience and, as we shall see, used 'The Rights of Woman' address to introduce his own 'Ça ira' into the theatre's proceedings the following month.

One eye-witness account exists of Burns's behaviour on 28 October 1792, but it was written forty years after the event by Charles Sharpe, who was eleven when he witnessed the commotion:

> I know he was most woefully indiscreet on that point, and I remember one proof. We were at the play in Dumfries, in October 1792 – the Caledonian Hunt being then in town. The play was "As You Like it"; Miss Fontenelle *Rosalind*, when "God Save the King" was called for and sung we all stood up uncovered, but Burns sat still in the middle of the pit with his hat on his head.

> There was a great tumult, with shouts of 'Turn him out!—shame, Burns,' &c., which continued a good while. At last he was either expelled or forced to take his hat off [. . .] This silly conduct all sensible persons condemned.[19]

Burns's biographer James Alexander Mackay suggests this account is coloured by hostility that had long existed between Burns and the Sharpe family.

Despite Burns's alleged involvement in the disturbance described above, his support for the theatre continued and was manifested in two addresses that he wrote for the actress Louisa Fontenelle (1769/73–1799). She had performed at the Covent Garden Theatre in London in 1788 and then during the winter season at the Theatre Royal, Edinburgh from 1789 to 1790. She married the Dumfries manager, Williamson, whom she accompanied to America in 1795. On her Dumfries benefit night, which took place on 26 November 1792, she played Little Pickle in *The Spoiled Child* (Isaac Bickerstaffe) and the lead in *The Country Girl* (David Garrick's version of Wycherley's *The Country Wife*), roles made popular by the comic actress Dorothy Jordan in London. Then, after a re-enactment of Drake's victory over the Spanish Armada, she recited the address which was entitled 'The Rights of Woman'. Acknowledging the current interest in the *Rights of Man* (Burns had a copy of Tom Paine's publication, but kept it at a friend's house), Burns's prologue commences with a highly political and potentially subversive introduction, perhaps precipitated by the events of 28 October:

> While Europe's eye is fixed on mighty things,
> The fate of Empires and the fall of Kings;
> While quacks of State must each produce his plan,
> And even children lisp The Rights of Man;
> Amid this mighty fuss just let me mention,
> The Rights of Woman merit some attention.

Although Paine's *Rights of Man* had circulated widely since its publication in 1791, his trial *in absentia* for the dissemination of seditious libel – he was eventually found guilty of treason and sentenced to be hanged – was due to take place in December 1792, thus making Burns's allusion highly topical. While there is a playful element in Burns's reference to this 'mighty fuss', the implicit reference to Paine is quite possibly a political act, diffused when he subsequently turns his attention to the rights of woman. Here he highlights the importance of protection and decorum as the first two rights and then defines a third right:

> For Right the third, our last, our best, are dearest,
> That Right to fluttering Female hearts the nearest;

Which even the Rights of Kings, in low prostration,
Most humbly own – 'tis dear, dear Admiration!
In that blest sphere alone, we live and move;
There taste that life of life-immortal love-
Smiles, glances, sighs, tears, fits, flirtations, airs;
'Gainst such a host what flinty savage dares-
When awful Beauty joins with all her charms,
Who is so rash as rise in rebel arms?

However, the final lines give the address a highly political tone, already implicit in the earlier reference to the *Rights of Man*, drawing on the French revolutionary catch phrase and song, 'Ça ira':

But truce with kings, and truce with Constitutions,
With bloody armaments and Revolutions;
Let Majesty your first attention summon,
Ah! ça ira! THE MAJESTY OF WOMAN!!![20]

'Ça ira', even within the context Burns was using it, was a highly inflammatory slogan. While there is no evidence that audiences took offence at the revolutionary implications in Louisa Fontenelle's address, Burns is being deliberately provocative.

Immediately prior to her benefit, Burns had written Louisa Fontenelle an adulatory letter on 22 November 1792 in praise of her talents:

> Madam,
>
> In such a bad world as ours, those who add to the scanty sum of our pleasures, are positively our Benefactors – To you, Madam, on our humble Dumfries boards, I have been more indebted for entertainment, than ever I was in prouder Theatres. – Your charms as a woman would insure applause to the most indifferent Actress, & your theatrical talents would secure admiration to the plainest figure. – This Madam, is not the unmeaning, or insidious compliment of the Frivolous or Interested; I pay it from the same honest impulse that the Sublime of Nature excites my admiration, or her beauties give me delight. –
>
> Will the foregoing lines be of any service to you on your approaching benefit night? If they will, I will be prouder of my Muse than ever. – They are nearly extempore: I know they have no great merit but though they shall add but little to entertainment of the evening, they give me the happiness of an opportunity to declare how much I have the honour to be
>
> Madam, your very humble servant.[21]

A second undated letter urges Louisa Fontenelle to look over the address, as Burns wishes to send it to a periodical publication. He requests her to oblige him by including *The Wonder or A Woman Keeps a Secret* (Susanna Centlivre) and *The Spoiled Child* as her benefit plays, then quotes from *Winter* by James Thomson, a dramatist and poet he much admired:

> Ah, what an enviable creature you are! There now, this cursed gloomy blue devil day, you are going to a party of choice spirits:
>
> "To play the shapes
> Of frolic fancy, and incessant form
> Those rapid pictures, that assembled train
> Of fleet ideas, never join'd before,
> Where lively *wit* excites to gay surprise,
> Or folly-painting *humour*, grave himself
> Calls laughter forth, deep shaking every nerve."
>
> But as you rejoice with them that do rejoice, do also remember to weep with them that weep, and pity your melancholy friend.[22]

Just over a year later Burns sent another 'Address' for Louisa Fontenelle to deliver on her benefit night. In his accompanying letter Burns wrote:

> Inclosed is the "Address", such as it is; & may it be a prologue to an overflowing House! – If all the Town put together, have half the ardour, for your success & welfare, of my individual wishes, my prayer will certainly be granted. – Were I a man of gallantry & fashion, strutting & fluttering in the foreground of the picture of Life, making the speech to a lovely young girl might be construed to be one of the doings of All-powerful Love; but you will not be surprised, my dear Madam, when I tell you that it is not Love, nor even Friendship, but sheer Avarice – In all my justlings & jumblings, windings & turnings, in life, disgusted at every corner, as a man of the least taste & sense must be, with vice, folly, arrogance, impertinence, nonsense & stupidity, my soul has ever involuntarily & instinctively, selected as it were for herself, a few whose regard, whose esteem, with a Miser's Avarice she wished to appropriate & preserve. – It is truly from this case, ma chere Madamoiselle, that any the least service I can be of to you, gives me most real pleasure – God knows I am a powerless individual. And when I thought on my Friends, many a heart-ach [sic] it has given me. But if Miss Fontenelle will accept this honest compliment to her personal charms, amiable manner & gentle heart, from a man too proud to flatter though too poor to have his compliments of any consequence, it will sincerely ob[lige] her *anxious* Friend, & most devoted humble servant.[23]

Burns continues to perform the role of the humble, melancholy (but perhaps infatuated) poet in this rather convoluted letter.

The address was performed at the Dumfries Theatre on 4 December 1793. Fontenelle tells the audience that, 'Still anxious to secure your partial favour', she has sought out a poet to write her 'a Prologue, Epilogue, or some such matter', but he has resisted her penchant for comedy, since these 'are no laughing times'. Nevertheless, she rejects both the melancholic man and his love-sick counterpart, concluding that merriment is the best policy.[24] Ironically, the poet Burns who wants a resurgence of serious Scottish drama here makes a case for comedy, at least if it is performed by Louisa Fontenelle. Perhaps too the address contains an implicit recognition his talent is more for comedy than tragedy. (Subsequently, Burns sent a copy of Louisa Fontenelle's address to Mrs Dunlop, informing her that 'We have had a brilliant Theatre here, this season; only, as all other business has, it experiences a stagnation of trade from the epidemical complaint of the Country – "WANT OF CASH".')[25] Burns also wrote a poem 'To Miss Fontenelle, on Seeing Her in a Favourite Character', although neither is the character mentioned nor the poem dated:

Sweet naivete of feature,
Simple, wild enchanting elf,
Not to thee, but thanks to nature,
Thou art acting but thyself.

Wert thou awkward, stiff, affected,
Spurning nature, torturing art;
Loves and graces all rejected,
Then indeed thou'dst act a part.[26]

In a similar vein he wrote a short verse in praise of the actress Elizabeth Kemble, wife of actor-manager Stephen Kemble, moved by her performance as Yarico in George Colman the Younger's *Inkle and Yarico* at the Dumfries Theatre in 1794.[27]

Burns's support of the Dumfries theatre also extended to canvassing local support for actors' benefits. Thus, on 10 January 1793 he wrote to David Staig, Provost of Dumfries, stating that

> Among the Company of Players here there is one to whose merits, as an Actor, you must be no stranger; his name is Guion. – Strolling comedians are a class of folk with whom you will readily believe I wish to have very little communication. – When Mr Guion came here, he was introduced to my acquaintance by a friend of mine in Edinburgh, a gentleman of distinguished

> character there who begged me to serve Guion in anything I could with propriety do. – I have found Mr Guion to be truly what my friend represented him, a man of more than common information & worth. His Benefit comes on tomorrow night – Now Sir – is there any periphrasis of Language, any circumlocution of phrase, in which I could convey a request without at the same time seeming to convey it, that your Lady & lovely daughters would grace my friend Mr Guion's Boxes. – Such a petition I have no right to make – Nay, it is downright impertinence in me to make it, but if I were in your rank of life & you mine I would forgive you such a fault.[28]

Burns made a similar plea to Maria Banks Woodley Ridell, Robert Ridell's sister-in-law, whose home he visited regularly and whom he frequently met at the theatre:

> You were so good as to promise me to honour my friend with your presence on his benefit-night. That night is fixed for Friday first: the play is a most interesting one! *The Way to Keep Him*. I have the pleasure to know Mr G [F. J. Guion] well. His merit as an actor is generally acknowledged. He has genius and worth which would do honour to patronage: he is a poor and modest man; claims which from their very *silence*, have the more forcible power on the generous heart.[29]

Guion was an admirer and acquaintance of the Edinburgh poet Robert Fergusson, whose work had inspired Burns, and occasionally published verse himself.

Given Burns's interest in the theatre and his exhortations on behalf of a Scottish national drama, it is perhaps surprising that he never wrote any full-length dramas himself. He certainly had a good knowledge of both contemporary and older drama, regularly referencing Shakespeare, but also authors such as James Thomson and John Home. A letter written to the bookseller Peter Hill in March 1790 asks him to look out for cheap or second-hand copies of dramatic works by Otway, Ben Jonson, Dryden, Congreve, Wycherley, Vanbrugh, Cibber, Macklin, Garrick, Foote, Colman or Sheridan, adding that he also needs a good copy of Molière in French. He says he especially wishes the work of any other good dramatists in their native language, comic authors chiefly, although copies of Racine, Corneille and Voltaire are also sought. While Burns is in no hurry for any of these works, the list implies a desire for easy access to the works of many major British and French dramatists.[30]

Burns's 'Prologue for Mrs Sutherland', implying the need for a new generation of major Scottish dramatists, suggests that perhaps he saw himself in this role. In 1788 he informed Robert Graham, through whom he hoped to obtain a position of excise man, that he was thinking of writing a drama:

> I am thinking of something in the rural way of the Drama-kind. Originality of character is, I think, the most striking beauty in that Species of Composition, and my wanderings in the way of my business would be vastly favourable to my picking up original traits of Human nature.[31]

Just over a year later he wrote to another of his patrons, Lady Elizabeth Cunningham:

> I have some thoughts of the Drama. – Considering the favourite things of the day, the two & three act pieces of O'Keefe, Mrs Inchbald &c. does not your ladyship think that a Scotish Audience would be better pleased with the Affectation, Whim & Folly of their own native growth, than with manners which to by far the greatest of them can be only second hand? – No man knows what Nature has fitted him for until he try; and if I after a preparatory course of some years' study of Men and Books, I should find myself unequal to the task, there is no great harm done –Virtue and Study are their own reward. – I have got Shakespeare, and begun with him; and I shall stretch a point and make myself master of all the Dramatic authors of any repute, in both English and French, the only languages which I know.[32]

Burns also discussed a possible subject for a drama with Ramsay of Ochertyre, to be called *Rob Macquechan's Elshon*, based on 'a popular story of Robert Bruce being defeated on the water of Caern, when the heel of his boot having loosened in his flight, he applied to Robert Macquechan to fit it; who, to make sure, ran his awl nine inches up the king's heel'.[33]

Despite intimations that he intended to write for the stage, Burns never completed any dramas and the representation of his published work on stage was largely contingent. *The Banks of Ayr* was set to music in his lifetime and became well-known, popularised originally by Sutherland's company. Posthumously songs originating from Burns works were included in various dramas; for instance, Isaac Pocock's version of Scott's *Rob Roy* (1818) included 'Auld Lang Syne' and 'Oh my Love is Like a Red Red Rose', sung by Francis Obaldiston, and 'A Highland Lad my Love was Born', sung by Diana Vernon. Pocock's adaptation was performed in 1818 at the Theatre Royal, Covent Garden and in 1819 at the Theatre Royal, Edinburgh, where it was phenomenally successful. In 1812 a 'Melo-dramatic entertainment, *Tam O'Shanter, and his mare Maggie*', based on Burns's poem, 'with a scotch overture – scotch music – scotch dresses – and scotch dances', was performed at the Theatre Royal Edinburgh.[34] A adaptation of the posthumously published 'The Jolly Beggars' was performed at the Caledonian Theatre, Edinburgh in March 1823.[35] A dramatisation of 'Tam o' Shanter', staged at London's

Coburg Theatre in 1820, was one of several London adaptations based on Burns's poem. However, Robert Burns's most significant contributions to Scottish theatre still rest on the existence of several published prologues and addresses, his support for the Dumfries Theatre Royal, evidence of visits to the theatre in Edinburgh and Dumfries, and his advocacy of a national drama.

Notes

1. Ian Brown, *Scottish Theatre: Diversity, Language, Continuity* (Amsterdam and New York: Rodopi, 2013), p. 82.
2. Ian Brown, 'Eighteenth-Century Scottish Drama and the Contestation of National Identities', *International Journal of Scottish Theatre and Screen* 8:1 (2015), p. 10.
3. For an overview of the rise of professional theatre in Scotland in the eighteenth century, see Adrienne Scullion, 'The Eighteenth Century', in Bill Findlay (ed.), *A History of Scottish Theatre* (Edinburgh: Polygon, 1998), pp. 80–136.
4. J. De Lancey Ferguson and G. Ross Roy (eds), *The Letters of Robert Burns Volume 1 1781–1789*, 2nd edn (Oxford: Oxford University Press, 1985), p. 92.
5. Prologue Spoken by Mr WOODS on his Benefit Night', in James Kinsley (ed.), *The Poems and Songs of Robert Burns Volume 1* (Oxford: Oxford University Press, 1968), pp. 330–1. Harley was the hero of Henry Mackenzie's novel *The Man of Feeling* (1771).
6. Ian Brown and Gioia Angeletti, 'Cultural Crossings and Dilemmas in Archibald Maclaren's Playwriting', in Christopher MacLachlan and Ronald W. Renton (eds), *Gael and Lowlander in Scottish Literature: Cross-Currents in Scottish Writing in the Nineteenth Century* (Glasgow: Scottish Literature International, 2015), p. 44.
7. 'Prologue Spoken at the Theatre of Dumfries', in Kinsley (ed.), *Poems and Songs Volume 1*, pp. 498–9.
8. Ferguson and Roy (eds), *The Letters Volume 2*, p. 3.
9. Ferguson and Roy (eds), *The Letters Volume 1*, pp. 465–6.
10. 'Scots Prologue, *For Mrs Sutherland's* Benefit Night, Spoken at the Theatre Dumfries', in Kinsley (ed.), *The Poems and Songs of Robert Burns Volume 2*, pp. 543–4.
11. Bruce Peter, *Scotland's Splendid Theatres* (Edinburgh: Edinburgh University Press, 1999), pp. 166–7.
12. Ferguson and Roy (eds), *The Letters Volume 2*, p. 12.
13. Ferguson and Roy (eds), *The Letters Volume 2*, pp. 22–3. Mrs Dunlop of Dunlop, a widowed grandmother, had entered into a correspondence with Burns after reading his poetry.

14. Ferguson and Roy (eds), *The Letters Volume 2*, p. 12.
15. Website of the Theatre Royal, Dumfries, URL https://www.theatreroyal-dumfries.co.uk/theatre-history (accessed 17 November 2019).
16. *Dumfries Weekly Journal*, 3 October 1792, cited in *Bruce Peter, Scotland's Splendid Theatres: Architecture and Social History from the Reformation to the Present Day* (Edinburgh: Polygon, 1999), p. 166.
17. Ferguson and Roy (eds), *The Letters Volume 2*, p. 173.
18. Ferguson and Roy (eds), *The Letters Volume 2*, p. 166.
19. Quoted in James Alexander Mackay, *Burns: A Biography of Robert Burns* (Edinburgh: Mainstream Publishing Company Ltd, 1992), p. 518.
20. 'The Rights of Woman – Spoken by Miss Fontenelle on her Benefit Night', in Kinsley (ed.), *The Poems and Songs of Robert Burns Volume 2*, pp. 661–2.
21. Ferguson and Roy (eds), *The Letters Volume 2*, pp. 160–1.
22. Ferguson and Roy (eds), *The Letters Volume 2*, p. 161.'Weep with them that weep' is from Romans 12: 15.
23. Ferguson and Roy (eds), *The Letters Volume 2*, pp. 262–3.
24. 'Occasional Address, Spoken by Miss Fontenelle, on her Benefit Night', in Kinsley (ed.), *The Poems and Songs Volume 2*, p. 721.
25. Ferguson and Roy (eds), *The Letters Volume 2*, p. 269.
26. 'To Miss Fontenelle, on Seeing Her in a Favourite Character', in Kinsley (ed.), *The Poems and Songs Volume 2*, p. 723.
27. 'On Seeing Mrs Kemble in Yarico', in Kinsley (ed.), *Poems and Songs Volume 2*, p. 746.
28. Ferguson and Roy (eds), *The Letters Volume 2*, p. 178.
29. Ferguson and Roy (eds), *The Letters Volume 2*, p. 177.
30. Ferguson and Roy (eds), *The Letters Volume 2*, p. 20.
31. Ferguson and Roy (eds), *The Letters Volume 1*, p. 314.
32. Ferguson and Roy (eds), *The Letters Volume 1*, pp. 464–5.
33. Robert Burns, 'Appendix to Biographical Sketch: Sketches by Mr Ramsay of Ochertyre', in *The Complete Works of Robert Burns*, ed. John S. Roberts (Edinburgh: William P. Nimmo, 1865), p. lxxii.
34. Barbara Bell, 'The Nineteenth Century', in Findlay (ed.), *A History of Scottish Theatre*, p. 140.
35. James C. Dibdin, *The Annals of the Edinburgh Stage* (Edinburgh: Richard Cameron, 1888), p. 341.

4

Burns and Music Hall

Paul Maloney

The music hall that emerged in Scotland's cities and towns in the 1840s and 1850s was a dynamic new entertainment format that attracted working-class audiences by offering a synthesis of old and new performances. Born in so-called 'free and easies', informal singing sessions sponsored by publicans, and in larger singing saloons, music hall, with its well-oiled conviviality and audience participation in joining in with the choruses of songs, quickly came to embody the outlook and tastes of urban audiences. In Glasgow by the late 1840s 'the music saloons extend[ed] from Buchanan Street to the Saltmarket, and in their several phases flourish alike in the East and in the West'.[1] By the 1880s an estimated 40,000 people a week attended the city's music halls.[2] Although an urban form, which was ostensibly about all that was fashionable and modern, music hall also offered important continuities with older, pre-industrial entertainments centred on the fair and the showground, recycling a wide range of traditional songs and performance material for a new urban context.

Establishing the place of Burns material in this performing mix, and the extent to which its performance and reception might have developed in the course of the music hall's many changes over the next eighty years, which saw it rebranded as variety theatre from the 1890s, is challenging. Press reporting of music halls tended to focus on performers' new repertoire; as Burns songs were regarded as standards, part of the body of Scottish songs, their inclusion was often not considered worthy of special comment. (We can, though, make informed assumptions: when a press review of the Milton Colosseum in Glasgow dated 26 January 1862 reports that 'The Scotch songs of Mr T Bishop, given in full Highland costume, are well received', we might expect them to include not only Jacobite songs, but also, given the season, very probably Burns.)[3]

From the 1850s, Burns's place in music hall seems to relate to questions of the control of his legacy, articulating with several contemporary debates concerning the role of music in popular culture and entertainment. These are, first, the question that musicologist and collector Gavin Greig raised, of whether Burns songs were really art music, rather than forming part of the body of traditional folk song of working people, which echoes similar questions about music hall's own status; secondly, the competition between sections of the temperance movement and the commercial music hall to appropriate Burns's creative legacy to their own ends; thirdly, the tendency to claim Burns songs for the concert platform, rather than popular stages, part of a wider drive by middle-class reformers to improve the quality of music available to working-class audiences.

First, while Greig describes the work of Burns, and of writers like Tannahill, Hogg and Scott, as 'book songs' which 'have never been the songs of the mass of the Scottish people', rather than true folk songs – essentially for their literary qualities and construction failing the test of easy singability – he makes an important distinction: that while the rural singer (he says 'rustic') 'will hardly himself sing the songs of Burns, he will sing *about* Burns *and* his songs, but it must be in lays which have got the folk-song hall-mark'. He gives as an example the success of 'The Cottage where Robbie was Born'.[4] Greig's argument is about rural society, and has been dismissed by some modern writers as being based on false assumptions about class that did not take into account the oral tradition from which many Scottish folk songs derived, or the relative cultural homogeneity of Scottish society.[5] But what is historically interesting – and useful – about his distinction is that it resonates with contemporary questions of whether music hall – which subsequently produced many songs about Burns, doing much to memorialise and celebrate his iconic status – was itself 'artificial', or rather the urban inheritor of the inclusiveness of older pre-industrial entertainments. We will return to this.

On the second debate, the temperance movement's claim on Burns did not deny the poet's love of drink, but embraced it as evidence of the all-too human fallibility of even this greatest of artists. The adoption of Burns as exemplar of the need for abstinence was reflected in Temperance Burns celebrations which, while celebrating his genius, lamented that 'the cruel power of the social glass laid hold of him, led him astray and cut short his days'. If in no sense an example to be followed, Burns remained 'a beacon of light [. . .] to all men flashing across life's ocean, telling the rocks and dangers ahead'.[6] The conclusion that 'If ever the duty of abstinence could be drawn and enforced from the life of any man it is from the life of Burns' was reinforced by temperance insistence that the poet had in his final days renounced his past life.

On the third area, his songs – or a sub-set of them – were featured by middle-class social reformers concerned to improve the discernment of Scottish audiences by raising the standard of musical appreciation. An 1860s article promoting plans for a Glasgow Orchestral Concert Society suggested: 'To those who are unacquainted with the fact, it will be surprising to learn how largely working people patronise such musical entertainments as are placed within their reach in our own city.'[7] However, because these entertainments were mostly experienced in music halls like the Britannia and Scotia, and largely consisted of 'comic singing and vulgar buffoonery', reformers quickly established popular concert series to promote 'more select music' or 'the spread of a purer taste'.[8] Burns songs were included in these concerts as part of the body of traditional Scottish songs and ballads, often listed as simply 'Scottish' or 'Scotch' items, but particularly featured in dedicated Scottish festivals and Burns concerts. There, whole programmes of Burns were performed by professional singers, often including music-hall artists.[9]

The initial popularisers of Burns on the concert stage were John Wilson (1800–1849) and John Templeton (1802–1886), classically-trained singers who presented his work in programmes of Scottish songs.[10] Wilson performed his 'A Nicht wi' Burns', one of his 'Scottish Entertainments', widely from 1843, while Templeton, who enjoyed an illustrious operatic career, appearing opposite Malibran at Covent Garden, achieved similar success with his 'Beauties of Burns' which, like Wilson's selections, were published as song collections. Both singers toured internationally, appearing extensively in North America, and were regarded as iconic performers. Moreover, in combining concerts and recitals with stage work and a strong identification with Burns commemorations, they provided a model of portmanteau careers that would be followed by their successor David Kennedy (1825–1886), who made his breakthrough singing at the 1859 Burns Centenary celebrations in Liverpool, and subsequent Scottish singers from Durward Lely (1852–1944) and J. M. Hamilton (1854–1939) to Robert Wilson (1907–1964) and Kenneth McKellar (1927–2010). Indeed, Scottish performers from the 1850s and 1860s on were happy to straddle different constituencies, combining engagements in music halls and singing saloons, and in concert parties touring rural areas, with appearances in concerts, soirees and social functions.

Burns in Popular Entertainment Culture

The presence of Burns's songs at concerts and soirees did not lessen their appeal in music hall, which, with different emphases, would have reflected his popularity in the 'rough' entertainment culture of popular theatre and fairground amusements to which music hall was related. Popular entertainments demonstrated Burns's appeal for working-class audiences through different media: stone figures of characters from 'The Cotter's Saturday Night' by the self-taught Anderson were exhibited at Glasgow Fair in 1844; the following year these or another set of statues of the same subject attracted 1,800 people to Gemmell's booth on their first night at the 1845 Glasgow Fair, proving markedly more popular there than with aristocratic audiences in the West End.[11] Meantime, popular visual culture, in the form of dioramas, illustrated talks and magic-lantern shows, attested to the popularity of Burns and his works across a range of subjects: Birrell's New Great Diorama of Scotland and Grand Scottish Concert presented amongst its topographical views 'The Land of Burns', showing Burns' Cottage, Alloway Kirk, Banks and Braes o' Bonnie Doon and Burns' Monument, and concluded with a grand finale of 'Auld Lang Syne' sung by the full company in Highland costume.[12] More biographically focused, a Grand National Entertainment at the Union Hall, Dundee in 1875 depicted 'The Land and Works of Robert Burns' with thirty-nine illuminated diorama views, alongside which appeared a soprano and tenor (who sang 'Ye Banks and Braes', 'Flow Gently, Sweet Afton', 'A Man's a Man', 'To Mary in Heaven'), a Scotch comic and a lecturer who recited 'The Cotter's Saturday Night' and 'Tam o' Shanter'.[13] On a more modest scale, the comedian James Houston (1828–1892) acquired a pair of magic lanterns with 200 slides and, with his wife as operator, worked up a successful descriptive lecture which 'teemed with racy anecdotes and humorous Scotch stories', songs and instrumental music, his lime-light view of the witches' dance in 'Tam o' Shanter' being 'one of the choicest, and the apt quotation from the poem itself, well merit[ing] the hearty applause with which it was received'.[14]

So too in popular drama. While Tam and Souter Johnny were popular characters in the booth theatres,[15] the licentious Cutty Sark was often a pretext for salacious displays of the female form, not only in the bawdier shows on Glasgow Green but even sometimes unwittingly in more upmarket theatres royal. There, middle-class theatregoers found it hard to reconcile anything approaching accurate stage depictions of Burns's character with contemporary mores: at one 1871 Glasgow pantomime of 'Tam o Shanter', sections of the audience were so offended by the 'scantiness' of Cutty's dress that they reportedly hissed the actress concerned on the first night, causing the management to tone down the scene, provoking a debate in the press.[16] In some other 'Tam' pantomimes Cutty was played dame-style by a cross-dressing male comic, thereby defusing the character's challenging sexual politics with a safer, more generalised knockabout misogyny.

Burns straddled and overlapped these two worlds – the politer, decorous environment of the public concert platform and the more raucous popular stages of the music hall and fairground. Reflecting this interconnectedness, representative of a cultural cohesion characteristic of Scottish society, performers often overlapped these different sectors, working in music halls and singing saloons whilst also appearing in a range of concerts, where Burns songs are more readily traceable.

Scotch Comics

Scotch comics of the 1860s to 1890s came from more diverse professional backgrounds and often made Burns material a central feature of their performances. Of these, James Houston and James Lumsden (1836–1899) were essentially concert singers and recitalists, who presented entertainments – often effectively one-man shows – where they recited, told stories and jokes, and sang a wide range of familiar Scots songs in which Burns featured prominently. Most came from working-class backgrounds – Houston had been an engineer, W. F. Frame (c. 1847–1919) a grocer in a family business – and used their memberships of professional networks which furthered Burns appreciation, particularly masonic and temperance organisations, as lifelong networks of influence. While Houston made great use of his masonic contacts and affiliation to trades bodies, Frame's status as a Good Templar and active churchman opened many doors.

Music hall's own promotion of working-class Burns appreciation was evident in a spate of songs calling for the raising of a statue of Burns in George Square, Glasgow.[17] While such campaigns are often identified with wealthy benefactors and business interests, these songs, published by the Poet's Box, a Glasgow printers which ran off penny broadsheet versions of the latest music-hall numbers, reflected support for a statue amongst working-class audiences, usually on the grounds of what was felt to be the social injustice of Burns's omission as the voice of the people. Often expressed in portmanteau songs providing 'what if?' musings on current issues of local concern ('In a Quiet Sort of Way', 'Shadows in the Stream'), the more assertive 'The Hale Jing-Bang' complained about the injustice of a statue of Walter Scott's being included in the square while 'Scotia's poet – is not exalted high':

> Nae doubt, at telling o' a story, Watty Scott he did excel
> But for a guid auld Scotch song, Rabbie Burns he beats the bell;
> And for touching the heart cords o' the folks he leeves amang –
> The immortal Burns he'll aye excel the Hale Jing-Bang.[18]

The protagonist of 'Camlachie Tam', written for the Britannia Music Hall around 1869, similarly looked 'roon a' the monuments' in George Square, but 'couldna see a stane ava to our auld frien' Rabbie Burns', concluding 'I'm sure I think its wrang / There's room for ane tae staun', / Tae see ane up immediately wad please Camlachie Tam.'[19] Scottish music-hall performers, who quickly became leading advocates of Burns performance and made sure they featured prominently in Burns anniversaries and festivals, were happy to embrace the overlapping spheres of influence of the different interests coalescing round Burns, which often played out to their professional advantage.

Frame used the same convivial tone ('Brither Scots, when freens meet, herts warm') in his 1898 speech at Carnegie Hall in New York, while Houston often referenced Burns in sketches and monologues such as 'Scottish Oatmeal', which, beginning 'Let epicures brag o' their Frenchified dishes', clearly drew on the Address to the Haggis.[20] Houston, a gifted recitalist and comic singer, was a long-time Burns advocate. At his concert at the Merchants Hall, Glasgow, in 1860, alongside turns from the city's singing saloons, he 'sang some of Burns' songs in a style that insured him several hearty encores'.[21] Houston went on to act in the national drama with great success – as Bailie Nicol Jarvie and Dumbiedykes – and was praised for his dame-style impersonation of the long-suffering Kate in a revival of 'Tam o' Shanter' at the Gaiety in Glasgow, 'causing much laughter by his faithful representation of Tam's masculine spouse'.[22] As skilled raconteurs and storytellers, Scotch comics like Houston and Frame constantly conjured up vividly drawn characters as vehicles for their songs and patter; it was a natural extension of their comic skills to bring Burns's characters to life in sketch form.

Tam and Souter Johnny were perfect vehicles for extemporising, being endlessly refreshable bar-room types – the Francie and Josie of their day – whom Scottish audiences adored. So, when Houston teamed up with the 'Tam' of the comic singer James Lumsden in a celebrated partnership as the characters, a resulting tour in the summer of 1878 – publicised as 'Tam O' Shanter and Souter Johnnie are Coming!!! ... Look out for the Cronies!!' – which took them as far north as Shetland, proved one of the highlights of their careers, even if Houston got into hot water in Lerwick by (he claimed) unwittingly impugning the character of an incensed local woman who shared the same name as a figure in his comic song 'Peter Carmichael', provoking a heated incident which Burns would surely have appreciated.[23]

These concert parties brought their own up-to-date music-hall innovations to the presentation of Burns. In a Lumsden entertainment, given by his Scottish Minstrels at Falkirk in 1875, the second half, entitled the 'Songs of Scotland', featured Lumsden and Houston, in character as Tam and Souter Johnny, acting as corner men in the familiar format used by blackface minstrel troupes: described as 'somewhat of a novelty', '"Tam" occupied the left and "Johnny" the right of the platform, the company being placed between, singing songs singly or together as called upon alternatively by the two presiding "worthies"', each song 'being introduced by a few lines of peasant rhyme' which 'kept the audience in the best of humour'.[24]

Willie Frame similarly harnessed the theatrical potential of Burns's cantata 'The Jolly Beggars', which he claimed in his autobiography to have performed 'for the first time in a music hall' in Sir Henry Bishop's musical arrangement, touring his version as the second half of his concert party's variety programme, in the spring of 1886 to venues including Arbroath, Forfar, Banff, Buckie, Elgin and Forres, before running it for a week at his own Frame's Royal Concert Hall in Glasgow. But, although Frame regarded it as a major achievement, 'The Jolly Beggars', which clearly lent itself to characterisation and staging, had been produced by music-hall performers on previous occasions.[25] An 1872 performance by the Queen's Minstrels at Hengler's Cirque in Glasgow was advertised as 'The first time in character', while the cantata had been seen in a music-hall context in London, at the Oxford Music Hall, as early as June 1862.[26]

Parodies, Sketches and Recitations

While Burns remained a useful standby resource for working professionals, nevertheless music hall, as a reactive medium that was all about fashion and the latest styles, also required a constant stream of new material to keep audiences diverted. One response was to utilise the familiarity of Burns songs in parodies which allowed them to be recast as topical material. Parodies, a key feature of burlesque and a stalwart of Victorian performing culture, were highly popular in music hall. While Scottish songs such as 'The Braes of Balquidder' were ripe for parodying ('Will ye come, lassie, come, / Tae the Braes of Balquither, / Say that ye'll come, lass, / But dinna tell yer mither.'),[27] Burns songs were particularly popular, and allowed for a range of satirical approaches. 'Comin Through the Rye', 'The Lea Rig', 'My Love is Like a Red, Red, Rose' and 'Sweet Afton' were all much parodied, an anonymous version of the last being typical of the style:

> Flow gently sweet river and don't mak' a noise
> My Mary is sleepin', so let us rejoice,
> An' if she waukens up – whit a riot you'll see:
> I wish she'd sleep on tae the day she dis dee.
>
> Thou blackbird wi' whusslin' alairms a' the place,
> I wish maist sincerely ye wid shut yer face;
> If you keep on whusslin' I'll no cry encore,
> For I'll get then whit I've got before.[28]

This typified one broad comic style, while others involved creative punning and wordplay. The opening of 'O' a' the Pairts in Pollokshaws' – a 'Parody on "O' a' the Airts the Wind can Blaw"' – runs:

Oh a' the pairts in Pollokshaws
I dearly lo'e the West,
'Twis there I gaithered hips an' haws,
An' hairret mony a nest.
I've been in countries whaur I couldna'
Settle doon because
This hairt o' mine wis ever wi'
The queer folk in the 'Shaws.

I left a female lassie there,
The brawest in the toon,
She weers a diamond ring o' mine---
It cost me hauf a croon.
O steer my barque tae Erin's Isle
Across the wattery sea,
An' tak' me back tae Shollokpaws,
An' Bonnie Bessie Lee.[29]

The semi-professional songwriters of *Barr's Professional* produced a stream of Burns parodies for the Scottish domestic market, but some originated further afield. 'Tarry Woo', performed by the Scottish-born star Charles Coborn (1852–1945) of 'The Man who Broke the Bank at Monte Carlo' fame, to the tune of 'Whistle o'er the Lave o't', which he sang at the Britannia in Glasgow 'with immense success', begins:

Noo, by my troth, ilk brither dear,
I trow ye're a' richt welcome here,
We'll prove to mirth our title clear,
But winna' prove the slave o't.
Dowf and dowie be his lot,
Whae'er denies a brither Scot,
Wi' helpin' haun' tae share a groat,
If want shall mak' him crave o't.

(Chorus)
Here's to the land o' bonnets blue,

Tartan kilts, and tarry woo';
Oh, for a waught o' mountain dew!
To toast the guid and brave o't.[30]

Some topical parodies riffed on political events – such as the later 'Joe Chamberlain, my Joe' – while others used the popularity of Burns's songs to promote reforming messages. 'The Templar's Address to his Band', subtitled 'Parody on "Scots Wha' Hae"', by Daniel Jeffrey, uses the stirring tune to blunt but powerful effect.

> Scots, who scarcely can get bread,
> Scots, whom boose has often led
> To a cheap and dirty bed
> 'Mang the lively fleas.
>
> Now's the day and now's the hour,
> While ye ha'e it in your power
> Gi'e your drinking habits o'er,
> Mend your crookit ways.
>
> You're a fool, but not a knave,
> See what money you could save,
> Drink leads to an early grave,
> And to poverty.[31]

A contrast to such proselytising was the nonsense style of James Curran (1863–1900), known as the 'Parody King' and the most famous exponent of these pieces, whose own 'Parody on "Scots Wha' Hae"', written for the exuberant Willie Frame, is just the sort of irreverent comic nonsense song in which Frame specialised.

> Scots wha hae, wa ha, wha hoo,
> See the price o' kippers noo,
> I'd like to eat a clapped doo,
> That's comin' through the pook. [fermented distillery worts]
> Wha for Scotlan's king or law,
> Wad ha'e such feeds as this ava?
> Better eat biled tatties raw,
> And lots o' guid soor dook. [buttermilk][32]

Comic recitations being highly popular, the influence of 'Tam o' Shanter' was widely evident. Its most enduring parody, 'The Goalkeeper's Ghost', remembered as pawkily rendered at benefit performances of the 1890s by Ritchie Thom, the former manager of the Scotia Music Hall,[33] transmutes the story to modern Glasgow. As the protagonist staggers home in the early hours past a graveyard as the clock strikes two, he sees a football match under way with the devil presiding as referee:

My heid, I think, began tae reel–
That kirkyaird look'd a fitba' field,
There stood the goalposts gapin' wide,
An' there the players--eleven-a-side;
An' crutches there for every man,
Forbye a ghostly ambulance van.
Wan goalkeeper there did staun,
A fireclay brick in ev'ry haun;
The ither business meant an' a',
Held in his fist a j'iner's saw.

But what wis referee – I look'd –
A tail he had an' horns sae crook'd;
I glowered--gey funny I did feel--
It wis his "Nabs" himself, the deil.[34]

Beyond these parodies, Burns's songs were adapted and repurposed for a wide variety of performing usages, their familiarity making the songs part of a body of popular work which felt like common property.

'The howff of genius': Burns and Music-Hall Culture

While we have discussed different impacts of Burns on music hall – through parodies, sketches and recycling of his songs – Burns also influenced its tone and style. The informal professional sub-culture of the Scottish music hall of the 1850s and 1860s, in these early years a cottage industry centred on the boozy conviviality of the singing saloons, had a very Burnsian feel to it. The Whitebait in St Enoch's Wynd, one of Glasgow's leading early singing saloons, was remembered as 'a howff of genius', frequented by 'the famous singers and authors and composers of the day, among whom were Hamilton Nimmo, the chairman, and Willie Jackson, a cello player, who wrote the tune of "The Lass o' Ballochmyle" and "The Dear Little Shamrock"'.[35] One anecdote concerned the poet Andrew Parks, a regular habitué, who, being hard up, met his friend John Fulcher there. Fulcher, taking some of Parks's lyrics, quickly knocked out a melody on the Whitebait piano.

> Thence they repaired to a music-seller's, and, after considerable haggling, sold their latest composition for a guinea, which was spent almost entirely that evening on a sumptuous repast. Thus was composed and launched into the world the popular national song 'Where has Scotland Found her Fame?'[36]

This sense of a free-spirited body of songwriters for whom Burns was an exemplar and inspiration was still evident in the 1890s, particularly among the circle associated with *Barr's Professional*, when the passing of several leading songsmiths produced tributes that linked them to the stream of earlier Scottish voices and Burns in particular.

A recurring theme involved material that imagines Burns brought back to life and bemused by the changes he encounters in modern society. One such piece of journalistic whimsy featured 'Tam o' Shanter Up-To-Date', a parody of the style of music-hall songs of the 1890s:

Round the town I went a strolling
Met the boys and soon was rolling
On a rare old fair old tiddley canter
All the girls were smiling winking
All the bobbies they were blinking
Shouting – 'Hi, there goes old Tam o' Shanter'

(Chorus – con amore)
I'm Tam o' Shanter, the pet of all the gels;
I'm Tam o' Shanter, the swelliest of swells.
You behold my changed condition
Since you read my first edition
Clear the way for good old Tam o' Shanter.[37]

Seventy years later the same idea inspired a 1970s sketch for Jimmy Logan (1928–2001), in which Burns, to the strains of 'Rantin' Rovin' Robin', walks back into Nancy Poosie's from the gents and tells his disbelieving drinking companions that he has returned from time travelling to Scotland centuries into the future ('Man, man I've been oot in the stars amang – twa hundred years'):

TAM: You're glaikit Rab or else you're fu'
A minute's sine or maybe two
You trotted out to find the loo
Quick as a fox
RAB: And I found myself with a Dr Who
In a wee police box.

Rab's stream of wry observations on contemporary society, and its social and sexual mores – which now say more about the social conservatism of Scotland in the 1970s than Burns's legacy – include that 'they hae this thing called the Welfare State' that 'pay[s] ye ower and ower again / A bonus for yer every wean'. When Nancy suggests Rab would have the system bankrupted in a year, he explains 'to make sure I could do nae ill / they brought oot something called the pill'. 'And do they give it to you free?' 'Aye, at the University.'[38]

Hector Nicol's (1920–1985) sketch, 'Rab and Mary', written for the Glasgow comedian Glen Daly (1920–1987), probably in the 1960s, similarly reimagined Burns encountering Heilan' Mary as a statue in a park. Entering to 'The Star o' Robbie Burns', Rab's opening gags are predictably one-note: ('I took her amang the corn riggs. She said "Yer awfi' quiet the nicht Rabbie. Say somethin' for goodness sake" . . . I said 'I'm jist groping for words" . . . She said "Well ye'll no' find them there"). Reunited with Mary, after speculating how McGonagall might have rendered some of Rab's poems ('Wee sleekit courin' timorous Moosie / I met thee in a council hoosie'), a closing song medley leads into reminiscence about times past:

RABBIE: Mary do you remember when
I took ye amang the ricks
And tore the elastic off yer blouse
And then I took ye doon by the gasworks
MARY: I remember it well
RABBIE: What a memory and Mary do you remember when
Ye said it was all a dream
Ye liked it so much ye didna scream
Mary you were wary in the good old days gone by
Do you remember?
MARY: Yes I remember . . .
RABBIE: Well Mary you're much older than I . . .

The up-tempo finale – to the Jolson song 'Swanee' – represents a Burns purist's nightmare:

MARY: Rabbie how I love ya, how I love ya
My dear old Rabbie
BOTH: We'd give the world to be
Among the folks in
Poosie Nancy's on the spree and
Drink a pint o' heavy, that's the bevy
We love tae savour
So take us back to Ayrshire once more
MARY: Rabbie's so contrary
RABBIE: Except aboot my Mary
BOTH: Take us back to Ayr once more.[39]

Burns Tribute Songs

As we have seen, music hall exploited Burns songs and poetry in ways that allowed for reinvention – in parodies, in comic sketches and through the comic dramatisations of Burns characters Tam and Souter Johnny. However, from the 1870s a genre of song emerged which was to become increasingly prominent in music hall and variety – tribute songs describing and celebrating Burns the man and icon. Focused on the increasingly mythologised person of Burns, and perhaps echoing Gavin Greig's suggestion, they marked a change from singing songs *by* Burns, to songs *about* him. By the 1890s, these included titles like 'Glorious Rabbie Burns', 'The Memory of Burns', 'The Grave of Rabbie Burns', 'The Name of Robert Burns Sounds Sweet', 'Burns and Tannahill', and recitations such as 'Famed Robert Burns' and 'Our Poet, Robert Burns'. Reflecting the wider promotion of Burns to the status of Scottish national icon, they focused on a range of preoccupations that mirrored rising public interest in the topography, landmarks and relationships associated with Burns appreciation.

The three most popular of these tributes reflected different aspects of this biographical focus. The most enduring, 'The Star o' Robbie Burns', written by James Thomson with music by the accompanist and songwriter James Booth, set the pattern for its many imitators by (loftily) depicting Burns as a low-born but heaven-sent genius, 'the ploughman lad' who 'wore the hodden grey':

> There is a star whose beaming ray
> Is shed on ev'ry clime;
> It shines by night, it shines by day,
> And ne'er grows dim wi' time.
> It rose upon the banks o' Ayr,
> It shone on Doon's clear stream –
> A hundred years are gane and mair,
> Yet brighter grows the beam.
>
> (Chorus)
> Let kings and courtiers rise and fa',
> This world has mony turns,
> But brightly beams aboon them a'
> The star o' Robbie Burns.

Stirringly elevating Burns to the Scottish and world pantheon, the song became a fixture at Burns festivities as the confluence of Burns appreciation and the Scottish music hall. (Although reportedly first sung at Hawick Burns Club in 1870, the published sheet music, rather in the face of that narrative, states it had been 'written and composed expressly for' the kilted tenor J. M. Hamilton (1854–1939), 'The Scottish Sims Reeves'.[40])

Beyond the romantic myth, the impact of these music-hall tributes was to project Burns as a national icon of Scottish patriotism. While some songs cast him as a radical figure, others firmly situated Burns within a Unionist lineage of soldiers, statesmen and literary figures. Tom McAusland's 'The Land Whaur I Wis Born', typical in surveying Scottish history as a parade of great men, intersperses heroes like Bruce and Wallace and empire-builders such as Lord Clyde, Sir John Moore, James Watt, Mungo Park and Dr Livingstone, with a Scottish literary pantheon which includes Scott and Tannahill, and in which Burns's is typically the crowning achievement:

> Ower the poetical world, I'm shair, each Scotchman should be full,
> When he thinks upon the happy thoughts of oor poet, Tannahill,
> Or Hogg, the 'Ettrick Shepherd' – shall that name e'er be forgot –
> Or the poetry or novels o' the far-famed 'Watty Scott.'
> And Rabbie Burns, oor native bard, his heart wis kind and true,
> And mony were the thochts he had as he stood langside the ploo;
> Ay, and roun' the banks o' Bonnie Doon Burns aft awoke his horn,
> And sang in praise o' Scotland's braes, the land whaur I wis born.[41]

The popularity of these tributes perhaps goes some way to affirming Gavin Greig's contention that the musical demands of Burns's own compositions set them apart from working songs. It is arguably true that while 'My Love is Like a Red, Red Rose' required sweet-voiced – or more skilled? – singers such as David Brown (fl. 1845–1880), 'the "Caledonian vocalist" of the early halls', or Wilson or Templeton before him, to do it justice, the stirring but musically more accessible 'Star o' Robbie Burns' was closer to the working aesthetic of music-hall chorus songs, which came with no such vocal benchmark. An appreciation of Harry Linn (1846–1890), the Scotch comic who wrote 'The Cottage Where Burns was Born', put this in context by bluntly asserting that 'He could not sing, but what of that! [. . .] the Scotia orchestra was thoroughly competent to execute the music and his voice, if somewhat reedy, was strong enough to fill the hall.'[42]

These tribute songs, promoting the poet as a romantic national icon, were part of the wider process of arrogating Burns into a constructed 'national' performance, combining tartan, Scottish songs and Highland music and dance, that emerged in the early twentieth century. Then, it was projected through representations in Scottish variety and popular theatre. This performance emphasised spectacle and visual appeal – the tartan and topography of Scottish landscape – the wildness of the Highlands and the Ayrshire countryside and landmarks associated with Burns. Much celebrated in magic lantern shows and dioramas, it achieved its apogee in popular theatre, in the National Drama, in the 'National' spectacles staged from the 1850s and in the Highland Glen scenes ubiquitous in Scottish pantomimes between the 1890s and 1950s, which crystallised this romantic constructed version of Scotland.

Burns and Rob Roy

Burns was a particular feature of *Rob Roy*, the most popular of the National Dramas, which embodied the contradictions of the hybrid Highland/Lowland identity by being, as Walter Freer remembered it, 'a strange mixture of a piece' that was 'half Jacobite and half Burns, and very Glasgow in atmosphere'.[43] Usually performed in Isack (Isaac) Pocock's (1782–1835) popular adaptation, 'Rob Roy MacGregor, or "Auld Lang Syne"', as 'an operatic drama in 3 Acts', it featured music by John Davy based on Scottish songs, providing a set score of airs, duets and choruses which were interpolated into the action and which, with regular additions and variations, were performed up to the 1930s, when Howard and Wyndham still presented annual Scottish seasons in Glasgow and Edinburgh.[44] Freer commented on the music that 'The story was turned and twisted so that songs that were particular favourites might be brought in,' adding 'The working people of Glasgow loved it.' The prominence of 'Auld Lang Syne' in this stage version has been credited as the source of the song's wider popularity.[45] Obligatory Burns items such as 'My Love is Like a Red, Red Rose' and 'Auld Lang Syne', were regularly augmented, with the actor playing the young hero, Osbaldistone, in a 1928 Aberdeen production singing 'The Lea Rig' and 'The Lass o' Ballochmyle', while his beloved, Diane Vernon, sang Scottish favourites 'Dark Lochnagar' and 'Cam Ye by Atholl'.[46]

But if there were no fixed rules, Burns's songs held their place. A potted music-hall sketch version of *Rob Roy* from 1903 further exaggerated this musical propensity by conveying the events of the story almost entirely through songs, paraphrasing well-known airs, ranging from Burns ('My Love She's but a Lassie Yet', 'Auld Lang Syne', 'A Man's a Man for a' That') and Scottish favourites ('Nae Luck aboot the Hoose') to, surreally, minstrel numbers such as 'Oh, Susannah', 'Yankee Doodle' and 'Nix My Dolly, Pals'. The drama reached its climax to the strains of 'Wait for the Waggon',

> 'Ask for mercy.' 'Never!' 'Then claymore,'
> Macgregor fiercely cries.
> A pass, a thrust, and Rashleigh kicks
> The bucket – then he dies.

The denouement achieved, the piece concluded with an address to the audience in Pocock's finale, 'Rob Roy Macgregor', set to a favourite Burns Air, 'Duncan Gray':

> Pardon now the bold outlaw,
> Rob Roy Macgregor, O!
> Grant him mercy, gentles a'
> Rob Roy Macgregor, O!
> Let your hands and hearts agree
> Set the hielan' laddie free,
> We will shout wi' muckle glee,
> Rob Roy Macgregor, O![47]

Performing Burns to the Diaspora

Up to the 1880s and 1890s Scottish music-hall performers closely identified with promoting Burns, such as Houston, Lumsden and Frame, retained strong links with working-class constituencies for whom Burns continued to be an important emblem of Scottish cultural identity. For these professionals, it was a logical extension of the fraternal communal appeal of Burns to expand their activities to perform to expatriate Scottish audiences overseas, particularly in North America. This was not a new impulse: earlier performers had explored the potential of the Scottish diaspora, using Scottish repertoire including Burns: Wilson and Templeton enjoyed great success in America and Canada (Wilson dying in Quebec), and David Kennedy toured extensively there, himself succumbing in Ontario in 1886, while the Scotch comics James Lumsden and R. S. Pillans toured Australia together in the late 1870s.

However, in November 1898 W. F. Frame took an eight-strong concert party on a five-month tour of the US and Canada. Opening in New York, they performed to an audience of 3,000 in Carnegie Hall, and went on to play concerts for Caledonian clubs and clan societies in industrial cities across the east coast, from Scottish centres such as Lawrence, Massachusetts (which Frame described as 'A Scotch city', full of people from Brigton), and Pawtucket, Rhode Island (which reminded him of Paisley), to Pittsburg, Cleveland, Philadelphia, Buffalo, Detroit, Hamilton, Montreal and Jersey City. But although the party – which as well as Frame included a soprano, contralto, tenor, violinist, Highland dancer, piper and pianist (James Booth, composer of 'The Star of Robbie Burns') – delivered a generic Scottish entertainment to a Carnegie Hall awash with Lion Rampant flags, the two subsequent highlight events were both huge 'Burns anniversaries'. In Toronto (to Frame 'the Scotch city of Canada'), they performed at the Caledonian Society's Burns Night, where 'three thousand countrymen of all classes, with their wives and weans, met to celebrate the

Scottish bard, and hear the songs of bonnie Scotland'. Following this, they played an even bigger Burns anniversary in Chicago, under the auspices of the local Scotch society, at the enormous Auditorium Theatre.[48] Frame recalled of the event that 'Burns and Frame were in everybody's mouth', that it was the largest audience to which he ever sang, and that they were joined on stage by a hundred Scotch children in kilts, who danced the Highland Fling.

Although Frame's entertainments were not simply Burns concerts, his framing of Burns within the context of a concert party variety entertainment – with a dancer, piper and humorous songs and stories – represented a high-water mark of the Burns music-hall tradition, casting Burns as part of a wider body of Scottish vernacular songs and ballads which, if it constituted the poet's commodification for a wider audience, also made his songs and readings accessible to the broadest potential constituency.

Frame returned to Scotland triumphant, but never visited America again. In contrast Harry Lauder's carefully orchestrated visit to the US in 1907, brilliantly planned by his agent William Morris, laid the foundations for his long-term success by systematically utilising the same network of Caledonian societies, Burns clubs and clan associations that Frame had touched on to galvanise the support of Scottish communities to generate publicity and ticket sales. While kilted Scottish acts remained popular in American vaudeville into the early twentieth century, Burns also retained a constituency and resonance with Scots-American communities: in Bradford, Vermont in October 1915 the Scottish Musical Comedy Company performed sketches of 'The Cotter's Saturday Night' and 'Tam o' Shanter'. Meanwhile, Lauder went on to twenty-two coast-to-coast tours of the US, which became the template for further visits to Australasia and the Far East.

By the early twentieth century Burns was venerated by Scottish variety theatre as a national icon, part of a constructed Scottish stage representation centred on tartan and Highland music and dance. But although Burns was the central bardic voice, in the post-war period the works themselves were largely reduced to shorthand signifiers – referenced in the titles of 1940s and 1950s tartan Winter Shows such as the Metropole's 'Abune Them A'' and 'Frae a' the Airts', and in the Palace Dundee's 'The Star o' Rabbie Burns' (1953). Howard and Wyndham's more up-market 'Five-' and 'Half-Past Eight' shows were to offer a 'Tam O' Shanter' ballet and a musical staging of 'The Immortal Memory', while their lavish 1960 Scottish pantomime *A Wish for Jamie* included a 'Red Rose' ballet sequence choreographed by Peter Darrell. But apart from medleys of Burns songs ('Songs from the Pen of the Immortal Rabbie Burns'), most post-war sketches – with titles like 'The Spirit of Burns', 'The Works of Burns', 'Comin' thro the Rye', 'The Burns Supper' and 'Poosie Nancy's Inn – modern version' – seem, however animated by the likes of Clark and Murray, George West, Tommy Morgan and Jack Milroy, to have been thin pretexts for generic comedy.[49]

The increasing tendency to sing *about* Burns rather than perform his work was representative of a wider change: a gradual shift away from the participatory performing culture by which Burns had been promoted to working-class audiences – particularly the masonic, temperance and trades union movements – as a shared cultural reference by an older generation of Scottish performers who were personally invested in Burns. Singing Burns and Scottish songs and ballads had continued to be a focus of music-hall careers. In the pre-World War One period the contralto Bertha Stuart (fl. 1906–1921), celebrated for her performances of 'Caller Herrin', sung with great sensitivity costumed as a 'comely fisher maiden' and in an appropriate stage setting, could still be advertised as 'the sweet singer of Burns's songs'.[50] There was also still Willie Frame: in 1914 his annual autumn tour of Scotland, now established for more than thirty years, featured alongside his pawky comic songs, a recitation of Burns's poem 'The Soldier's Return'. A poignant choice, it became the focus of his press slogans like 'Hear Frame read Burns' "Soldier's Return."'; '"Frame and Burns" (Says the Press) "What a success, The Soldier's Return"'; and 'Frame Saturated wi' Burns'. The following March his appearances as 'Scotland's Own Comedian' at the Olympia Bridgeton and Glasgow Pavilion featured special Burns Nights at which Frame gave 'a synopsis, "Happy Moments with Burns"', and recited 'Tam o Shanter'. But this affinity now belonged to an earlier age. Perhaps more representative was that the Scottish tenor J. M. Hamilton, who had scored a success on his debut with Burns's 'To Mary in Heaven' at the Good Templars' Harmonic concerts, ended his career famous for singing 'The Star o' Robbie Burns'.[51]

By the interwar period, variety theatre had moved to a veneration of Burns which saw imaginative, committed performances of his work largely reduced to shorthand references in the titles of sketches, scenas and tartan winter shows. Burns Nights remained a bastion of engaged amateur performance, and Scots songs remained popular. But variety theatre's own decline – after World War One, and then, terminally, from the 1950s – perhaps together with the move away from live performance to cinema and radio, mirrored the growing distance between the social and cultural world of Burns's time and the urban circumstances of twentieth-century living, and saw an increasing loss of the performance skills and shared references that had connected audiences and performers in the past.

Notes

1. *Glasgow Theatrical Review*, 10 November 1847, p. 19.
2. *Evening News & Star* (*Glasgow Evening News*), 29 April 1887, p. 4.
3. *Era*, 26 January 1862, p. 12.
4. 'Folk-Song of the North-East. IX. Burns and Folk-Song', part of a series of articles written for the *Buchan Observer* between 1907 and 1911, in

Gavin Greig, *Folk-Song in Buchan and Folk-Song of the North-East* (Hatboro, PA: Folklore Associates, 1963), no through pagination. I am grateful to Adam McNaughtan for this reference, and for his assistance in lending materials for research on this chapter. Greig misquotes the title of the song, written by the Scotch comic Harry Linn, which is actually 'The Cottage where Burns was Born'.

5. Sheila Douglas, 'Burns and the Folksinger', Burns Conference, Strathclyde University, January 1996: https://www.arts.gla.ac.uk/STELLA/STARN/crit/burns.htm
6. Letter, 'A Nicht wi' Burns', *Fife Free Press*, 9 February 1895: Mitchell Library Scrapbook, 'Newspaper Cuttings. Robert Burns', G154850, p. 200.
7. 'Concerts for the Working Class', *Glasgow Sentinel*, 21 January 1865, p. 4.
8. Ibid.
9. So, for example, an 1845 Saturday Evening Concert included, alongside items by Mendelssohn, Bellini, Donizetti, Mehul, Arne and Mercadente, Miss Amelia Hills singing 'I'm o'er Young to Marry yet' and 'John Anderson, my Jo'. An 1864 Grand Concert at Wishaw included 'Whistle and I'll Come to thee, my Lad' and 'Tam Glen', while an advertisement for a 'Great Burns Night' at the City Halls in January 1887, part of the Saturday Evening Concert series, promised an extravaganza with 'Burns's songs, Burns's poems' and 'Burns's "Jolly Beggars"', with ten named soloists singing twenty-five listed Burns songs, including 'There was a Lad', 'Logan Braes', 'Dainty Davie', 'Man was Made to Mourn', 'Craigie Burn Wood', 'My Heart is Sair', 'Bonnie Wee Thing', 'Ca' the Ewes' and 'The Jolly Beggars'. See *Glasgow Citizen*, 15 November 1845; *Hamilton Advertiser*, 21 January 1864; *Glasgow Herald*, 21 January 1887.
10. See J. Wilson McLaren, *Edinburgh Memories and Some Worthies* (London and Edinburgh: W. & R. Chambers, 1926), pp. 136–49; Peter Ross, *The Scot in America* (New York: Raeburn Book Co., 1896), pp. 336–7.
11. 'Glasgow Fair', *Glasgow Citizen*, 13 July 1844; Tracy C. Davis, 'Let Glasgow Flourish', in Richard Foulkes (ed.), *Scenes from Provincial Stages* (London: Society for Theatre Research, 1994), pp. 98–113.
12. Programme, Royal Assembly Rooms, Torquay, 6 July [1874], Birrell's New Great Diorama of Scotland and Grand Scottish Concert. Author's collection.
13. Advertisement, *Dundee Courier*, 28 December 1875. James Lumsden, who presented annual festivals of Scottish music commemorating Burns in Edinburgh for some twenty-eight years was, by the 1890s, similarly including in them 'a musical and pictorial entertainment' entitled 'The Life and Land of Burns', with magic-lantern views which he described.
14. *Evening Citizen*, 21 October 1872 and *Evening Star*, 14 November 1873, quoted in James Houston, *Autobiography of James Houston, Scotch Comedian* (Glasgow and Edinburgh: John Menzies and Wm Love, 1889), pp. 116–19.

15. Alasdair Cameron, 'Popular Entertainment in Nineteenth-Century Glasgow', in Karen Marshalsay (ed.), *The Waggle o' the Kilt: Popular Theatre and Entertainment in Scotland* (Glasgow: Glasgow University Library, 1982), pp. 5–12.
16. While the *Glasgow Herald* reviewer blamed the attention-seeking of the actress, Miss Anderson, suggesting that 'however true to the original, the scantiness of her habiliments in Alloway Kirk may have been, it undoubtedly offended the taste of the audience'. Yet, letters to another paper defended the actress and production, one stating that 'Miss Anderson's "Cutty Sark", about which so much has been said, was simply perfect, ie, in exact accordance with the witch given us by Burns.' See *Glasgow Herald*, 12 December 1871 and 'The Cutty Sark Controversy', *North British Daily Mail*, 21 December 1871, p. 5.
17. Contained in the Poet's Box collection in the Mitchell Library, these include 'Camlachie Tam' (29 June 1872); 'Shadows in the Stream' (10 July 1869); 'The Statues in the Square' (26 February 1870); 'In a Quiet Sort of Way' (3 August 1872); 'The Hale Rick-Ma-Tick' (2 November 1872), 'The Hale Jing-Bang' (8 November 1873); 'The Working Man that Pays for A' (29 January 1876).
18. 'The Hale Jing-Bang' (8 November 1873), Poet's Box, 1001, Mitchell Library. For such songs see also Paul Maloney, *Scotland and the Music Hall, 1850–1914* (Manchester: Manchester University Press, 2003), p. 49.
19. 'Camlachie Tam', written and sung by Harry Linn, Poet's Box, 403, Mitchell Library. Although dated 29 June 1872, the verse on Rossborough taking over the Britannia suggests the song was written in 1869.
20. See Houston, *Autobiography*, pp. 191–2.
21. *Glasgow Sentinel*, 25 February 1860, p. 4.
22. *Glasgow Evening News*, 18 May 1881; quoted in Houston, *Autobiography*, p. 69.
23. Houston, *Autobiography*, pp. 81–7; see also Jill Farleigh Tattam Wolfe, 'Fellow Travellers: James Lumsden's and James Houston's Summer Tour to the Highlands and Northern Isles, 1878', *UPSTAGE: A Journal of Turn-of-the-Century Theatre* 5 (Winter 2012/13), http://www.oscholars.com/Upstage/issue5/articleshub5.htm [accessed 13 July 2020].
24. From *Glasgow Evening Star* and *Glasgow Evening Citizen*, quoted in an advertisement for Falkirk School of Arts' opening concert by Lumsden's Original Scottish Minstrels, *Falkirk Herald*, 21 October 1875, p. 1.
25. James Lumsden had included a performance in a Burns anniversary concert for Edinburgh Burns Club at the Music Hall, with a company that included the Glasgow Scotch comic W. H. Lannigan, repeating the piece in March in his 'A Nicht wi' Burns' presentation of Lumsden's Popular Scottish Concert in Selkirk.
26. For Hengler's, see *Glasgow Herald*, 22 January 1872, p. 1; for Oxford Music Hall, *Glasgow Sentinel*, 'Letter from London', 28 June 1862, p. 4.

27. 'Will Ye Go? Ay-Or-No? Air-"The Braes o' Balquidder"' (no author), from *Scotch Parodies*, (pink) song booklet (undated, incomplete copy, no title page), publ. D. R. Burnside, 50 Stockwell Street, Glasgow. (A full-page advert in a second Burnside songsheet from McNaughtan's collection, 'Hame o' Mine', which lists the parodies featured, confirms that this is issue 1 of *Scotch Parodies*.) I am grateful to Adam McNaughtan for generously making this and other material available.
28. 'Parody on "Afton Water"' (no author), from *Scotch Parodies*, (pink) song booklet (undated, incomplete copy, no title page), publ. D. R. Burnside, 50 Stockwell Street, Glasgow. I am grateful to Adam McNaughtan for generously making this material available.
29. *Scotch Parodies*, issue 1, (pink) song booklet (undated, incomplete copy, no title page), D. R. Burnside, 50 Stockwell Street, Glasgow.
30. *Barr's Professional Gazette & Advertiser* (hereafter *Professional*), no. 209, 6 September 1890. The lyrics were followed by a note stating the song 'was written many years ago by a Scottish clergyman at Liverpool, and sung at an anniversary held there in commemoration of the birthday of Robert Burns'.
31. *Professional*, no. 207, 9 August 1890.
32. 'Parody on "Scots Wha' Hae"'. Written by James Curran, sung by W. F. Frame 'with immense success', *Professional*, no. 214, 15 November 1890.
33. *Scottish Referee*, 17 November 1902.
34. 'The Goalkeeper's Ghost' was published in the *Scottish Referee*, 11 February 1895, when the lines were reported as having been 'exhibited on the premises of a popular ex-international goalkeeper', by a correspondent who signed himself 'A.M.'. When it was republished in *Barr's Professional* in 1903, the author was revealed as the songwriter Alex Melville: *Barr's Monthly Professional Song Writers' & Singers' Journal*, no. 12, June 1903. The poem was subsequently recorded by John Walker in 1911 as 'The Goal-Keeper's Ghost', pts 1 and 2, for the Columbia Rena label (ColRena 1695); see Bill Dean-Myatt, *A Scottish Vernacular Discography, 1887–1960* (Hailsham: City of London Phonograph & Gramophone Society, 2013).
35. *Evening Times*, 20 October 1908, p. 2.
36. Ibid.
37. 'A Night Out with the Immortal', *The Glasgow News*, 26 January 1899 (n.p.).
38. 'Rabbie Burns', Royal Conservatoire of Scotland Archives, Jimmy Logan Collection. JL-91ff 2. Performed by Logan with Peter Morrison in the 'Songs for Scotland' summer show at His Majesty's Theatre Aberdeen in 1977, see *Aberdeen Press & Journal*, 21 June 1977 (n.p.). Handwritten

changes and alterations to a second copy of the typescript in the archive confirm the sketch was revived in 1984.

39. 'Rab and Mary, a Scottish Fantasy'. Typescript. I am grateful to my friend, the late William Gallacher, for kindly making this and other material available to me.
40. 'The Star o' Robbie Burns', words by James Thomson. Music composed by James Booth. 'Written & Composed Expressly for Mr J. M. Hamilton, The Scottish Sims Reeves & sung by him with unbounded applause'. Mozart Allan, 60 South Portland Street, Glasgow. See also Clark McGinn, *The Burns Supper: A Concise History* (Edinburgh: Luath Press, 2019), p. 219. The two other most popular tribute songs mentioned were Harry Linn's 'The Cottage Whaur Burns Was Born', and the older 'Burns and Highland Mary'.
41. 'The Land Whaur I Wis Born'. Written by Tom McAusland and sung by R. C. McGill. *Barr's Professional Song Writers' & Singer's Journal*, no. 13, July 1903.
42. *Professional*, no. 204, 28 June 1890.
43. Walter Freer, *My Life and Memories* (Glasgow: Civic Press Ltd, 1929), p. 79.
44. *Rob Roy Macgregor or, "Auld Lang Syne"*. An Operatic Drama in 3 Acts by Isack Pocock'. French's Acting edition no. 38 (London and New York: Samuel French Ltd, no date [*c.*1923?]).
45. For analysis of Pocock's adaptation see Ann Rigney, *The Afterlives of Walter Scott* (Oxford: Oxford University Press, 2012; paperback edn 2017), pp. 65–74. For the full stage history of *Rob Roy*, see H. Philip Bolton, *Scott Dramatised* (London and New York: Mansell, 1992). The role of Pocock's version of Rob Roy in popularising 'Auld Lang Syne' is discussed on p. 163.
46. *Aberdeen Press & Journal*, 8 May 1928, p. 11.
47. 'Rob Roy, or, The Days of Auld Langsyne', *Professional*, no. 18, December 1903.
48. Frame reported the auditorium (incorrectly) as holding 10,000; the actual figure was 4,200. W. F. Frame, *W. F. Frame Tells His Own Story* (Glasgow: Wm Holmes, 1907), pp. 90–118.
49. Crace Clark and Colin Murray (1905–1995 and 1904–1989 respectively) were a popular husband and wife double act in Scottish variety, known as 'Mr and Mrs Glasgow'. George West (1890–1963), Tommy Morgan (1898–1958) and Jack Milroy (1915–2001) were Glasgow comedians who appeared extensively in pantomime and variety.
50. Stuart also regularly followed with 'The Star o' Robbie Burns'. See Bertha Stuart advertisement, *Era*, 30 January 1909. Also *Era*, 20 February 1909.
51. Freer, *My Life and Memories*, p. 80.

5

'But to our tale': 'Tam o' Shanter' on Stage

Paul Maloney and Adrienne Scullion

In February 1876 a pantomime version of 'Tam o' Shanter', written by the jobbing dramatist and actor William Lowe (fl. 1862–1916), was produced at the Opera House Kilmarnock. The adaptation and its staging were enthusiastically received by a local newspaper which suggested 'the good folks of "auld Killie" never saw a pantomime better put on the stage, and more effectively performed'.[1] It found the libretto 'adheres in many cases most closely to the original, and bristles with point and repartee, many of which, especially those of a local nature, bring happy and decided hits'. The review praised 'the machinery, stage effect-dresses and music' and thought the 'scenic effects [. . .] exceedingly good, on the whole faithful to nature, and beyond what Kilmarnock audiences are accustomed to see'.

Notwithstanding that this is pantomime, the idea that Scottish audiences of the time could have experienced Burns's poem through a style of production which, although very different, felt culturally familiar enough to seem and feel authentic to the spirit of the original, is something that bears exploring. Whilst a modern focus on the poem's literary and oral qualities may forefront its potential performative nature, the production and reception of the Kilmarnock pantomime suggests the Victorian audience's openness to a freer dramatic adaptation which focused on the theatricality of the narrative's visceral excitements. The spectacle of the supernatural effects, the domestic humour and conviviality of the alehouse scenes, the cross-dressing of Kate, the Landlady and even Cutty Sark, which leant themselves to the inclusion of local references and topical jokes, as well as the breathless culminating chase, all met the demands of the contemporary popular stage and its emerging favourite, the pantomime.

Performance History

Lowe's version of 'Tam o' Shanter' was first produced at the Theatre Royal Greenock in December 1865 as *Tam o' Shanter: or, Caledonia, Queen of the*

Heather, and Auld Clootie, and the Witches of Alloway Kirk.[2] Whilst not described as a pantomime, it was, nevertheless, advertised in seasonal terms as a 'Grand National New Year's Burlesque' and was produced to meet demand for what a Greenock newspaper termed as 'something [. . .] of a light and pleasing character for the festive season'.[3] The piece's function as a seasonal and partly satirical entertainment was confirmed by printed advertisements that referred to it as a 'Grand, Allegorical, Paradoxical, Poetical, Pleasingly Practical Burlesque, adapted from the celebrated Poem by Robert Burns'.

In contrast to this seasonal role, Lowe's adaptation next appeared in June 1868 in Glasgow at James Baylis's huge Royal Colosseum Theatre in Cowcaddens where, following performances of *The Merchant of Venice*, it was presented as a 'Grand National Extravaganza', now titled *Tam o' Shanter; or, The Brig o' Doon!*[4] That production was a popular hit with Glasgow audiences, running throughout the month, and was revived for further performances the following year. The adaptation resurfaced, again successfully, in February 1873 at Macfarlane's Dundee Music Hall and Opera House where it was now referred to as a 'Scottish Burlesque'.[5] The fourth iteration came at the Opera House Kilmarnock in February 1876. There it was titled the 'Grand Scottish Pantomime of *Tam o' Shanter*', with the script in the Lord Chamberlain's collection being subtitled 'An Original Burlesque by William Lowe', with the production also now called a pantomime in press reviews, and on a surviving printed daybill, which also gives the time of the last train for Ayr after curtain down.[6]

As pantomime became increasingly popular, from the mid-nineteenth century, Scottish theatres began producing their own homegrown pantomime stories which often drew on characters and episodes from Scottish history and literature. These Scottish stories ranged across several types of subject: for example, the foundational myths of Scottish cities as represented by pantomimes such as *Let Glasgow Flourish; or, The Fairy of St Mungo* (1868) and its sequel *Edina, White Hart of the Lothians* (1869), and characters pulled from popular authors such as the Paisley poet Alexander Wilson and Walter Scott, whose Watty and Meg and Rob Roy respectively both received pantomime treatments. But the Scottish subject which proved most popular as a source for pantomime, and which most readily lent itself to stage adaptation, was 'Tam o' Shanter'.

In addition to Lowe's four productions, 'Tam o' Shanter' enjoyed a number of other different pantomime incarnations. Not surprisingly, given the dramatic potential of its famous climactic chase, it was readily adapted by circus managements for equestrian productions: for example, in London in 1843 Astley's Royal Amphitheatre produced a 'Comic Christmas Equestrian Pantomime' entitled *Harlequin Tam o' Shanter and his Steed Meg; or, The Witches of Alloway Kirk*[7] and in Edinburgh in December 1851 a 'comic Christmas pantomime' was presented at Pablo Franque's Royal Amphitheatre on Nicholson Street as *Harlequin Tam o' Shanter and his Steed Meg; or, The Witches of Alloway Kirk and the Fairies of the Magic Thistle*.[8] Conventional pantomime versions of 'Tam o' Shanter' also proved popular in Edinburgh (1858–9), Coatbridge (1866) and Glasgow (1845), where a spectacular production of J. S. Strachan's version at the Theatre Royal in 1871–2 was given sumptuous settings by William Glover.[9]

Lowe's 1876 version of 'Tam o' Shanter' for Kilmarnock was the first of his adaptations to be termed a pantomime, having previously been promoted to the public as a 'Grand National New Year Burlesque', a 'Grand National Extravaganza' and a 'Scottish Burlesque'. Was this the same piece; or was the script substantially rewritten for each outing to reflect these different formats and genres; or was it essentially the same script, simply represented under different titles to reflect changing theatre fashions; or was it the case that the development of Lowe's script through these different iterations, partly evidenced by surviving editorial alterations to the manuscript script, throws light on the themes and facets of Burns poem which Lowe chose to emphasise and heighten as a means of maximising the piece's appeal for contemporary Scottish audiences?

As well as being an experienced and capable actor, Lowe was a busy playwright, working as an embedded company dramatist who brought with him his skills and back catalogue of past stage adaptations when he moved between engagements with different stock companies. His involvement as a member of the acting company meant that he could write to suit the companies and theatres he joined or worked for, adding topical and local material as required. Given that he usually performed in these pieces – at Greenock Lowe took the role of Auld Clootie and in Dundee and Kilmarnock he played Tam himself – he may also have had a hand in producing or stage managing them.

Lowe's early pieces – including an adaptation of Alexander Wilson's *Watty and Meg*, a Burnsian domestic comedy about a rowing couple based on a popular comic poem, and a version of Burns's 'Hallowe'en' – were usually burlesques, a form that, arising out of the earlier fairy extravaganzas, added text that combined parody with topical allusions and extravagant punning, essentially many of the elements of pantomime without the harlequinade.[10] This distinctively Victorian genre emerged as a mainstay of contemporary popular theatre also encompassing the notion of a 'national' burlesque. Drawing on the conventions and dramaturgy of the popular, fairground-located touring theatres known as 'geggies', with a repertoire that celebrated figures from Scottish history, folklore and literature such as William Wallace, Mary Queen of Scots, Warlocks of the Glen, Scottish Chieftains, Gilderoy and Wandering Steenie, and the Scottish National Drama, with its dramaturgical basis in stage adaptations of the works of Walter Scott, the national burlesque specifically referenced patriotism. It did so through entertainments that drew on elements of Scottish music, history and nationhood to evoke and celebrate Scottish identity.

Lowe, in writing his successful national or Scottish burlesques, consciously alluded to older popular forms in ways designed to evoke old associations. His 'Grand Christmas and New Year Burlesque *Bonnie Dundee*', performed at the Dundee Music Hall over Christmas 1872–3, was subtitled *Hogmanay and Yule o' Yore; or, The Yerl and the Lily of Tay* and was advertised, tongue in cheek, as including 'for the first time on any stage, the Ancient Scottish "Guizer Masque"', with advertisements promising 'all the fun of a pantomime'.[11]

Against this backdrop, 'Tam o' Shanter', with the figures of Tam and Souter Johnny as iconic Scottish folk archetypes, may be understood as a highly appropriate vehicle for burlesque depictions of Scottish cultural identity, which was always flagged as a key criterion for success. A reviewer of Lowe's first *Tam o' Shanter* at Greenock enjoyed the production but regretted 'that there seems not to be two Scotchmen in the company to whom can be allotted the parts of Tam o' Shanter and Souter Johnny'.[12] This was not an issue two years later at the Royal Colosseum in Glasgow, a huge barn of a theatre that held 4,000, where both the Scottish elements, and the poem's status as a literary treasure were given what seems to have been received as proper consideration: as a Glasgow critic wrote, 'Scottish music, song and dances, always so attractive, are largely introduced, and Tam otherwise has been put upon the stage with great care and attention, backed out by the exertions of a numerous corps de ballet.'[13]

The Kilmarnock Pantomime

The British Library manuscript of Lowe's Kilmarnock *Tam o' Shanter*, inscribed 'licensed 25 February 1876', is a fair copy of a script that has undergone adaptation for several different theatres, as evidenced by an amount of editorial changes in the form of crossings-out and overwriting, and by the adding in of alternative topical material.[14] The thrust of the changes seems to be that the older, probably original burlesque script in the style of the fairy extravaganza – which had fairy characters, in the person of Caledonia, a national deity representing Scotland, and her attendants, to balance the witches and diabolical Clootie – has been expanded to include the extra elements required for pantomime. The cast list suggests an expanded range of secondary immortal characters, the scenario seems to have been expanded in places, in particular with extra topical material, and, although not included in the British Library text, press advertisements and reviews make clear that the production had also acquired the prerequisite of any Victorian pantomime, a harlequinade.[15]

The cast of characters is listed as: the Immortals, made up of Caledonia, Queen of the Thistle, and her attendants Heatherbell, Thistlebloom, Roseleaf and Fernleaf; the Demons consisting of Auld Clootie, alias Nick, and his minions Smokefume, Pitchdark, Impereill, Firebrand and Redhot; and the Mortals, Tam o' Shanter, Souter Johnny, the Landlord, Kate, Cutty Sark, the Landlady and Meg the Mare. The *Kilmarnock Standard* reviews confirm that, while Lowe himself played Tam, the roles of Kate (Mr Dobson), Cutty Sark (Mr Walmisley) and the Landlady (Mr Courte) were all played by cross-dressed male actors, with Dobson's portrayal of the long-suffering Kate being found 'all the more effective by his perfect command of the west country lowland dialect'.[16]

Lowe's scenario tells the story in eight scenes beginning with the introduction of the demons, immortals and mortals. Firstly, in a 'gloomy cave' Auld Clootie summons Cutty Sark to tell the assembled demons and imps that Tam is carousing in Ayr and of his plan to lure him to Alloway Kirk and capture him. Topical jokes include punning references to crinolines and ladies' fashions and Lord Dundreary, the title figure in Tom Taylor's popular play *Our American Cousin* (1858), before the imps take a deoch an doris, execute a Demon Dance and exit. The next scene introduces the alternative forces of good and is set in the 'Heather Home of Caledonia', where Caledonia enters drawn in her Lion Rampant car, 'decorated with thistles and emblems of Scotland', to the strains of 'The Campbells are Coming' to warn the assembled fairies of Clootie's plot against Tam. As they depart for Alloway Kirk to foil Clootie's plans, the scene 'Burns Dream Realised' is shown upstage and backed by a chorus of 'Tam O' Shanter Shall Be Free'. The next scene brings the story into the world of the Mortals and to the kitchen of Shanter Farm where Kate laments her neglect by Tam and even looks forward to life with a new husband. In the song 'Comin' through the Rye' she details her prospects for a new lover:

> If Tam deserts every night
> He'll find out bye and bye
> Some other one will steal his right,
> When comin' through the rye.

To the strains of 'Auld Lang Syne', Clootie tells Kate he comes to rid her of her faithless husband, who 'now in toddy glasses / pledges names of ither lasses'. When he tells her of the trap at Alloway Kirk, and his use of Cutty Sark, Kate agrees to the plan and declares herself so joyous that she 'could reel e'en with the deil'. She and Clootie duet and dance to the 'Cameronian Rant', revelling in Tam's terrible fate. Then, to a 'Spirited Dance', Clootie carries Kate off stage.

The fourth scene reveals Tam and Johnny in the pub. They are putting the world to rights, railing against the encroachment of industrial technology on the Souter's shoemaking craft and speaking disparagingly of witches and deils. In a scene of song and reels, Clootie enters and frightens the company off one by one until he comes face to face with Tam who just manages to escape. Accompanied by 'demonic music' and lightning, Clootie exclaims, 'By mystic spell and magic quirk, / Convey me now to Alloway Kirk' and the scene immediately transforms to depict Alloway Kirk where the demons and witches dance until Tam is seen at the upstage window and shouts out 'Weel done Cutty Sark ye limmer / Way but ye're a supple kimmer'. A Demon flies up to the window where Tam strikes him and, with lightning all around, disappears back into the night. Clootie exhorts all to follow Tam: 'Up demons follow me your chief / Our hunting cry be catch the thief.'

In another exterior scene, 'Near the Brig o' Doon', Tam enters to the sounds of 'hurried music', mounted on Meg and telling the audience that 'The spirits of the nether regions are after me in hellish legions [. . .] here they come in pell mell bustle.' As Cutty, the witches, demons and Clootie rush on stage, a gauze panorama of flying imps is drawn on and Clootie galvanises his forces for a last attack: 'The swiftest gets the grey mare's tail. / The losers get Greenock gaol.' They rush off to storm music and the gauze panorama is removed as the action cuts to the Brig o' Doon. One by one Meg knocks down four pursuing demons, then jumps over them, circus style, and gallops off. Cutty or, the stage directions suggest, a double, flies down to the bridge and grabs the mare's tail. Half the horizon cloth at the back is illuminated showing 'aerial demons', suggesting figures revealed suspended aerial ballet-style. Clootie and the witches on the bridge join in a concerted piece, a reprise of 'Sally Come Up', while Cutty, holding on, insists Meg will never pass and, of course, pulls off her tail. As Caledonia appears, the other side of the transparent horizon cloth is illuminated to reveal 'the Genii of Good'.

This huge effect-filled scene cuts back to Kate in her kitchen contemplating being free of Tam. In a song, 'Nobody's Child', which accounts suggest was possibly cut in performance, she looks forward to captivating other men:

Oh won't I swell down Argyle Street
And be admired by all
I'll wear a chignon will defeat
The Belles of Sauchiehall.
For I will have a husband, and I will have a lover
For I'm a widow now, for I'm a widow now

Then, in a chorus song, possibly referencing the first number, Kate, anxious for confirmation of Tam's fate, reads various different papers – the *Glasgow Weekly Mail*, the *Evening Citizen* and the *Evening Post* – before concluding:

I know the reason now of this,
Clootie my Tam has chanced to miss.
Clootie on Tam was bent on ill,

But Tam had a Glasgow Sentinel.
None of the papers mention Tam.
Oh what a weary wretch I am.

With a clap of thunder, a parcel is thrown onstage, containing Meg's tail and a letter from Clootie, explaining that Tam has temporarily escaped him. Tam enters, chased by Clootie, Cutty Sark and the witches. Brandishing a poker Tam adopts a heroic pose: 'Behold the sword o' Nicol Jarvie / Now Kate my lass behind me glide,' only to be thunderstruck by Kate's rejoinder: 'Na' faith I'm on the deil's side.' All seems lost for Tam when Caledonia enters – 'Through vampire trap C':

A peace with you I never fear
'Tis peace with them – to audience – that I revere.
Without your welcome all is sad
But with it we are truly glad.
Then friends come nightly 'neath this dome
And see your Caledonia's Home.

The stage directions indicate a 'Change Scene' that reveals 'Caledonia's Home – fairies x [cross] centre, a pedestal with inscription "Burns". "Scots Wha Hae" played. Statue of Burns Rises. Fame descends & crowns it with laurel. Grand tableau. Red Fire. Finale "Corn Riggs"', and the appeal from Caledonia to the audience that:

We hope we've pleased you all my friends
And trust you'll come tomorrow oh.
For Tam o' Shanter here defends
All hearts from aching sorrow oh.
Curtain

What intrigues in Lowe's scenario are the elements of the story that he chooses to emphasise within this popular, pantomime format. Lowe located the Tam story within this Scottish popular theatre genre and drew heavily on Burns's influence by combining the story with the tropes of the genre, which include: the incorporation of dame-style drag performance, playing up the underlying sexual frisson of men playing women; a heightened dramatic and visual portrayal of the supernatural; theatrical and scenic effects alongside pacey physical theatre and humour; and the incorporation of local and topical material.

Lowe's *Tam o' Shanter* is a perfect encapsulation, a perfect fit, for this style of popular theatre, as it combined a powerful supernatural storyline, which could be heightened by the scenic spectacle in which Victorian playhouses specialised, and the provision of two characters – Tam and Souter Johnny – who were already well established as transcendent, timeless figures in Scottish popular culture, whose scenes provide perfect opportunities for refreshing with contemporary allusions and topical references. The additional element, the addition of Burns's songs, inserted into the dramatic context somewhat in the manner familiar from modern tribute musicals, was a further gain.

Language and Characters

Lowe's adaptation eschews any substantial quotation from Burns's poem but retains enough well-known phrases and familiar turns of phrase and Scots words. For example, Clootie's opening speech to his assembled demons shows Lowe's pragmatic style of blending phrases from the original poem with couplets advancing the exposition and scene-setting that were typical of popular drama and pantomime of the time:

> Cease this clatter
> And list to this important matter.
> This was the market day at Ayr
> Tam o' Shanter still is there
> Out on the spree, wie Souter Johnny,
> His ancient, trusty drouthy crony.
> Now as he mounts auld Meg his mare
> We'll raise a storm he scarce can bear
> And fill the air with lightning flashes
> And make him livid, pale as ashes
> As he rides home we all will lurk
> Within the walls of Alloway Kirk
> And by our arts will draw him to us
> Where he will come and slyly view us
> When out we'll sally, seize and bind him
> We'll have his heart if we can find him.

Caledonia, on her entrance, similarly combines exposition with well-known phrases from the poem:

Thistlebloom	Tam will make his wife a martyr.
Caledonia	Tam in her has got a tartar,
	he gets it when he dares to roam
	Kate in the sulks now sits at home
	gathering her brows like gathering storm
	nursing her wrath to keep it warm.

Given their familiarity, the incorporation of these well-known phrases represented the minimum threshold of audience expectation for a performance text of 'Tam o' Shanter'. But elsewhere Lowe uses familiarity with the text to play with or embellish phrases and impact. An example is his playful addition to Tam's exclamation at the sight of the witches dancing at Alloway Kirk: 'Weel done Cutty Sark ye limmer / Way but ye're a supple kimmer.' Audiences might have similarly appreciated his punning switch of Burns's 'Lowping and flinging on a crummock / I wonder didna turn thy stomach' to Cutty's line after being butted by Meg in the chase, 'Oh Clootie send me home to Cumnock / That mare's head has upset my stomach.'

The key to this licence was the piece's presentation as a Scottish burlesque, which allowed for punning and satirical juxtaposing in ways which we would associate with pantomime. It was a style of character-based vernacular theatre in which Lowe was a skilled exponent as a performer, having being highly praised in the character roles of the National Drama, including Bailie Nicol Jarvie. Indeed, at an 1864 benefit performance for his wife at Airdrie, where both were members of the company, Lowe read Burns's poem of 'Tam o' Shanter' from the stage, a sure indicator of its audience appeal.[17]

Topicality

The topical and local material in the script, important in productions often badged as 'written by the author expressly for this theatre', included a requisite quota of sight gags and puns, one involving one of the demons dressed as the protagonist of Tom Taylor's hit play *Our American Cousin* and referencing the actor Edward Sothern who was the famous creator of the eponymous role:

Clootie There shut up you, Lord Dundreary.
You are a *northern* not a *Sothern*.

But the familiarity of Burns's poem also allowed for more telling topical references, particularly to contemporary Scotland and the changing industrial world. Costume and fashion also provided pretexts for punning:

Clootie Oh here she is both lank and lean
(*to* Cutty) Cutty, where's your crinoline?
Cutty Crinoline is out of fashion
So I've forgone the vulgar passion
The fashions of the day are vile
I re*vile* them, I often smile
To see the girls walk out with fellows
Just like two handled umbrellas.

Cutty Sark's eponymous costume is also teased by Kate:

> Cutty Sark! here's deevilish thrift
> That even tries to rob a shift
> Cutty Sarks should be forgotten,
> Considering cheapness now of cotton.

Later Clootie's prejudices about the garment provoke Cutty to defend her West of Scotland roots:

> Clootie Beware my inauspicious frowns
> I should not like to treat you basely,
> Because your Granny dwelt in Paisley.
> Cutty Well I am Paisley born and bred,
> and I have also learnt and read.
> 'Twas there my Granny in a lark
> Bought me this famous cutty sark.
> Ne'er did she think when sewing the stitches
> That it wad grace a reel of witches.
> I never had a garment stronger.
> Clootie It might have been a little longer.r

Jokes about skimpy shifts aside, references including material about local news and places such as Paisley, Greenock and Glasgow, and familiar events and personalities, were a key part of the appeal, not just of pantomime, but of reimagining Burns's story in a contemporary urban Scottish context. Tam himself, an unlikely anti-heroic national icon, is described by Caledonia as 'spreeing in Ayr' while

> His wife at home sits in the dumps
> But Tam yet does not stir his stumps
> But boasts of Greeks and Roman Rienzi
> and vents his oaths on Forbes Mackenzie.

Resentment at the 1853 Forbes Mackenzie Act, which introduced Sunday closing and limited the opening hours of public houses, was entirely apposite for Tam as a character; and the bonhomie of Tam and Souter Johnny's ale house scene, with its boozy conviviality, was ideal for the sort of rambling discursive banter that allowed for the inclusion of whatever topical concern was on the characters' – and audiences' – minds. Part of the same discussion involves changes to life brought about by industrial working practices and their impact on Souter Johnny's craft of shoemaking:

Tam Johnny this is glorious weather
To get awa your rotten leather.
Souter Ah me! I'll have to change my calling
My trade is getting quite appalling,
These times have blasted my pursuits,
Folks wear Dick's gutta percha boots.
I'll lose my all ere long is past
And wie my awl off goes my last.
Landlady This is a sample o' your makin
Eh? Souter ye deserve a smackin.
When I gaed 'oot to buy our supper
Aff came the nethers frae the uppers.
Then I promised you a peltin.
Tam Aye like your shoon he needs a weltin.
Souter Haud ye're tongues gie ow're your deevin [nagging]
An' honest man maun get his livin,
Hand labour now is poorly reckoned
Machine work first class hand work second.

The constant punning, and mention of 'gutta percha', an early latex rubber, may be typical of such stream of consciousness. However, Tam and Souter Johnny's status as timeless everyman figures, whose very saloon-bar aimlessness made them perfect vehicles for endlessly refreshable topical humour, is stretched when the discussion shifts to weightier topics of improvement and education, as in a passage designed to meet the 'national' tone of celebrating Scottish achievement:

Tam Improvements now are all the rage
We live in truth a glorious age.
The time of literature and lore
By minds augmented more and more.
This city to the south sends forth
Their Borealis from the north.
No wonder that our lights shine there
For northern lights shine everywhere.
Souter Oh that results because our nation
Predominates in education
Tam Souter man you are discerning.
Yes it is true it comes of learning.

	Some say our education's bad
	For 'tis far better than I had.
	I say by all means teach our youth
	The principles of love and truth
	But in my mind to write and read
	Has naught to do with sect or creed.
Souter	Let men in parliament mind that.
Tam	Souter Johnny stop your chat.
	The people must mind state affairs
	The nation's well fare must be theirs.

This rather self-conscious change in tone becomes clearer in the context of Lowe's adaptation as a Scottish 'national' burlesque pantomime promoting Burns's place in Scottish culture.

Spectacle

Visual spectacle was, from its inception, a key part of the appeal of Lowe's *Tam o' Shanter*, with the settings of the Greenock production being described as 'really magnificent [and] among the best scenes being the Heather Bell Howe, the Brig o' Doon and the grand closing scene'.[18] The staging's spectacular elements may have been scaled up two years later in Glasgow to meet the requirements of the barn-like Royal Colosseum, which termed itself 'The Great Theatre' and advertised the production as a 'Grand National Extravaganza', with a 'New Grand Fairy Ballet' featuring Mademoiselle Ferena Stussy and a 'greatly augmented corps de ballet'.[19] If this is the 'Grand Ballet' that is crossed out in the Kilmarnock script, kinetic choreographic elements nevertheless remain very evident in that version and production, suggesting a vigorous musical staging. For example, Clootie's first scene climaxes with witches engaging in a demon dance; Clootie and Kate gleefully celebrate Tam's impending fate by singing and dancing to the pipe tune the 'Cameronian Rant'; and, in the Ale House scene, the singing of the glee 'Willie Brewed a Peck o' Maut' culminates in a 'spirited Scotch reel' during which Clootie enters to scare the company off one by one.

Scenic and choreographic elements also come together in one of the story's dramatic highlights, the witches' Sabbath at Alloway Kirk. One of the remarked-on features of Lowe's version was its treatment of the subject in a manner that befitted a poem regarded as a national literary treasure. Perhaps with this significance in mind, the stage directions, which give a vivid impression of the action and *mise en scène*, suggest that the designs for settings like the Ale House should be based on illustrations in the collected edition of Burns; specifically the directions state 'See plate in Burns works'. The transformation from the Ale

House into Alloway Kirk, singled out as impressive at Greenock, was evidently planned as a dramatic *coup de theatre*; the stage directions state:

> Gong – Scene changes, Being transformed to Alloway Kirk. Demonic music. This scene is changed by means of flaps – Green mediums on lights. Witches, demons and Cutty Sark enter simultaneously with the change.[20]

The ensuing scene was vividly described by the *Kilmarnock Standard*, which reported that 'the auld kirk is depicted with all the weird and ghastly occupants mentioned in the poem, and that 'Full scope has been given to the addendum of "An mair o' horrible an' awfu' / Which e'en tae name wad be unlawful".'[21] As the witches' Sabbath gets under way, Clootie pipes the company in a 'Grand Witch Dance' and the 'Band imitation of Bagpipes strike[s] up'. Tam appears and, as he delivers his exclamation to Cutty Sark, a 'demon flies up to window', the first of a sequence of special effects that follow his escape and the demonic pursuit.

Taken collectively, these effects remind us of the appeal of this version of the Tam story and that, for the Victorian audience, this worked as narrative theatre and as a piece of popular drama in which visual and dramatic effects were utilised to bring alive and heighten the supernatural storyline. This may have reached a different audience from that which read the poem in print and would have made an impact in promoting the poem and its story beyond its life on the page by renewing its appeal in contemporary popular culture.

After a front cloth scene *en route* to the Brig, in which Meg head-butts Cutty, a new scene, possibly added for the pantomime version, specifies that 'a gauze panorama is drawn on' – that is pulled across the width of the stage – 'representing flying imps, etc'. The panorama is then drawn off to reveal 'The Brig o' Doon', specified as 'practicable from L to R'. The meaning of this – that it is robust enough for the cast to stand on and use in the action – becomes clear when first Tam appears on the bridge. The stage directions then specify that Cutty Sark flies down 'worked by the wings' to alight on it, with the directions also suggesting that in 'The former part of this scene a double can impersonate Cutty Sark'. During the mid-bridge struggle for Meg's tail – and again the directions advise 'see plate' as in see the illustration in the collected works – 'Half the horizon cloth at back becomes illuminated showing aerial demons', suggesting that members of the company are flown suspended upstage, as in an aerial ballet, during which struggle 'Sally Come Up',[22] a popular minstrel song, is performed. As Meg's tail is pulled off, and Caledonia appears to intervene, 'the other half of the horizon is now illuminated showing the Genii of Good', suggesting further 'flown' aerial appearances, this time by the forces of good. The staging, therefore, is drawn not just from Burns's descriptions but also from illustrated print versions of the poem as well as using all the tools of spectacle available to the Victorian playhouse.

Indeed, such visual spectacle was expected by contemporary theatre audiences. Although there is no mention of the harlequinade in the Kilmarnock script – not surprisingly, as it was treated as a discrete episode, and usually performed by a separate, specialist troupe – the transition into its magical fantasy world remained an important focus of pantomime spectacle in general and in this performance too. Advertisements boasted of the 'enormous outlay' expended on it and a reviewer described the unveiling of this scenic coup when, 'at a wave of the fairy wand, the humble cottage disappears in the dazzling brightness of the gorgeous transformation scene. The harlequinade succeeds with the Clown and Pantaloon in their comicalities'.[23] All the pantomime tropes, including those drawn from the obligatory harlequinade, were legible in this pantomime 'Tam o' Shanter'.

Celebrating Burns

Pantomime convention also required a prologue in which immortal characters representing the forces of good and evil set out to intervene in the human world, framing the mortal story and characters as pawns in a battle between higher forces. In the case of the pantomime *Tam o' Shanter*, the poem's supernatural subject already involved devils and demons and made this element an easy tool with which to include the forces of good. The fact that the benevolent deity, Caledonia, 'Queen of the Thistle', is a national figure who personifies Scotland and Scottish identity, conflates the moral cause of goodness with that of Scottish national identity. Moreover, the stakes are higher in that Tam is not only being protected for his own right but also as a creation of Scotland's national poet, Burns. As Caledonia states in her opening exposition:

> Auld Clootie full of rage now turns,
> against a hero of our Burns,
> Now for respect for our great poet,
> We'll use our power, and quickly show it,
> and set at nought Auld Hornie's banter
> to rescue drunken Tam o' Shanter.

The veneration extends also to the poem's Ayrshire landscape and locations:

> The places there are sacred soil,
> Hallowed by Burns, there did he toil
> There where he struck the muse's lyre

That bade the earth list and admire,
There roused his mind in heavenly theme
And saw fame's radiance round him gleam
Behold! our national poet's dream.

Saving Tam, therefore, means saving Burns and, through him, Scotland's voice and even nationhood.

The focus on Burns himself as national bard also received an extra, reflexive twist in this Kilmarnock production. Lowe included a calculatedly flattering reference to the special place of Burns in the town's cultural politics. This involved a spoken prologue eulogising the poet, followed by a new song entitled 'Burns', written by Lowe and sung by Caledonia, that does not appear in the British Library script but was reproduced in the *Standard*, 'respectfully dedicated to James McKie by the Author'.[24] The Kilmarnock-born McKie (1816–1891), a famous Burns publisher and collector, was a leading campaigner for commemorative statues of Burns in Glasgow and Kilmarnock, and a prominent and popular figure in the town.[25] The spoken eulogy incorporated as part of the pantomime was received 'with great favour' by local audiences and McKie was reportedly so delighted that he presented Miss Pitt, the actress playing Caledonia, with a two-volume set of the poet's works.[26]

The idea that a popular staging of 'Tam o' Shanter' also functioned reflexively as a celebration of Burns and his iconic status in Scottish (and here Ayrshire) cultural life, reflected a tendency to veneration that saw the figure of Burns increasingly featuring in music-hall songs, and his life and work increasingly abrogated into an iconography of Scottish national identity centred on tartan, Highland music and dancing, to which were added Burns's own songs and poetry. This conflated iconography was evident from Caledonia's initial entrance 'Drawn on her Rampant Lion car, decorated with thistles and emblems of Scotland', to the strains of 'The Campbells are Coming'.

Lowe had previously utilised such visual tableaux, notably in *Watty and Meg*, his pantomime version of the well-known comic poem by Alexander Wilson which he adapted for the Theatre Royal Paisley in December 1865 and subsequently also produced in Dundee. In it Lowe provided a set piece representation in which a 'dolphin' oracle responded to questions posed by Caledonia, her answers being conveyed by cubes featuring the letters of the alphabet, arranged by junior members of the cast: the responses, after 'Happy New Year', 'Palmerston', the theatre manager, and 'The Press' continued with eulogies of Paisley and its own literary icons:

A local sentiment let's nourish;
Quick march.
(*Letters form* LET PAISLEY FLOURISH!)

Our nation's honour, letters show it;
The Scottish bard, the songster poet.
(Letters form TANNAHILL!*)*

Let honour be paid to more than one –
Quick, change your form, favour show to none.
(Letters form WILSON!*)*[27]

In Lowe's *Tam o' Shanter*, the stage directions state that the pantomime's concluding setting, 'Caledonia's Home', revealed a pedestal inscribed 'Burns': as 'Scots Wha Hae' is played a statue of Burns rises and the figure of 'Fame' descends to crown it with a laurel, followed by a 'Grand tableau' with 'red fire' and 'Corn Riggs'.

Conclusion

'Tam o' Shanter' was an ideal, archetypal subject for a burlesque, national pantomime, in that it provided plenty of opportunities for punning and local topical humour. The fact that the poem was so well-known allowed the adaptor to presume the audience's knowledge of and familiarity with the text and therefore there was a degree of licence to play with juxtaposed phrases and quotations in a nuanced way that added an extra level of sophistication to the punning and wordplay. The pre-existing supernatural storyline meant that the burlesque pantomime convention of framing the narrative as a moral struggle between mortals and immortals was easy to accommodate by simply adding in the forces of good – in the person of a benevolent deity and her fairies – and was given a twist by the fact that the forces of goodness were here represented by Caledonia, a figure who personified Scottish national identity. Moreover, the story's iconic status and familiarity as a latter-day folk subject allowed for a reflective approach, in which the objectives of the moral struggle – set out in the opening scenes – go beyond 'saving' the character of Tam to celebrating Burns himself and his status as Scotland's national poet. This conflation of the forces of goodness with Caledonia, and the moral struggle with the defence of Burns's legacy, makes the poet himself the true focus of the production, as demonstrated in the final 'Grand tableau'.

The defining qualities of Burns's poem, the energy and vivacity, the dramatic imagery of the piece, with its supernatural aspects, and above all its sheer vernacular force, make it inherently theatrical. Added to which, contemporary audiences took a much broader, more relaxed view of the relative integrity of literary adaptations of favourite pieces.

Notwithstanding that this is a pantomime, the reception accorded to the Kilmarnock 'Tam' suggests that Scottish audiences of the time would have experienced Burns's poem through a style of production which felt culturally familiar enough to seem and feel connected to the spirit of the original. Indeed, in pantomime production, the theatricality of the narrative's visceral excitement made for a celebration of quintessentially Victorian Scottishness.

Notes

1. *Ardrossan and Saltcoats Herald*, 19 February 1876, p. 5.
2. Advertisement, *Greenock Telegraph and Clyde Shipping Gazette*, 29 December 1865, p. 3.
3. Advertisement, *Greenock Advertiser*, 2 January 1866, p. 3; review, *Greenock Telegraph and Clyde Shipping Gazette*, 30 December 1865, p. 2.
4. Advertisement, *Glasgow Evening Citizen*, 1 June 1868, p. 1.
5. Advertisement, *Dundee Courier*, 12 February 1873, p. 1.
6. Advertisements, *Kilmarnock Standard*, 12, 19 February 1876, p. 2.
7. 'Astley's Royal Amphitheatre. Proprietor & manager Mr W Batty. Comic Christmas Equestrian Pantomime entitled *Harlequin Tam o' Shanter and his Steed Meg; or, the Witches of Alloway Kirk*'. British Library Add 42971, ff. 2–30. Produced 26 December 1843.
8. 'Tam o' Shanter Pantomime, Amphitheatre Edinburgh, License sent 24 November 1851, W.B. Donne'; 'Edinburgh, Pablo Franque's Royal Amphitheatre, York Hotel, Nicholson Street, Edinburgh. A new Comic Christmas Pantomime entitled *Harlequin Tam o' Shanter and his Steed Meg; or, the Witches of Alloway Kirk and the Fairies of the Magic Thistle*'. British Library Add 43038A, ff. 207–13.
9. *Glasgow Herald*, 12 December 1871, p. 4.
10. Michael E. Booth, *Theatre in the Victorian Age* (Cambridge: Cambridge University Press, 1991), pp. 194–202.
11. See advertisements in *Dundee Courier*, 23 December 1872, p. 1 and *Dundee Advertiser*, 27 December 1872, p. 1. For this production Lowe himself played the star role of Matilda Towhead and performed an overture on the penny tin whistle.
12. *Greenock Telegraph and Clyde Shipping Gazette*, 30 December 1865, p. 2.
13. *Glasgow Evening Citizen*, 2 June 1868, p. 3.
14. British Library Add 53162. 'Tam o' Shanter by W. Lowe. Licensed 25 February 1876'. Inside sheet, 'Tam o' Shanter, an original Burlesque by William Lowe Esq'. The last page of the manuscript, numbered 37 on the top right, has, at the bottom under the final 'Curtain', a handwritten cartouche drawn in ink stating 'J. R. Shaw, call boy, Colosseum Theatre Glasgow, May 1869'.
15. See 'The Pantomime – Tam O' Shanter', *Ardrossan and Saltcoats Herald*, 19 February 1876, p. 5. The harlequinade connected the contemporary

Victorian pantomime with its *commedia dell'arte* roots via a slapstick or at least mimed scene using archetypes including the lovers Harlequin and Columbine, the foolish or gullible father-figure Pantalone and the Clown and Pierrot.

16. *Kilmarnock Standard*, 19 February 1876, p. 2.
17. *Era*, 12 June 1864, p. 11.
18. *Greenock Telegraph and Clyde Shipping Gazette*, 30 December 1865, p. 2.
19. Royal Colosseum advertisement, *Glasgow Evening Citizen*, 3 June 1868, p. 1.
20. British Library Add 53162. 'Tam o' Shanter by W. Lowe. Licensed 25 February 1876'. Inside sheet, 'Tam o' Shanter, an original Burlesque by William Lowe Esq'.
21. *Kilmarnock Standard*, 12 February 1876, p. 2.
22. 'Sally Come Up' (1862), with its refrain 'Sally come down the middle', was composed by E. W. Mackney and arranged by Frederick Buckley (1832–1864) for Buckley's Serenaders, a leading American minstrel company run by his British-born father James Buckley.
23. *Kilmarnock Standard*, 12 February 1876, p. 2.
24. As reproduced in the *Kilmarnock Standard*, 'Burns' was 'Sung by Miss Fanny Pitt in Mr Wm Lowe's Pantomime on "Tam O' Shanter" and respectfully dedicated to James McKie Esq., by the Author':

    In counsel met the Sacred Nine,
    Their theme the minstrel song;
    'Choose we,' they said, 'a northern shrine
    For Scottish King of Song.'
    Fame, summoned to proclaim their choice,
    With rapture-hastened wing
    Reach'd Ayrshire, and with trumpet voice
    Nam'd Burns as Minstrel King.

    Earth brightened with his thoughts divine,
    All charms claim'd his control,
    His pen hath left on every line
    An impress of his soul.
    His spirit sings in all his songs,
    His sighs breathe in sad strains,
    His words still wage a war 'gainst wrongs,
    His pity yet soothes pains.

    For laurelled-chaplet on his brow
    Each land hath sent a leaf;

The last, stripp'd from Parnassian bough,
Fame gave our songster chief.
Time drifts all nations to the dust
And age each age inurns;
But proof against oblivion must
Remain the lays of Burns.

Kilmarnock Standard, 19 February 1876, p. 2

25. For McKie, see Christopher Whatley, *Immortal Memory: Burns and the Scottish People* (Edinburgh: John Donald, 2016).
26. 'Lorgnette', *Glasgow Evening News*, 16 February 1876, n.p.; McKie Collection scrapbooks, Dick Institute, Kilmarnock.
27. Libretto, *The New Pantomime of Watty and Meg by W. Lowe* (Paisley, 1865).

6

'O what a glorious sight': Performing Identity and the Burns Supper

Ronnie Young

Robert Burns's 'Address to a Haggis' puts performance at the heart of the Burns Supper. In the long history of the poem's reception, this text has acted as the centrepiece of the dinner held each January to commemorate the anniversary of the poet's birth on 25 January 1759, in effect giving a ready-made performance script for the serving of the haggis, the main dish of any self-respecting Burns Night. The poem can also inject some drama into what is otherwise a largely ceremonial public event. In some respects, the addressing of the haggis stands in contrast to the lines as they were first received by the public via their appearance in the 'Edinburgh' edition of *Poems, Chiefly in the Scottish Dialect* in 1787. There, Burns attempts to communicate verbally to the reader, through specific metaphor and simile, the sensory aspects of the dish, encouraging them actively to visualise the haggis bursting open 'Warm-reekin, rich'.[1] At a Burns Supper, the same lines function quite differently. They act as cue for the orator to slice up a haggis in the flesh and for the audience to receive this ritual offering as prefaced by Burns's poetic appetiser. Burns's mock-heroic stylings have through repeated performance become central to remembering a bona-fide national hero – quite the elevation for an indecorous apostrophe to oats and offal.

Though the 'Address' is a centrepiece of Burns Night celebrations, it acts as only one element in a wide range of performances associated with the anniversary dinner, from standard songs and bespoke recitals, through to toasts, speeches and outward affirmations of 'loyalty' and patriotism. Some clubs have even gone so far as to dramatise the entire evening, as in the case of the Plymouth Burns Club in 1956, which linked the 'Immortal Memory' and 'poetry and songs by various Club members [. . .] by a script specially written for the occasion, while the introductory music for the songs was being played softly as a background'.[2] These wider performances are important elements to consider.

Yet to explore the Burns Supper in terms of performance, we can go beyond the dramatic, the musical and rhetorical to show how such aspects intersect with more pervasive types of cultural 'performativity' related to cultural identity, as a means of performing communal co-dependency, cultural authority and 'imagined' nationhood. As Ann Rigney claims in her account of the global centenary celebrations of Burns in 1859 – a key moment in history for moving the Burns Supper towards becoming an annual event – the commemoration of Burns can be understood within the wider 'performative turn' in memory studies, or what she describes as a shift 'from products to processes, from static "sites" to performances [in which] attention turns both to embodied practices of remembrance and to the idea of remembering as a form of social action: a way of intervening in the world'.[3] The survival of cultural memory, in other words, can be seen not only through relatively stable artefacts such as texts but through cultural re-enactment and an 'ongoing willingness to reproduce'.[4] For example, we can make assertions about Burns's role in elevating haggis from a regional to national dish and in turning it into a symbol of Scottish national identity, but does that come directly from the text itself, or through annual public commemoration of Burns? Taking her cue from Benedict Anderson, Rigney suggests how the idea of reading the 'Immortal Memory' at exactly 6pm across the globe during the 1859 centenary encouraged the kind of imagined (actual time differences were ignored) 'simultaneity' that Anderson saw as central to building a sense of national identity.[5] Taking my cue from Rigney, I want to elaborate on her outline of the Burns centenary celebrations as 'embodied communities' to consider later enactments of identity through the tradition of the Burns Supper. Much recent work has been carried out into the emergence of the cult of Burns in the nineteenth century, a time, of course, when commemoration gained a global spread through Scots diaspora and colonial activities, but also when the elements we now see as part and parcel of the anniversary dinner are still evolving.[6] I aim to examine the period following this expansion, from the 1890s to the century following, when the ritual elements 'bed in' – roughly what Clark McGinn, in his recent comprehensive history of the Burns Supper, calls the 'bureaucratic period'.[7]

Ceremonial and Processional Performance

Lisa Wood has suggested that 'Writers at the end of the eighteenth century in Britain used food figuratively as a way of negotiating a number of cultural and social issues, including gender, class, race, revolution, and nationalism.'[8] In 'To a Haggis', Burns negotiates these issues by describing the positive effects of haggis in terms of mass consumption by an imagined community of hardy labouring-class Scotsmen. In the tradition of the Burns Supper, such concerns are subject to annual re-enactment, and, as I suggested above, have effectively become a performance script for the centrepiece of the supper. Popular guides to hosting a Burns Supper, for instance, tend to insist upon the symbolic cutting of the haggis timed to coincide with the specific lines:

His knife see rustic Labour dight,
An' cut you up wi' ready sleight,
Trenching your gushing entrails bright,
Like ony ditch;
And then, O what a glorious sight,
Warm-reekin', rich! ('To a Haggis', lines 13–18)

In his *Ultimate Burns Supper Book*, McGinn goes so far as to outline two different approaches to the ritual of cutting the haggis, the 'poetic' and 'dramatic' addressors,[9] the former simply taking their cue from the line 'an' cut ye up', while for the latter McGinn suggests a number of actions to accompany different lines of verse. The 'dramatic addressor' might, for example, explain the line 'as lang's my arm' by indicating the length of their arm or the Scots word 'hurdies' by patting their behind; they might lift the haggis to show its weight within the 'groaning trencher'; and of course there are a number of gestures associated with the knife, including the wider enactment of the Scot 'haggis-fed' warrior, and representative of a hardy fearsome race, who grabs the knife and twirls it over his head, acting out the dismemberment of enemies to the lines:[10]

But mark the Rustic, haggis-fed,
The trembling earth resounds his tread.
Clap in his walie nieve a blade, [strong grasp]
He'll mak it whissle;
An' legs an' arms, an' heads will sned, [lop off]
Like taps o' thrissle. [thistle] ('To a Haggis', lines 37–42)

The poem thus becomes the focal point of a ceremony in which we witness the wider public performance of Scots martial prowess, national resilience and even global reputation.

In popular published guides to the Supper, then, ritual performance of standard elements is an indispensable part of the event, during which these elements take on a larger symbolic and communal function. A typical evening might be described as beginning with the Selkirk Grace (once erroneously attributed to Burns); the first course is followed by piping in of the haggis, then the 'Address'; main and dessert courses are followed by a standard series of toasts: the Loyal Toast, the 'Immortal Memory'; the 'Toast to the Lassies' and 'Reply to the Laddies'; and it is capped off by all participating in singing 'Auld Lang Syne' (often to a series of ritualised movements).[11] Where early accounts of Burns Suppers were often *descriptive* – Lockhart's outline of an anniversary dinner held in Edinburgh in 1819, for example[12] – such guides tend towards the actively *prescriptive* by promoting observance of established forms and a rigidly codified set of essential components. The ceremony of piping in the haggis, for instance, appears to have evolved as part of nineteenth-century St Andrews Dinners, crossing over to Burns's Suppers with some assistance from Scots military regiments. There is some evidence to suggest that the ritual itself was treated as a humorous event,[13] a kind of 'mock-procession' befitting Burns's mock-heroic address. Yet, such associations sometimes do not cross to popular guides to the Burns Supper, which can be comparatively reverential in their treatment of the haggis ritual. Rennie McOwan's advice to beginners outlines an elaborate haggis 'Procession' including the order in which to process and who can participate. Here, the pudding itself takes on the almost sacramental function of embodying Burns, whereby '[t]he Haggis is really meant as a symbol. It is a reminder to us of the life of Robert Burns and the type of food he would have eaten two centuries ago'.[14] There are similar religious undertones to Nancy Marshall's description:

> The Haggis ceremony begins when the Chairman is signalled from the kitchen that all is ready. He asks the company to stand to receive the haggis and the piper or fiddler then leads in the chef carrying the haggis aloft, followed by a third person with two bottles of whisky. They march around the room to the top table, while the guests perform a slow handclap. The platter is placed on the table in front of the Chairman, who invites the chef and piper to join him in a glass of whisky to toast the haggis. Together they raise their glasses in the Gaelic toast '*Slainte mhath*' [. . .] – your good health. The chef and piper then leave the proceedings (the piper rejoining his table) and the company take their seats. The Chairmen or an invited guest then recites 'To a Haggis'.[15]

Barbara Kirshenblatt-Gimblet and Brooks McNamara outline typical elements of what they call 'Processional performance': a means of getting from A to B which includes ceremonial features that distinguish it from ordinary movement, such as dress and music, and an accessible symbolism readily comprehended by the audience. 'Through its symbols,' they add, 'the procession formalizes and dramatizes some event of importance to the community.'[16] The commemoration of Burns is clearly such an event, yet what Marshall's account of the 'Haggis ceremony' suggests is that, above and beyond the commemoration of

Burns, the performance of 'Scotland' is of particular communal importance here. We have an instantly recognisable symbolism – from kilted piper through to the ceremonial carrying of whisky – which immediately signifies 'Scotland' to spectators. The insistence upon a Gaelic toast might even suggest that this is the Scotland of 'Invented Tradition', whereby an ersatz nineteenth-century Highlandism becomes representative of the nation as a whole.[17] The stereotypical trait of (predominantly male) conviviality fuelled by the over-consumption of alcohol was established as a marker of Scottish identity through popular memory of Burns as early as the nineteenth century.[18] Far from simply acting as a way to get a recognisably 'national' dish out of the kitchen and onto the plates of diners, then, the ceremony of the haggis becomes a symbolically overdetermined communal imagining of nationhood. Far from being simply a trivialising symbol of tartanry, the haggis is, as Joy Fraser argues, a contested symbol 'generative of multiple and often competing meanings and perspectives on Scottishness'.[19]

Immortal Memories of Scotland

The ritual performances linked to the annual commemoration of Burns from the 1890s onwards can be viewed as an example of what Rigney calls 'embodied practices of remembrance', in which the idea of Scotland as a past or place to be recovered has become intrinsic to the social commemoration of Burns. A ballad penned by James Adams, MD, for 'recital on the 25 January and 21st July', published in *The Burns Chronicle* in 1896, adopts the common motif of diasporic longing for homeland in which Burns Night provides occasion for 'Leal brither Scots, in distant lands, / Their fondest memories twine, / Of Home, of Love, of Friendships dear, / With his songs of Langsyne'. Indeed, studies of the role of empire and diaspora in spreading the commemoration of Burns points to such factors as nostalgia in places as far apart as India or the United States.[20] Yet there is more to the commemoration of Burns as national symbol than the sentimental longing of expatriate Scots in distant lands. The Reverend Hugh MacMillan's 'Immortal Memory' speech at Greenock around the same time as Adams's verse shows a different aspect of how the popular memory of Burns becomes conflated with the revival of a national past in the present:

> It is well to have such commemorations as this, if only to keep in remembrance our nationality. At one time, not so long ago, Scottish names connected with the Scottish capital were at the head of our English Literature, and Edinburgh was in truth the Modern Athens. England, by the attraction of its superior wealth and political importance, is gradually assimilating our country to its own likeness. In such circumstances, we are called upon to

> maintain and assert our individuality as a nation and a country with greater zeal and resoluteness than ever. And the best way of doing so is, not by echoing the parrot-cry of 'Justice to Scotland' in regard to its political interests, but by such commemorations as this, which fan the fire of our patriotism through our homage to our great national poet. Scotsmen are cosmopolitan, and Scottish blood everywhere has a peculiarly cohesive property; and in every country under heaven our kinsmen tonight meet together, and while they do speak with rapture of what Robert Burns has done for their native land.[21]

The key point here is that, for MacMillan, annual re-enactment of Burns Suppers keeps Scottish culture alive and distinct as a sentimental idea rather than political entity. Notably, he rejects political solutions at a time when the question of Home Rule is very much on the political agenda.[22] The anniversary, in other words, suffices as a mass cultural outlet for patriotic Scottish feeling without having to trouble with the messy business of constitutional change, and cultural re-assertion acts as surrogate for political self-determination.

What such sources suggest is that the 'Scottishness' on display during the 'bureaucratic period' is not singular and can involve performance of an identity that in differing contexts can be at once Scottish and British, provincial and imperial, regional and global. Burns Suppers across the world display an often-complex negotiation between different kinds of identities, including the civic, national and patriotic. Elizabeth Buettner, for example, has explored the multiple overlapping identities linked to Scottishness in colonial India in the 1920s, where St Andrews Night – then a more prominent display of Scottish identity than the Burns Supper – gave opportunity also to reinforce British identity and Scotland's role in empire.[23] Ann Rigney questions the notion that the kind of self-image constructed in cultural memory 'relates to the "unity and particularity" of a given group' by proposing that celebration of Burns involves 'appropriation by multiple, often over-lapping communities'.[24] As she concludes

> [Burns's] immensely broad appeal created a convivial platform in which multi-layered identities were displayed in an increasingly globalized world, inhabited by people who were themselves often boundary-crossing migrants. At times their frame of reference was very broad indeed.[25]

The evidence from diaspora communities would appear to bear out her point about intersecting social 'frames' of identity. Indeed, examples from the New World reveal a palimpsest of identities enacted through a supper recast presumably to suit audience tastes in the host nation. At the ninth Burns Anniversary of the Springfield Caledonians in Glendower Hotel, Springfield, MA on 25 January 1892, performances included spoken 'sentiments' titled 'America' and 'Scotland' and musical performances of Burns's 'Rantin' Rovin' Robin' along with sentimental remembrances of homeland in the 'Scottish Emigrant' song 'I am Lying on a Foreign Shore' and the popular faux-Burns ballad 'Scotland Yet':[26]

They tell o' lands wi' brichter skies,
        Where freedom's voice ne'er rang,
Gie me the land where Ossian dwelt,
        And Coila's minstrel sang –
For I've nae skill o' lands, my lads
        That kenna to be free –
Then Scotland's vales, and Scotland's dales,
        And Scotland's hills for me,
I'll drink a Cup to Scotland yet,
        Wi' a' the honours three.[27]

Ending the evening with a company recital of 'The Star-Spangled Banner' alongside Carolina Oliphant, Lady Nairne's Jacobite song 'Will Ye No Come Back Again', then 'Auld Lang Syne', asks guests to perform the kind of complex patriotic identifications that are also evident in later US suppers. A similar template seems to have been followed at other suppers by the Springfield Caledonians, with 'Rantin' Rovin' Robin' starting the evening followed by speeches or 'sentiments' about Scotland and America and popular Scottish ballads. At their twelfth Burns Anniversary of 1895, performances included Burns's 'O' a' the Airts the Wind can Blaw', John Fulcher's 'Where hath Scotland Found her Fame'[28] and traditional song 'Annie Laurie', with solos on mandolin and guitar. It might be noted that the American accent to this evening is reflected in the dinner menu, a haute cuisine affair with oysters, consommé and salmon and an occasional nod to Caledonia with a couple of options – 'Mutton Broth' and 'Scotch Punch' – but without the couthy pretensions sometimes witnessed at US suppers. Instead, celebration of local provenance featured strongly with turkey from Vermont, 'Escalloped Oysters, a la Newberg' and 'Pommes de Saratoga'.[29] At the fourteenth Burns Anniversary in 1897, the performances were similarly Scots in spirit yet American in execution. Musical performances of 'Rantin' Rovin' Robin' again kicked off an evening which included singing of the popular ballad about Highland Mary, 'Bonny Mary of Argyll' and 'The Land of the Leal' by Carolina Oliphant. To add to the overlapping frames of cultural reference, an intriguingly hybrid 'selection of Scottish melodies' was played on the mandolin, an instrument then becoming popular in America through Italian immigrant communities.[30]

Performing Patriotism

If we move forward a century to see what is happening at the other end of the 'bureaucratic period', examples from the New World diaspora community again show the modification of (by this time more stable) Burns Supper rituals, and suggest an even more complex negotiation between intersecting national identities via a format that invites both public signification of Scottishness and civic performance of one's patriotic duty as a citizen of the host nation. Clan Cameron No. 7's programme for their supper held in 1984, for example, depicts photographs of an earlier anniversary in which formal Highland dress is much on display.[31] There is perhaps nothing surprising here, but it pays to remind ourselves that it is in part due to diaspora societies in North America that we see the adoption of Highland dress – the sartorial signifier of 'invented' Scottishness – at the commemoration of Burns the Lowland Scot.[32] The clan's supper menu follows the laws of performative Scottishness with a Scottified 'Fairin' of Scotch Broth and Roast Beef', yet even in this Burnsian Brigadoon, one cannot ignore the material reality of contemporary US consumer culture: the menu thoughtfully includes tea, coffee or 'Sanka', a major US brand of instant decaff.[33]

The overlapping frames of cultural identity are only too evident in the Burns celebrations of Clan Cameron No. 7. Their Burns Supper of 1982, for instance, was held in Cranston, Rhode Island on 23 January in a suitably 'hybrid' venue of the Cranston Portuguese Club Hall. Though Clan Cameron No. 7 was instituted in 1883, its 'Burns Committee' was formed only in 1962, and this was their nineteenth supper after the first in 1963. It had, however, since its inception involved a number of diaspora societies linked with the Providence Caledonian Society, including the Daughters of Argyle, the Daughters of Scotia, the St Andrews Society and the 'British Subcommittee' of Rhode Island Heritage. In the order of ceremony, this gathering of the clan societies piled patriotic identity upon patriotic identity. The evening commenced with two national anthems, 'The Star-Spangled Banner' followed by 'God Save the Queen', which set an overarching frame of national reference in which later performances of conventional Scottish songs appeared. Therefore, the performance of an imagined community of Scots descent allowed by the Burns Supper takes place within the context of a very real US citizenship, reaffirmed through the opening ritual of patriotic song, while the tributes to the British monarch which punctuate the evening add another layer of complexity. The 1982 supper itself is mostly conventional – 'The Star o' Robbie Burns', the 'Selkirk Grace', 'Piping of the Haggis', 'Toast to the Lassies' and so forth – but it is the very conventionality that brings dissonance. In tradition, the Loyal Toast enacts allegiance to the reigning monarch (as in the example of Bridgeton club's toasts early in the century to the '"The King," "The Queen," "The Prince of Scotland and the Royal Family"').[34] Yet here the Loyal Toast to Her Majesty Queen Elizabeth II is preceded by a quite different expression of loyalty to the president of the USA. Even given the sartorial and culinary Scottishness on display, we nevertheless see the ritualised performance of a complex diaspora identity, one grasping for a distant past yet inexorably bound by present circumstances and criss-crossed with other forms of civic and patriotic identification.

Across the border in Canada, there are similar examples of the public celebration of Scottish heritage within overlapping frames of performative identity. The Winnipeg Burns Club's anniversary dinners, for example, present a mix of Scottish cultural signifiers with Canadian civic identity and a hybrid 'settler' identity. Their 1956 dinner treated guests to performances of 'A Red Red Rose', 'Lay your Loof in Mine Lass', 'Ye Banks and Braes' and 'My Braw John Highlandman', as well as a 'selection of comic Scottish Songs'. Yet toasts were also offered 'to Canada, the land we live in' and – equally appropriate for an event whose head table included both the lieutenant governor and premier of the Manitoba province and the US vice-consul – to 'Oor Guid Neebor to the South'. The response by 'the lassies' was given, we are told, by 'a descendent of the old Selkirk settlers', one Margaret E. Bayer, whose reply was apparently a polyglottal performance of 'pidgin' settler identity 'all the more amusing since it was rendered in the old Red River dialect, a mixture of Scottish, English, French and Cree Indian languages'. Keen to show 'the cosmopolitan nature of the gathering', the reporter to *The Burns Chronicle* notes that a Swede responded to the Canada toast, that the guest speaker was English, and that the singer was a 'Canadian of Ukrainian descent', concluding 'Who was it said the Scottish people were clannish?'[35] One of their later anniversary dinners of 25 January 1982 mixed typical elements of the Burns Supper with civic displays of patriotic loyalty, opening with the Canadian national anthem, and again incorporating the President's Toast to 'Canada the Land we Live in'.[36] Such practices do not appear to have been uniform among Canadian clubs. The Edmonton Scottish Society's Burns Night of 23 January 1988, at which editor James Mackay gave the 'Immortal Memory', did not include the Canadian anthem, but a toast to 'The Twa Lands' was given by the British consul general, as well as the standard toast to the queen, in an otherwise typical night of Scottified fare and Scottish country dancing.[37]

What these diasporic performances remind us is that the kind of Scottishness on display can happily co-exist as a cultural enactment within a larger distinctly non-Scottish frame of civic and political life. Nigel Leask, for instance, has shown how an 'approved' version of Scottish cultural tradition was expressed and encouraged within the British Empire. His analysis suggests how one might offset the other, how the inconvenient fact of Scots' active and disproportionate role within the British Empire could be compensated for with a belief in spreading the notions of 'Caledonian' liberty stemming from Burns.[38] We see something of this theme enacted by the Caledonian Society of Colorado Springs, who framed their 'Burns Banquet' as an opportunity to remember ancestors who 'with their lives laid the foundation for freedom and liberty not only for Scotland but for other lands'.[39] Other Burns Suppers suggest how a performative version of Scots 'liberty' can sit comfortably with present-day colonial structures. Centenary celebrations in New Zealand in 1896 included an 'Immortal Memory' in Dunedin which foregrounded the 'civilising' effects of Scotland abroad: 'In every quarter of the globe – Europe, Asia, Africa, and America – wherever Scotchmen have penetrated, or civilisation obtains, men and women are joining you, and with uplifted voices proclaiming that the Poet's memory is hallowed in their hearts for ever.'[40] Colonial tributes compiled for the *Burns Chronicle* around the onset of World War One claimed 'Burns is one of the assets of Empire', whose 'democratic song', 'A Man's a Man' expresses the 'spirit' that moves the 'persevering colonist', and one of the collected tributes from New Zealand boasts that 'earth's remotest ends are, at thy name, / In sympathetic bonds brought side by side'.[41] At the 1956 anniversary in Dunedin, the message of universal brotherhood of which William H. Brown, past president of Dunedin Burns Club, spoke becomes a 'gospel' (note the missionary connotations of the phrase) whereby Burns's proto-democratic strain is reinterpreted as justification for the extension of British territorial sovereignty:[42]

> For over thirty years in New Zealand I have attended anniversary celebrations around 25th January and have heard the gospel according to Robert Burns proclaimed again and again-the brotherhood of man irrespective of creed, race or colour-and invariably my thoughts have turned to the Treaty of Waitangi. What Burns would have done in certain circumstances if his life had been lived under different conditions or perhaps in a different age has often been discussed and debated. Perhaps I may venture further into the realms of conjecture and say that Burns would have strongly approved of the Treaty of Waitangi and found much to admire in this young democracy being established in the far away Pacific.[43]

Through a clumsy rhetorical sleight of hand – annual commemoration 'invariably' leads to thoughts of the Antipodean constitution – Brown reads the 1840 Treaty of Waitangi as extending democracy to a new nation, and as consistent with the word of Burns who, it seems, would have approved of a treaty which established British colonial government in the fledgling colony of New Zealand.

If, then, the Burns Supper has long offered occasion for Scots to publicly perform such aspects of civic identity as patriotism then it has frequently ensured that such patriotism is put in service of British imperial interests or acts as a simultaneous means of performing loyalty to the Crown. In the decades following the 1896 centenary celebrations, the Burns Supper appears to have been particularly attuned to moments of national 'crisis'. On the death of Queen Victoria on 22 January 1901, The Edinburgh Ninety Burns Club abandoned its anniversary dinner 'in accordance with the national mourning for Her Majesty'; while the Sunderland Burns Club 'as loyal Scotsmen' lamented 'the great loss the nation has sustained', forthwith suspended all entertainments, and sent a letter of condolence to the new king.[44] Cancellations of Burns Suppers intensified with the onset of World War One. At that time, a letter from the president of the Burns Federation noted either suspension of activities or cancellation of the anniversary dinner alone among a number of Burns Clubs. One such federation member, the Moorpark Burns Club, cancelled their 1914–15 schedule and donated membership subscriptions to war funds. Others such as Hull turned their anniversary dinner into a 'Scottish Concert in aid of the Belgian Relief Fund'.[45] The 'Immortal Memory' delivered at a supper held in Sunderland – to which soldiers stationed nearby were invited – was a 'clarion call to Scotsmen to follow the example of Burns himself' and his love of country, a 'love which inspires the patriotic zeal which makes Scotland stand out as one of the largest contributors in men and money at this momentous time in the history of our country'.[46] By 1917, this contribution appears to have paid dividends in the lives of members wounded or killed in action being reported by federated clubs.[47] By 25 January 1919, the London Robert Burns Club was still mobilising Burns's message in service of a triumphant British Empire, paying tribute to Burns's 'spirit of liberty, equality and fraternity' as 'the negation of the hateful, and, fortunately, discredited doctrines of Prussia', offering a military toast (a common feature of suppers) to 'The British Imperial Forces' that praised the important contribution of the 'Scottish race' to Empire, and proposing an Immortal Memory focused upon the armed services and Burns's sympathy for soldiers.[48]

Horizontal Comradeship

That the assertion of Scottishness at Burns Suppers has often worked happily within the larger frame of British interests should perhaps come as little surprise. As Rigney argues '"Britishness" is in effect a Scottish invention: a broad social frame that, by allowing Scots to retain their cultural distinctiveness without being politically independent, also paved the way for their mass complicity in British imperialism.'[49] Pittock and Whatley have outlined how a 'unionist nationalism' has been a feature of Burns Suppers since the nineteenth century, wherein we see 'performance as a celebration of communal solidarity linked not to present issues but to a narrative of shared historical inheritance, revivified not solely through public acts of memory dedicated to heroes, but by other factors' such as 'a shared present simultaneously realised with the celebration of a shared past, and the selection of poetry (and sometimes objects) which underpinned certain key Scottish (often gendered) national values'. Here, the authors highlight how 'drink [. . .] convivial association, loyalty to locality, egalitarianism, meritocratic ambition and a distaste for inherited power, became closely associated with Burns'.[50] One might read the Burns Supper in this context in terms of the performance of an imagined horizontal comradeship,[51] which presents a temporary alignment of national communal interests regardless of actual social or political divisions. As phrased by the secretary of the Glencairn Burns Club during the 1896 centenary celebrations, 'And now in cottage, as in lordly hall / Thy soul inspiring, mind-enriching themes, / Alike the peasant and the prince enthral.'[52] The Burns Supper, in other words, temporarily collapses class distinctions in order to bring Scots together in a moment of simultaneous national communion.

Yet, for all the enacting of 'a man's a man for a' that', existing social structures can remain firmly in place. An account of the 1896 celebrations in New South Wales, for example, exemplifies the strict observance of hierarchy that has sometimes framed the displays of egalitarian sentiment typical of Burns Night:

> The Governor was received by a guard of honour, consisting of eighty-five men and four pipers from the Scottish Rifles, under Lieutenants Grieve and Machardy. The pipers played the Royal salute and escorted his Excellency into the room, followed by the Premier [. . .] As the Governor took his seat between Dr. MacLaurin (who presided) and Mrs MacLaurin, the orchestra of the Permanent Artillery, located in the gallery, played the National Anthem. Immediately on the chairman's left, sat Mrs McCormick and the Premier.[53]

Archaeologists point out that the ritual activity of feasting is often associated with ideological power, expressing social structures such as status, gender, or age through such things as the social seating or the behaviour on display in such a way that can either support or challenge them.[54] Far from collapsing class distinctions, then, the Burns Supper can work within such structures to merely temporarily suspend class hostility. For the London Robert Burns Clubs writing during the Great War, such suspension would unite them with the prestigious London Burns Club: 'We are in the midst of a war which is breaking down convention and levelling men of all classes in society, and which is making men realise more than ever the absolute truth of the Poet's dictum: "A man's a man for a' that".' Harry Lauder's reply from the London Burns Club tellingly turns this vision of fraternity into a specifically imperial camaraderie: 'That man to man, the Empire o'er, / Shall brothers be for a' that.'[55]

The calcification of existing social structures as something occurring between 'men' and 'brothers' should not go unnoticed. Though women have long been admitted to anniversary dinners, practice has been uneven. For their dinner of 1913, 'Ye Cronies Burns Club' of Govan boasted that 'on this occasion we had the ladies with us and they enjoyed themselves immensely'.[56] Other clubs have chosen an exclusively male format for their anniversary dinner. Hull Burns Club opted for a 'smoking concert' – a traditionally male-only form of popular entertainment – to raise funds for British prisoners of war as the form of their 1916 anniversary dinner.[57] The whist drive held for their anniversary celebration the following year was presumably more inclusive,[58] yet the concert format exemplifies how performances at Burns Suppers have traditionally included elements of male performativity in audience and attenders. McGinn notes women joining as equals in Burns Suppers following World War One,[59] though not universally, and the ritual activities associated with the Burns Supper have also tended to embed existing gender divisions and disparities of power. For the first hundred years of the Burns Supper, it appears that a woman giving a speech was far from the norm, and the reply from the lassies – responding to a traditional toast which itself encourages those women present to identify with persistent gender stereotypes – seems only to have been a feature since the 1920s.[60]

If the commemoration of Burns has thus imagined change through the kind of inversion of social hierarchy expressed in his radical anthem, Burns anniversary dinners have often given a chance for participants, regardless of their gender or status, to act out a Scots identity associated with working-class men. The haggis, set as peasant dish par excellence in contrast with the high-status French ragout, is a symbol of reverse social mobility. It is not the only 'egalitarian' dish to have been served at suppers held by Burns Clubs throughout the twentieth century. An alternative supper which appears to have formed part of the standard club calendar for a while was the 'tattie and herrin' supper', a dish of flaked salt herring bulked out with potatoes with the reputation of being a frugal meal.[61] A song written around the Crimean War reveals its working-class credentials, and an intriguingly similar association between diet and the hardiness of ordinary Scotsmen as warriors as 'To a Haggis':

> Noo a pound in the week, you maun aye be content
> Ten bob tae lay by for the claes and the rent
> Half a croon ye aye can be sparin'
> Ye've aye seven and sixpence for tatties and herrin'
> [. . .]

When the Queen wanted someone tae fecht wi' her foes
It wisna awa' tae the lowlands she goes
But awa' tae the hills where the brave an' the darin'
The lads that were fed upon tatties and herrin'[62]

In the opening years of the twentieth century, the tattie and herrin' supper appears to have become a regular alternative supper in the Burns calendar. The Rosebery Burns Club appears to have held one in April 1903 and also 1905,[63] as did the Western Burns Club.[64] The Greenock Burns Club resolved to hold a St Andrews Night tattie and herrin' supper for session 1904–5 'for the furtherance of Burns [sic] idea of brotherhood',[65] suggesting that this additional supper in the calendar offered further occasion for the public performance of Burnsian egalitarianism. The Tam o' Shanter Burns Club had not one but two tattie and herrin' suppers in the season 1912–13 and another in October of the following year.[66] When war broke out, Helensburgh Burns Club's annual tatties and herrin' supper sold tickets to raise money for the Belgian Relief Fund[67] and herrings were even sent to the Western front to enable soldiers to celebrate Burns Night in true Scottish style.[68] Although this is a rare occasion when the herrin' supper appears to have merged with Burns Supper proper, there are other examples where the dish was served as part of the anniversary dinner. The 1914 Burns Supper menu from Hourston and Sons of Ayr includes 'Potted herrin' and tatties' among its extensive menu of 'Biled Cod', 'Briests o' Chuckies', 'Sheip Heid', 'Bubbly Jock wi' Soo's Leg' and other culinary examples of performative Scottishness.[69] Like the haggis, the tattie and herrin' supper could perform a similar function of providing symbolically Scottish sustenance in a ritual aimed at celebrating ordinary life and embodying horizontal camaraderie.

As 'embodied performance' therefore, the Burns Supper allows communal imagining of a Scottish identity through the rituals associated with, yet often obliquely evolved from, the annual commemoration of Scotland's national poet. Yet examples from home, diaspora and other communities show the way in which this public assertion of national identity is never a simple sentimental performance of a singular 'Scottishness'. The Burns Supper has often shown a negotiation between different frames of civic and patriotic identification, and in doing so, it has displayed an adaptability to different circumstances that acts as a counterpoint to the apparent codification of ritual elements associated with the event throughout the twentieth century. The Burns Supper can also be said to be central to the performance of Scotland's self-image as a nation of egalitarian values, and its history can reveal an inclusive phenomenon which brings in different people from different parts of the world; but part of that story must include how the Supper has at times acted in the service of considerably less progressive forces.

Notes

1. Robert Burns, 'To a Haggis', in *The Poems and Songs of Robert Burns, Vol. 1*, ed. James Kinsley (Oxford: Oxford University Press, 1968), pp. 310–12, line 18.
2. *The Burns Chronicle* (1957), p. 150.
3. Ann Rigney, 'Embodied Communities: Commemorating Robert Burns, 1859', *Representations* 115 (2011), p. 77.
4. Ibid.
5. See Benedict Anderson, *Imagined Communities: Reflections on the Origin and Spread of Nationalism*, rev. edn (London and New York: Verso, 2006).
6. See, for example, Mary Ellen Brown on the development of and 'elaboration' upon the Burns Supper in *Burns and Tradition* (London: MacMillan, 1984), pp. 117–39.
7. Clark McGinn, *The Burns Supper: A Comprehensive History* (Edinburgh: Luath, 2019), p. 21.
8. Lisa Wood, '"Wholesome Nutriment" for the Rising Generation: Food, Nationalism, and Didactic Fiction at the End of the Eighteenth Century', *Eighteenth Century Fiction* 21:4 (2009), pp. 615–30 (pp. 615–17).
9. Clark McGinn, *The Ultimate Burns Supper Book* (Glasgow: Bell & Bain, 2006), pp. 73–7.
10. Ibid., pp. 75–7.
11. For an outline of the 'bureaucratic' formalities of the supper, see McGinn, *The Burns Supper*, p. 158.
12. John Gibson Lockhart, *Peter's Letters to his Kinsfolk* (1819) (Glasgow: Thomas Nelson, 1952), letters 4 and 5.
13. McGinn, *The Burns Supper*, pp. 273–6.
14. Rennie McOwan, *Robert Burns for Beginners* (Castle Douglas: Rowan Tree Printing, 1995), p. 60.
15. Nancy Marshall, *The Chambers Companion to the Burns Supper* (Edinburgh: Chambers 1992), p. 31.
16. Barbara Kirshenblatt-Gimblett and Brooks McNamara, 'Processional Performance: An Introduction', *The Drama Review* 29:3 (1985), pp. 2–5 <www.jstor.org/stable/1145648> [accessed 26 November 2019].
17. Hugh-Trevor Roper, 'The Highland Tradition of Scotland', in Eric Hobsbawm and Terence Ranger (eds), *The Invention of Tradition* (Cambridge: Cambridge University Press, 1983), p. 15.
18. See Murray Pittock and Christopher A. Whately, 'Poems and Festivals, Art and Artefact and the Commemoration of Robert Burns, c.1844–c.1896', *Scottish Historical Review* 236 (2014), pp. 63–4.
19. Joy Fraser, 'A Taste of Scotland? Representing and Contesting Scottishness in Expressive Culture about Haggis' (unpublished doctoral thesis, Memorial University of Newfoundland, 2011), p. 172.

20. See Christopher A. Whately, 'Robert Burns, Memorialization, and the "Heart-Beatings" of Victorian Scotland', in Murray Pittock (ed.), *Robert Burns in Global Culture* (Lewisburg, PA: Bucknell University Press, 2011), p. 212.
21. Quoted in John Cairney (ed.), *Immortal Memories* (Edinburgh: Luath, 2003), p. 169.
22. See, for example, Hansard on the Commons motion on Home Rule held in Westminster on 9 April 1889. <https://api.parliament.uk/historic-hansard/commons/1889/apr/09/home-rule-for-scotland> [accessed 28 November 2019].
23. Elizabeth Buettner, 'Haggis in the Raj: Private and Public Celebrations of Scottishness in Late Imperial India', *Scottish Historical Review* 2 (2002), pp. 212–39.
24. Rigney, 'Embodied Communities', p. 85.
25. Ibid., p. 95.
26. 'Ninth Burns Anniversary [held by] Springfield Caledonian Club' (New York Public Library Digital Collections) <https://digitalcollections.nypl.org/items/510d47db-2283-a3d9-e040-e00a18064a99> [accessed 11 October 2019].
27. 'Broadside Ballad Entitled "Scotland Yet"' (National Library of Scotland) <https://digital.nls.uk/broadsides/view/?id=15017> [accessed 24 January 2020].
28. 'Broadside Ballad Entitled "Where Has Scotland Found her Fame"' (National Library of Scotland) <https://digital.nls.uk/broadsides/view/?id=16042> [accessed 24 January 2020]. Attributed to Fulcher in David Baptie, *Musical Scotland: Past and Present* (Paisley: J and R Parlane, 1894), p. 58.
29. 'Twelfth Burns Anniversary [held by] Springfield Caledonians' (New York Public Library Digital Collections) <https://digitalcollections.nypl.org/items/510d47db-2793-a3d9-e040-e00a18064a99> [accessed 11 October 2019].
30. 'Fourteenth Burns Anniversary [held by] Springfield Caledonians' (New York Public Library Digital Collections) <https://digitalcollections.nypl.org/items/510d47db-2c72-a3d9-e040-e00a18064a99> [accessed 11 October 2019]. On the mandolin in America during the period, see Jean Dickson, 'Mandolin Mania in Buffalo's Italian Community, 1895 to 1918', *Journal of World Anthropology: Occasional Papers* 2 (2006), pp. 1–15.
31. 'The Twenty-First Annual Burns Supper, Celebrating the 225th Anniversary of the Birth of Robert Burns, Rhodes-on-the-Pawtuxet, Cranston, Rhode Island, Saturday, January 28, 1984', Edinburgh, National Library of Scotland, PB8.209.285/12.

32. Clark McGinn, 'Vehement Celebrations: The Global Celebration of the Burns Supper since 1801', in Pittock (ed.), *Robert Burns in Global Culture*, p. 199; cf. Murray Pittock and Christopher A. Whatley, 'Poems and Festivals, Art and Artefacts and the Commemoration of Robert Burns, *c.*1844-*c.*1896', *Scottish Historical Review* 93:1 (April 2014), pp. 56–79 (p. 66).
33. 'The Nineteenth Annual Burns Supper Celebrating the 223rd Anniversary of the Birth of Robert Burns', Edinburgh, National Library of Scotland, PB8.209.285/13.
34. *The Burns Chronicle* (1918), p. 120. An outline of the range of toasts given at Burns Suppers throughout their history appears in Mary Ellen Brown, *Burns and Tradition*, pp. 126, 130.
35. *The Burns Chronicle* (1957), p. 125.
36. '75th Anniversary Burns Supper, Marlborough Inn, Winnipeg. Monday, January 25, 1982', Edinburgh, National Library of Scotland, PB6.209.238/24.
37. 'Burns Night', Edinburgh, National Library of Scotland, PB5.209.570/14.
38. Nigel Leask, '"Their Groves o' Sweet Myrtles": Robert Burns and the Scottish Colonial Experience', in Pittock (ed.), *Robert Burns in Global Culture*, p. 173.
39. *Burns Chronicle* (1914), p. 160.
40. *Burns Chronicle* (1897), p. 130.
41. *Burns Chronicle* (1915), pp. 56–9.
42. On the Treaty of Waitangi see <https://www.waitangitribunal.govt.nz/treaty-of-waitangi/signing-of-the-treaty/> [accessed 29 October 2019].
43. William H. Brown, 'Burns and New Zealand', *The Burns Chronicle* (1958), p. 69.
44. *Burns Chronicle* (1902), p. 119; (1903), p. 112.
45. *Burns Chronicle* (1915), p. 165, p. 168, p. 174; cf. McGinn, *The Burns Supper*, p. 182.
46. *Burns Chronicle* (1916), pp. 103–6.
47. See the Club Notes in the *Burns Chronicle* of 1917. Sunderland Burns Club notes attendance by wounded soldiers (p. 136), while Ye Cronies Burns Club records some twenty-three members missing or killed in action (p. 146).
48. See the *Burns Chronicle* (1920), pp. 46–57.
49. Rigney, 'Embodied Communities', p. 91.
50. Pittock and Whatley, 'Poems and Festivals', p. 69.
51. A term used by Benedict Anderson to describe the nation as imagined community.
52. James Laing, 'Centenary Tribute to the Memory of Robert Burns', *Burns Chronicle* (1896), p. 98.

53. 'United Highland Haggis Supper', *Burns Chronicle* (1897), p. 124.
54. Katheryn Twiss, 'The Archaeology of Food and Social Diversity', *Journal of Archaeological Research* 20:4 (2012), p. 364.
55. *Burns Chronicle* (1918), pp. 110–12.
56. *Burns Chronicle* (1914), p. 161.
57. *Burns Chronicle* (1917), p. 148.
58. *Burns Chronicle* (1918), p. 123.
59. McGinn, 'Vehement Celebrations', pp. 200–1.
60. McGinn, *The Burns Supper*, pp. 362–4.
61. *Dictionary of the Older Scottish Tongue*, 'tatties and herrin' <https://dsl.ac.uk/entry/snd/tattie [accessed 23 July 2020]
62. Norman Buchan and Peter Hall, *The Scottish Folksinger: 118 Modern and Traditional Folksongs*, new edn (London: Collins, 1978), p. 26.
63. *Burns Chronicle* (1903) p. 115; (1905), p. 107.
64. *Burns Chronicle* (1905), p. 111.
65. Ibid., p. 112.
66. *Burns Chronicle* (1914), pp. 152–3; (1915), p. 161.
67. *Burns Chronicle* (1915), p. 161.
68. McGinn, *The Burns Supper*, pp. 183–4.
69. 'Burns Anniversary. Celebrated Jany. 26 & 27, 1914', Edinburgh, National Library of Scotland, HP2.90.119.

7

Burns, Public Ceremonial and Civic Scotland, *c.*1796–*c.*1914

Christopher A. Whatley

In the numerous industrial cities and towns of Britain during the 'long' nineteenth century, the period with which this chapter is primarily concerned, spectacular pageants, parades and processions were commonplace. They marked royal birthdays, coronations and visits, as well as certain anniversaries, and often preceded the opening of prestigious public buildings and the unveiling of statues and monuments. Amongst the functions of such carefully choreographed dramatic spectacles – some of which were 'invented traditions' – was a desire on the part of the civic authorities to create social cohesion through (mainly) joyful celebrations in what were often stressed urban communities.[1] Across the country urban rulers strove to encourage orderly, consensus-building civic ceremonials, thereby engendering loyalty, obedience and co-operation.[2] By ritualistic and performative means they reinforced prevailing hierarchies of power and authority. Burgh trades – anxious to assert their rightful place within urban communities, also organised and marshalled their own parades for the kinds of civic occasions mentioned above.[3] Typically, marchers on processions of this kind carried banners, bannerettes, emblems and other devices, in recognition of their visual and emotional potency for the purposes of ideological declamation, but also to commemorate and memorialise.[4]

Public Ceremonials

In the Scottish context some attention has been paid to Burns ceremonials. But mainly those held indoors, the countless Burns Suppers held on or near the date of Robert Burns's birthday on 25 January, a 'tradition' dating back to Ayr in 1801, although on that first occasion the supper actually took place on the anniversary of his death, 21 July. These tended to be small-scale, as in the early years; attendance numbers were restricted by space and the quasi-masonic format of the proceedings.[5]

We know much less about rituals devoted to Burns open to the public. In the century after Burns's death in 1796 they attracted hundreds if not thousands of participants and tens of thousands of onlookers, as has been revealed by the pioneering investigations of Alex Tyrrell and Ann Rigney.[6] The level of participation is not in itself so significant; monster crowds were a distinguishing feature of most public gatherings of any moment in Victorian Britain. However, even allowing for the difficulty contemporaries had in estimating with any degree of accuracy crowd sizes, some of the Burns-related celebrations seem to have been amongst the biggest large-scale participatory events in Victorian Scotland.[7] The first of these was in 1844, the Burns Festival at Alloway, Ayr. The last on such a scale was in Dumfries in 1896/7, as well as the two centennial celebrations that followed, in 1859 and 1896 (respectively, the centenary dates of the poet's birth and death). In passing I will allude to the ceremonies that accompanied the inauguration of Burns memorials: the monuments in Dumfries and Ayr, and the flood of statue building between 1877 and 1914.

On all of these occasions the orator (or orators) and oratory – how speakers performed – were important in galvanising and inspiring audiences, and some of this will be reported below. However, many – most – of those present in crowds of several thousand might hear only snatches of speeches, made inaudible above the general hubbub; speakers were without modern means of amplification. The satirical *Punch* magazine, represented when the Kilmarnock Burns statue was inaugurated in 1879, described the platform proceedings as having 'a private and confidential character, as far as the general public is concerned'.[8] The unveiling of the Burns statue in Dumfries's packed Church Place in 1882 – 'no more than a dumb show to all but a few hundreds in the immediate vicinity' – was another occasion when the main speaker's eloquent address, this time the fifth earl of Rosebery's, had to be read afterwards. Full verbatim reports of what was said (and sometimes what had been intended to be said but had not) appeared in local newspapers and other published accounts.[9]

At least of equal importance therefore – for participants as well as onlookers – were mnemonics, that is visual prompts including performative contributions to the ceremonies; how Burns was represented in the iconography of the many banners marchers held aloft, and in the slogans they displayed, along with other symbolic messages. Material culture of this kind, its value for historians as well as its problematisation has hitherto been largely focused on reform politics in Scotland and elsewhere in the British Isles.[10] However, the investigative tools applied in that context can usefully be extended to Burns demonstrations.[11] Our understanding of what Burns meant to contemporaries may by this means be enhanced; it takes us beyond text (what has been written about him, his work and his legacy) towards an appreciation of his appeal to the visual senses of those looking on.

I will also attempt briefly to assess the significance of these occasions, and thereby add another dimension to our understanding of Burns's place in Scottish society in the nineteenth and early twentieth centuries.

Processions Portrayed

The outdoor procession was an integral part of all of the Burns-centred commemorative events just outlined. Processions wended their way through villages and towns which were decorated with a profusion of flags and, sometimes, temporary triumphal arches, topped by appropriate mottos from or devices representing characters from Burns's poems or songs. One of the arches that spanned the road at Ayr's Townhead in 1844 was a large-scale wooden representation of 'Tam o Shanter' and 'Souter Johnnie' seated, enjoying their 'reaming swats that drank divinely'. Over time it became increasingly common for couthy characters from Burns's poems to make their appearance on such occasions. At Laurencekirk in Aberdeenshire in 1859 for instance, 'We had Tam o' Shanters and Duncan Grays in abundance and even the famous Willie who brew'd his maut [. . .] Even the de'il himself was not left unrepresented [. . .].'[12] 'Tam o Shanter', Burns's evocation of the pleasures and pitfalls of drink-infused conviviality was the most frequently publicly performed of his works in the nineteenth century, with on some occasions virtually entire communities turning out to watch as Auld Nick and his coven of witches danced before Cutty Sark chased Tam on his grey mare Maggie down so many Scottish streets.[13]

Little of the visible ornamentation was random, but rather carefully calculated to convey by visual signifiers their creators' or sponsors' messages. Responsibility for the decoration of streets and buildings was usually assumed by the civic authorities who worked hand in hand with property owners, such as hoteliers, innkeepers, shopkeepers and owners of public works.

The arrangements made by the town council of Dumfries for the Burns centenary in January 1859 were fairly typical, even if those concerned were, as custodians of the place where Burns had last lived and was buried, 'determined to excel, if not by their numbers, by their fervency' all other similar celebrations that were held across Scotland, England and overseas to mark the one hundredth anniversary of Burns's birth.[14] With burghs like Dumfries having become the voice of the post-1707 'stateless nation', what has been called 'town patriotism' was arguably even more important a motivator for organisers of such civic rituals in Scotland than in Victorian England.[15]

Along Dumfries's streets were three lines of arches, 'twelve in number, four being visible in each range when viewed from either of the three sides'. Triumphal arches were classical structures, in former times erected mainly in Edinburgh to welcome Scottish monarchs, and most recently for Queen Victoria's first visit to and tour through Scotland in 1842. Those erected in Ayr only two years later were the first in Scotland for a commoner. The Dumfries arches were decorated with evergreens and flags, while the principal triple arches which 'towered for a considerable height above the rest' were topped by flags bearing the name 'Burns', along with inscriptions, one of which read, 'He'll be a credit to us a', / We'll a' be proud o' Robin', the other, 'Preserve the dignity of man with soul erect, / And trust the universal plan will all protect'.

The procession itself was planned with military precision. Start and finish times, the route, halts, insignia, mottos used and the music (to be played by seven bands) were all laid down in advance. Predetermined too was the order of the procession. At the front were to be the magistrates and town councillors, followed by various trades bodies and occupations (even the 'Drapers' Assistants' took part), employees from the burgh's principal workplaces and, at the rear, the carters on horseback. Participants were to walk four abreast.[16]

Preparations could take weeks. Suitable boughs and greenery had to be found for the arches. Flags and banners required to be designed, sewn and painted, and exhibits of various kinds made. Enterprising silversmiths and the like struck commemorative medals for those with the wherewithal to purchase them and worn with pride by spectators and participants alike.[17] Publishers raced to print new editions of Burns's poems and songs for both the upper and lower ends of the market – the latter provided for at the time of the unveiling of the statue of Burns in Glasgow in 1877 by a 'People's Statue Edition' with paper covers costing one shilling.[18]

Civic leaders recognised that on days like these the eyes of the world could be on them. The depth of public as well as private devotion to Robert Burns in the land of his birth intrigued and puzzled outsiders, above all the London press. In July 1896 no fewer than seventy reporters descended on Dumfries to cover the anniversary of the poet's death.[19]

But it was the Burns centenary in January 1859 that topped the lot. Hardly anywhere in Scotland was not in some way touched by an event that in terms of numbers, fervour and extent was quite unprecedented.[20] Town councils usually took the initiative, sometimes prompted to do so by local Burns clubs; there was frequently an overlap in the personnel of the two bodies. It was only exceptionally where at the last minute some public-spirited individual or organisation, determined that their community should not be left out or seen as less enthusiastic about Burns than a neighbouring town or village, organised some kind of 'demonstration' of affection.[21] (Globally, there may have been up to 17,500 celebrations of some kind or other.)[22] 'We have had dinners, suppers, gatherings, and balls many a time,' it was reported of Dufftown on Speyside, 'but never anything equal to this. Excitement, enthusiasm, gossip, and scandal were at their highest pitch for weeks [. . .].' 'Never has Dunfermline, even in periods of greatest political fervour, witnessed a more enthusiastic demonstration,' a correspondent there noted. No public event, it was said of Lauder, 'has created so much stir here within the living memory of the oldest inhabitant'. But the same could have been said – and often was – of thousands of other towns, villages, hamlets and even smaller settlements. In Auchterarder it was clearly a red-letter day, with it being reported with some satisfaction that a dinner in the Railway Inn attended by all 'grades of society' had been conducted with 'utmost decorum', despite three-quarters of those present having 'never been present at a public dinner before'.[23]

In the rural districts, small bands of farmers, ploughmen and other agricultural workers gathered to process and celebrate in inns or even barns; fittingly, in Stonehaven it was 120 farmers of the Mearns on horseback who formed the procession.[24] Shops and offices closed early, as sometimes did public works, such as factories and warehouses. Announcing what was a day of national celebration in those places that had them were towns' music bells, which rang out constantly as in Linlithgow, or at pre-arranged times, as happened in Stirling. Elsewhere it was brass and flute bands that kicked off the proceedings. In places less well-endowed aurally, or additionally as darkness fell, celebratory bonfires were lit – borrowing a tradition associated with the monarch's birthday: this happened for example in Biggar in Lanarkshire, Blairingone in Fife, Dalbeattie in Kirkcudbrightshire and Patna in Ayrshire.

Participation, Paternalism and Politics

The procession that was marshalled for the Burns Festival held on the banks of the river Doon in August 1844 to mark the fact that for the first time in many years all three of the poet's sons had been on Scottish soil – provided the template others followed. In some respects what happened at Ayr was borrowed from the parades that had been features of Scottish burgh life in former times. For one witness of the Ayr procession, in which shoemakers from Ayr itself and the surrounding villages had determined to participate, 'the most striking part [. . .] was the [recently revived] pageant of King Crispin, which was got up with great splendour, and had a fine effect'.[25] In Irvine in January 1859, the procession was led by the town's carters riding on horseback, a practice that began in the seventeenth century, at the burgh's annual Marymass fair – the origins of which were medieval.[26] Similarly drawing deep from the pool of local custom was Kirkcudbright, where again in 1859 the procession, after having been addressed on the subject of Burns by one of the burgh's bailies, paraded to the town's common where members of the trades 'shot for the "siller gun" and the "silver arrow"', a centuries-old tradition.[27]

Leading the way in the Ayr procession in August 1844 was the band of the 87th Fusiliers, with the parade itself being headed by the magistrates and town

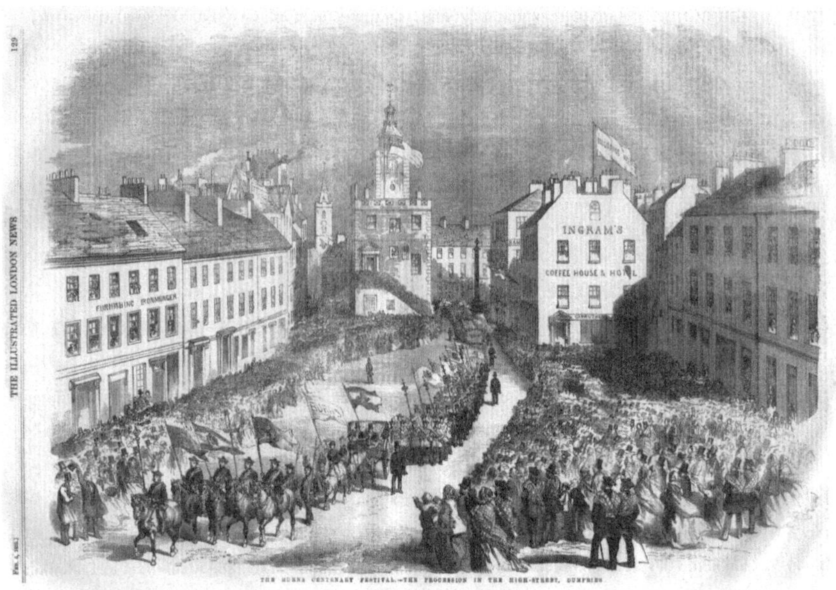

Centennial procession, Dumfries, January 1859 (*Illustrated London News*, 5 Feb. 1859, p. 132).

councils of Ayr and nearby burghs, 'with numerous bodies of Freemasons, Odd Fellows, and other trade societies, accompanied with bands of music etc, etc.'

The country's freemasons rightly claimed Burns as one of their own, arguing that the 'propelling power' and inspiration for the poet were the notions of independence and brotherhood that lodge membership instilled.[28] From the outset, therefore, freemasons were a ubiquitous feature of public festivities associated with Burns. Indeed, at the laying of the foundation stone of the architect Thomas Hamilton's monument to Burns at Alloway in January 1820 masonic lodges from throughout Ayrshire formed the body of the procession, their presence ordered by the 'most Worshipful Master of Mother Kilwinning Lodge, and as such Grand Master of the Ayrshire District'. The ceremony itself – held 'amidst a vast concourse of people, and a respectable assemblage of Ladies and Gentlemen of the County' – was conducted in accordance with full masonic rites.[29] The freemasons' influence can be seen too in processions in subsequent years which took place in the evening, by torchlight (a prominent feature of masonic marches), as at Inverkeithing in 1859 where the 'brethren of St John's' were accompanied by 'the representatives of the different trades, carrying banners etc'.[30] Freemasons would continue to have a presence at most Burns public ceremonials throughout the rest of the century – although less prominently later.

Even in 1844, however, outside observers remarked more on the presence of farmers, ploughmen and shepherds, the last-named being 'equipped with their plaids and crooks', along with the blue Kilmarnock bonnets they removed when bowing as they passed Burns's birthplace. The gesture, homage to an ordinary man rather than a magistrate, laird or lord, was significant, and may have been the first time this had happened in Scotland. The three-deep, mile-long procession made its way to the site near the river Doon, beneath the recently built Burns monument at Alloway, where the festivities were to culminate.[31]

An aspect of the Ayr festival worth noticing, as it recurred at similar occasions thereafter, was the enthusiasm amongst artisans and other sorts of working people to take part. In fact, once trade associations became aware that a Burns ceremonial was to take place, they clamoured to be included. Arguments about the order in which the various trade societies and workplaces should appear were usually resolved by ballot. In virtually all of the Burns processions from 1844 until 1914 the trades were the most prominent and usually the most numerous of the participants.

In one sense Burns was incidental. The organised trades, by the nineteenth century, were increasingly focused on their friendly society function, their collective strength and consequently their independence from the state, which they proudly proclaimed – dressed in the clothes associated with their occupation (such as bakers in white shirts, black vests, white aprons and red nightcaps) and carrying with them the implements associated with their respective trades and, often, examples of their products.

Capturing this is the following extract from a description of the procession that preceded the unveiling of Dundee's Burns statue in 1880:

> At the head of the second column were the Operative Masons, who mustered a strength of 400, and had the band of the Arbroath Rifle Volunteers. As in all other cases, the trade flag took precedence of everything else. It bore the motto, "We join to protect, not injure," and was followed by a display of the tools used in the trade.[32]

By such means on Burns parades, as on more overtly political demonstrations throughout the century, working people proclaimed the intrinsic worth of their labour.[33] As the editor of the *Dumfries and Galloway Standard* remarked at the time of the unveiling of the Burns statue in Dumfries in 1882, 'Burns was one of their [the working classes] best friends, and sang the dignity of labour, and of man as man irrespective of earthly rank, as no-one did before or has done since [. . .].'[34]

Similar sentiments were expressed and loudly cheered by those in the 25,000 crowd who could hear, at the unveiling of Sir John Steell's Burns statue in Dundee in October 1880. This was when Frank Henderson, newly elected as one of the town's two Liberal MPs and the main speaker, declared that the 'Scottish working man became transformed' through two of Burns's ideas: 'the essential dignity of his labour and the possible nobility of his life'; thereby, the 'coward slave' struck off his chains, and 'stood erect in the dignity of his manhood'.[35]

Noticeable too at Ayr, but elsewhere too, was the orderliness of the proceedings. In large part this was due to self-policing on the part of the trades, anxious to convince onlookers and the country's legislators of their respectability. Even so, the authorities worried about the potential there was for disorder amongst such vast numbers of working people – either in the processions or the watching crowds. To make sure nothing untoward happened, the bigger processions were heavily policed.[36] Drunkenness was a constant threat, while 'juveniles' were inclined to exploit the opportunity the festivities provided for them to light fires, throw fireworks and engage in other mischief late into the night.

Arguably as important in accounting for the orderliness of Burns as with other working-class parades was the 'new' paternalism adopted from mid-century in many places by employers and the civic authorities, which in its turn inculcated deference and the 'fiction' of community – in this case structured around Burns-love.[37] Shrewd employers recognised the industrial relations benefits of granting time off to their workers to participate in Burns-related rituals, or of contributing to the costs, as in January 1877 when the proprietor of Glasgow's Saracen Foundry supplied a band to accompany his workmen who were going to take part in the procession that preceded the unveiling of the city's Burns statue. Similarly, town councils and their allies exploited opportunities to earn the goodwill of their citizenry in the name of Burns by enhancing social provision. This could take the form of, for example, a new public fountain or by leading campaigns for statues of the people's poet. Older paternalistic gestures were in evidence too, as at Stranraer, also in 1859, where a 'procession of nearly 400 of the deserving poor [. . .] walked to the cross' where they were given a quartern loaf each, along with a supply of tea and sugar, to 'give them a happy evening', Lord Stair's way, it was reported, of honouring the 'centenary of the Great Peasant'.[38]

While some crafts paraded only devices and slogans advertising their own skills, handiwork and collective values, many more, including contingents from local workplaces incorporated Burns into the visual language of the processions. Banners carried titles of and lines from Burns's poems and songs, along with declarations of pride in the poet. Burns, upheld as a man who had achieved immense success and fame regardless of his relatively humble background, was someone with whom working people strongly identified, and looked to as an exemplar for the artisan class as a whole. By identifying with Burns they were at one with the Victorian Liberal zeitgeist; the labouring poor as fully fledged citizens, meriting due respect, the public space they commandeered in processions 'a visual analogue of the vote'.[39] In Scotland Burns's exalted political status was on a par with that of William Gladstone MP – as a leader and embodiment of the formerly excluded who were now 'enlisted in the armies of the just'.[40] Indeed, on the many demonstrations calling for extensions of the franchise – in 1884 for example, when there were more than 300 – phrases taken or adapted from Burns's poems were commonplace on the banners and placards carried by marchers.[41] For the centenary in 1886 of the publication of the first, 'Kilmarnock' edition of Burns poems, which attracted a crowd of some 30,000 people, not only was the Burns monument in Kay Park festooned, so too was the nearby Reformers Monument: as the 'immortal bard was himself a reformer when to enact that part was dangerous [. . .] it was appropriate that the Reformers Monument should be lavishly decorated with evergreens and floral wreaths'.[42] Burns and the cause of electoral reform were as one.

But adulation for Burns encompassed more than this: to the Scottish people, opined the editor of Dundee's *Courier & Argus* in October 1880, Burns 'stands in a different category from all other men, from every son of Scotland, however illustrious'.[43]

Parsing Processional Performance

Music was crucial; processions were noisy affairs. Cacophonous too, as the several bands rarely played the same tune concurrently. The organisers of the 1882 procession that would precede the unveiling of Amelia Hill's statue of Burns in Dumfries reckoned there should be a band of some kind for every 250 marchers.[44] As the marchers to Alloway in 1844 gathered, they were regaled by a handful of pipers – in full Highland costume. (As hinted too by the 'Welcome Royal Charlie' message emblazoned atop the triumphal arch attached to Ayr's 'Auld Brig', the festival was pan-Scottish and in its iconography drew on the Jacobite strand in Scottish history, something Burns had warmed to.)[45] The selection of music performed is revealing. Unsurprisingly, airs and songs associated with Burns were commonly played as marchers wended their way to their destination; 'Duncan Gray', 'The Birks o' Aberfeldy', 'Green Grow the Rashes' and 'My Love She's but a Lassie Yet' were amongst the musicians' repertoire. Nostalgia – including the reification of the Scottish countryside and the Burns's vivid depictions of scenes from everyday life not quite lost – was an important aspect of his popular appeal.[46] On the festival site by the river there was an emotionally charged mass rendition of 'Ye Banks and Braes o' Bonny Doon'.[47] 'Auld Lang Syne' too had an airing, prior to a previously unannounced enactment of 'Tam o Shanter' – complete with a full flight of witches.

However, much attention in 1844 as on other occasions was paid by observers to the prominence of 'A Man's a Man'. It was with this rousing song that the procession had begun. And it would do so with great frequency over the next half century; the battle cry of the 'people' – the emergent middle classes as well as the working classes – as they sought to establish a foothold within the constitution which hitherto had been the preserve of aristocrats and the landed interest. In the driving seat at Ayr in 1844, the last's representatives preferred instead to allude to works such as 'The Cotter's Saturday Night', with its stress on Christian piety and the stoicism they believed was a chief characteristic of the country's rural poor.[48]

It was Burns's democratising principles that had prompted the call made in 1858 by Colin Rae Brown of Greenock Burns Club for a demonstration of unity behind the 'creed', 'A Man's a Man' on the hundredth anniversary of Burns's birth on 25 January 1859. Burns by this time had been adopted not only as 'the poet of the Scotch', but the global representative of this 'one great democratic idea and formula'.[49] Accordingly this was a recurring theme on the centennial day, both through the singing of 'A Man's a Man' and as the core message of many after-dinner speeches.[50] Its force intensified thereafter, with the sentiment being 'conspicuously flaunted' as the 'legend of the day' amongst a display of evergreens mounted on a lorry drawn by nine horses belonging to the city's carters, at the head of the monster procession in Glasgow on 26 January 1877 that preceded the inauguration ceremony for George Ewing's Burns statue in George Square.[51]

Displayed too were other devices that linked Burns directly with the demands for the practical application of the democratic principles he had articulated. Thus, even in the small Borders village of Denholm in January 1859, the centennial celebrations began with the instrumental band going round the village, accompanied by 'villagers bearing the standards which have "braved the battle and the breeze" of many a political conflict of days gone by'.[52] Similarly, visible in the processions that, for example, preceded the unveiling of Burns statues in Glasgow and Dumfries, in 1877 and 1882 respectively, were tradesmen carrying flags that looked 'as if they had more than once done duty in the cause of Reform', a reference to the campaign to extend the franchise in 1831–2.[53] Links with the reform movement's genesis were maintained right until the end of the century, with the workers from Dumfries ironworks in July 1896 carrying with them an 'old Chartist flag, with the inscription "Scotland shall be free"' – the 'low key nationalism' of this particular artefact underscoring the assertive sense of Scotland the nation that was evident on numerous Burns demonstrations and at celebratory dinners and meetings.[54] That processions were sometimes mustered at locations where reform meetings had taken place or from where protest and other political marches had begun – Glasgow

Green and Dundee's Magdalen Green, for instance – is likely to be part of the same radical heritage narrative.[55]

But there were places where Burns's democratic sentiments were ignored, at least as far as visual displays or reported speeches are concerned. We referred earlier to 1844. In 1859 in Jedburgh, where the centenary of Burns's birth was celebrated 'with great enthusiasm' 'A Man's a Man' was not listed amongst the music played by the brass band, nor, apparently, was it mentioned by any of the speakers at the dinner held in the Black Bull Inn. Instead, reference was made to Burns's genius, his associations with the burgh and the countryside around, his nature poems and his patriotism.[56] In this regard Jedburgh was far from unusual; just as Burns had many voices, so did his proselytisers.

Equally important as a factor that lay behind Burns's enormous popularity was his role in rescuing by recording, promoting and adapting Scottish song. One of the most prominent street decorations in Dumfries in July 1896 was a large banner strung high across the road quoting Burns's fellow poet Thomas Campbell's epithet, 'High Chief of Scottish Song', in silver letters against a red background.[57] It was this and his association with Scottishness (manifest in part through his use of Lowland dialect) itself that endeared him to many of those who marched in processions and applauded when platform speakers extolled Burns as Scotia personified.

The most visible symbol of this was the thistle – Scotland's national flower. On 6 August 1844 it was a giant, 8-foot-tall thistle on a board carried shoulder high by the box-makers of Mauchline that both astonished and delighted the platform party that included Archibald, 13th Earl of Eglinton, Professor John Wilson and other dignitaries as well as Burns's relatives, and the massive crowd of onlookers. Wilson's theatrical ardour (he attempted to clasp the thistle to his chest as it passed by) was not feigned: with Eglinton and other leading Scottish Tories he was part of a cultural nationalist movement that soon developed into a campaign in defence of Scotland's interests at a time of growing state centralisation at Westminster, under the auspices of the National Association for the Vindication of Scottish Rights.[58] Thistles were much in evidence thenceforth, as at the Dumfries centennial in 1896 where large specimens of the plant were sited at each side of the door of the house in which Burns had died.[59]

Heather was fairly commonplace. Daises too were frequently seen. This was another flower identified with Burns, with many being set in stone and bronze in those statues where he was modelled holding one example of the 'modest, crimson-tipped flow'r' he had immortalised in verse. Eye-catching in the demonstration in Kilmarnock in August 1886 to mark the centenary of the initial publication of Burns's poems was a group of between 150 and 200 'young ladies' each of whom was carrying a wreath of daisies.[60]

At a time when the prevailing political culture in Scotland was what has been termed unionist-nationalist, that is a potent pride in Scotland nesting within a secure unionist framework and an active partnership in the British imperial project, the proliferation of union flags on buildings private and public is unsurprising. It is notable that in Ayr on the morning of the Burns Festival in August 1844 those who had stayed in town the previous night noticed that at 'earliest dawn the union-jack was floating from Wallace Tower'.[61] Another fluttered above the tented pavilion beside the Doon. In the very different environment of an entertainment in Leith in 1859, organised by the employees of Fullarton's print works, a portrait of Burns hung over the platform, flanked by devices carrying the words 'Scots wha hae wi'Wallace bled', and 'A man's a man for a' that', while at the foot of the room 'floated the Union Jack'.[62] In Dumfries in 1882 at the unveiling of the Burns statue there was what was described as a 'spontaneous' display of flags. These included royal and Scottish standards, and numerous Union Jacks, including one in Glasgow Street, on which were two verses, the first of which hailed Burns as 'Scotland's greatest son'. The second verse ran:

> We'll hoist the Union Jack on high,
> An' shout out three times thrice
> In memory of the brain and pen
> That wrote for liberty.

The liberty narrative was commonplace in Scottish political culture, drawn from Scotland's (and England's) myth-history of vanquished foes and as unconquered peoples. It was in this vein that 'Scots wha Hae' was frequently praised not only as a song for Scotland but one that would be sung 'from the Lizzard to the Tweed [. . .] while ever liberty shall hold her reign in Britain'.[63] Not unusual therefore were devices that represented and conjoined Scotland, England and Ireland. Such a banner had been prepared for the 'Working Men's Festival [of Burns]' in Falkirk in January 1859, while the 'principal flag' carried in the procession in Dumfries in 1882 was a bed quilt comprising a design made from 15,000 pieces of cloth that represented a thistle, rose, shamrock and leek – along with 'Tam o Shanter'.[64]

Notwithstanding the harmony that seemed to prevail on such occasions, there were of course tensions. The 1844 festival was criticised by radicals and, from a different angle, by representatives of the Presbyterian churches especially, most notably Hugh Miller of the Free Church; Burns, he raged, may have been a genius, but 'too often prostituted his talents to serve the cause of irreligion and immorality'.[65] Ministers stayed away. In 1859, concern was expressed about the appropriation by the upper classes of the Burns centenary celebrations, the 'starched stateliness' of whose dinners were neither attractive to nor affordable by most working people. It was, wrote one critic, 'the people alone who can truly keep the birth-day of Robert Burns [. . .] and claim him as one of themselves'.[66] Indeed, in Dumfries in 1882, as plans were being finalised for the inauguration there of Mrs D. O. Hill's statue of Burns, the trades threatened not to take part if a proposed grandstand around the plinth and statue was erected. This they argued would 'place the favoured classes above the heads of the other people'; as a result, only a part platform was put up, with a low barricade to protect the provost, speakers and other dignitaries.[67] Not everyone took Burns so seriously. Joining the procession for the Glasgow Burns statue unveiling in 1877 was a party of students from the university who, in mockery of the trades' 'emblems of industry', carried their gowns on walking sticks and their books on the end of umbrellas, while instead of singing 'honked and yelled', inducing angry remonstrances from spectators before they were removed by the Foresters and the police.[68]

Yet ruptures that might have marred public celebrations of Burns were carefully managed. The Ayr Festival of 1844 was a potential powder keg, given the background rumblings of radicalism, and the fear that rural rioting of the sort that had ignited in East Anglia and other parts of the south of England would spread to Ayrshire. But by celebrating Burns as coming from the 'bosom of the people' who was also a product of Scotland, speakers were able to conflate the two popular ideas, while by the aural and visual means described earlier, divisions based on class and social standing were transcended. Indeed, the organisers' masterstroke, it was remarked, was that a peer, Lord Eglinton, should have been appointed to chair 'the commemoration of a Peasant'. Old paternalism. Consequently, 'All ranks, from side to side of social life, thus bound and fused together on the illustrious occasion.'[69] The melding agent at the heart of that fusion was the consolidation of a renewed sense of Scotland the nation.[70]

By mid-century, Liberal values had become hegemonic, underpinned by the Liberal Party's political ascendancy following the Great Reform Act. Eschewed were the languages of class and class war.[71] Accordingly, there was now little quarrel with the democratic sentiments Burns had espoused and much admiration amongst the bourgeoisie for his commitment to notions of independence, from the state and of the mind.

Nevertheless, there were fissures within Scottish society that no amount of elite-led choreography over Burns could overcome. The norm following the public part of any Burns demonstration was that the various parties divided – usually on the basis of class and associational loyalties – for their own celebrations indoors. Cupar, Fife, provides a typical example, when in January 1859 the 'working men' held a supper in the Guild Hall, chaired by a book-binder, which was followed by a dance that went into the small hours. 'The more aristocratic part of our citizens', it was reported, attended a dinner in the County Hall, the five hours of which was spent listening to toasts, numerous addresses and songs.[72] In larger towns there were even more separate events, as at Ayr where they ranged from a County Hall ball for the 'most influential townsmen', a gathering of the local legal establishment along with county landowners and eminent guests from elsewhere in Scotland, through a freemasons dinner in the Corn Exchange to a soiree organised by the Ayr Working Men's Reform Association where the sole focus was on Burns as the herald of manhood suffrage.[73]

Even so, it seems reasonable to conclude that the periodic, consensus-building celebrations of Burns discussed in this chapter may have contributed, in ways hitherto overlooked, to the remarkable stability of Scottish society during the nineteenth century. By identifying in public with Burns, first Tory then Liberal politicians and their allies, lord provosts and other prominent citizens including some employers were able to command the respect of their Burns-loving townspeople. Involvement in large-scale community-based celebrations of Burns, civic leaders thought, was good for the soul, improving, elevating and a reminder of what Dundee's *Courier & Argus* called 'the diviner element in our nature' rather than 'trades and professions [. . .] counting rooms and factories, however important these, in their place, are'.[74] Burns and how he was publicly promoted, celebrated and represented, it can be argued, was a carrier in distinctively Scottish terms of ideals and values attributed to him, and above all helped to impart a new-found confidence in and preparedness to celebrate Scotland and Scottishness.

Notes

1. Eric Hobsbawm, 'Mass-Producing Traditions: Europe, 1870–1914', in Eric Hobsbawm and Terence Ranger (eds), *The Invention of Tradition* (Cambridge: Cambridge University Press, 1983), pp. 263–307; Patrick Joyce, *Work, Society and Politics: The Culture of the Factory in Later Victorian England* (London: Methuen, 1980), pp. 276–82.
2. Joyce Ellis, 'Regional and County Centres 1700–1840', in Peter Clark (ed.), *The Cambridge Urban History of Britain, Volume II 1540–1840* (Cambridge: Cambridge University Press, 2000), pp. 696–7.
3. Simon Gunn, *The Public Culture of the Victorian Middle-Class: Ritual and Authority in the English Industrial City 1840–1914* (Manchester: Manchester University Press, 2000), pp. 163–86.
4. Nicholas Mansfield, 'Radical Banners as Sites of Memory: The National Banner Survey', in Paul A Pickering and Alex Tyrrell (eds), *Contested Sites: Commemoration, Memorial and Popular Politics in Nineteenth-Century Britain* (Aldershot: Ashgate, 2004), p. 81.
5. Clark McGinn, *The Burns Supper: A Concise History* (Edinburgh: Luath Press, 2018).

6. Alex Tyrrell, 'Paternalism, Public Memory and National Identity in Early Victorian Scotland: The Robert Burns Festival at Ayr in 1844', *History* 90:1 (2005), pp. 42–61; Ann Rigney, 'Embodied Communities: Commemorating Robert Burns, 1959', *Representations* 115 (Summer 2011), pp. 71–101.
7. Christopher A. Whatley, *Immortal Memory: Burns and the Scottish People* (Edinburgh: John Donald, 2016), pp. 1–23.
8. *Punch*, 13 September 1879.
9. *Dumfriesshire & Galloway Herald & Register*, 8 April 1882; *Dumfries and Galloway Standard*, 19 April 1882.
10. For example, Nick Mansfield, 'The Contribution of the National Banner Survey to Debates on Nineteenth-Century Popular Politics', *Visual Resources* 24:2 (2008), pp. 133–43.
11. Mark Nixon, Gordon Pentland and Matthew Roberts, 'The Material Culture of Scottish Reform Politics, *c.*1820-c.1884', *Journal of Scottish Historical Studies* 32:1 (2012), pp. 28–49.
12. James Ballantine, *Chronicle of the Hundredth Birthday of Robert Burns* (Edinburgh and London: A. Fullarton & Co., 1859), p. 259.
13. See, for example, Ballantine, *Chronicle*, pp. 169–72.
14. *Illustrated London News*, 5 February 1859; Rigney, 'Embodied Communities'; Leith Davis, 'The Robert Burns 1859 Centenary: Mapping Transatlantic (Dis)location', in Sharon Alker, Leith Davis and Holly Faith Nelson (eds), *Robert Burns and Transatlantic Culture* (Farnham and Burlington, VT: Ashgate), pp. 186–205.
15. Joyce, *Work*, p. 278; on Scotland see Graeme Morton, *Unionist Nationalism: Governing Urban Scotland, 1830–1860* (East Linton: Tuckwell, 1999), pp. 189–200.
16. Philip Sulley, *Robert Burns and Dumfries, 1796–1896* (Dumfries: Thomas Hunter & Co., 1896), pp. 49–53.
17. Murray Pittock and Christopher A. Whatley, 'Poems and Festivals, Art and Artefacts and the Commemoration of Robert Burns, *c.*1844-*c.*1896', *Scottish Historical Review* 93:1 (April 2014), pp. 56–79.
18. Dick Institute, Kilmarnock, McKie Collection, Section XIII, Scrapbook, 1876–7, James Gibson to James McKie, W. Wilson to James McKie, 18 December 1876; James Gibson to James McKie, 13 January 1877.
19. *Burns Centenary 21st July 1896 Great Demonstration at Dumfries* (Dumfries: Thos Hunter & Co., 1896), p. 31.
20. Whatley, *Immortal Memory*, pp. 1–23, 79.
21. See, for example, James Ballantine, *Chronicle*, pp. 334, 357.
22. Murray Pittock, '"A Long Farewell to All My Greatness": The History of the Reputation of Robert Burns', in Murray Pittock (ed.), *Robert Burns in Global Culture* (Lewisburg, PA: Bucknell University Press, 2011), p. 32.
23. Ballantine, *Chronicle*, p. 170.

24. Ballantine, *Chronicle*, pp. 172–3, 394.
25. *Londonderry Standard*, 14 August 1844; Bob Harris and Charles McKean, *The Scottish Town in the Age of the Enlightenment 1740–1820* (Edinburgh: Edinburgh University Press, 2014), p. 438.
26. See John Strawhorn, *The History of Irvine: Royal Burgh and New Town* (Edinburgh: John Donald, 1985).
27. Ballantine, *Chronicle*, p. 311.
28. *People's Friend*, 20 November 1872.
29. National Trust for Scotland, Robert Burns Birthplace Museum, minutes, 'Monument to Robert Burns', 1814–1845.
30. Ballantine, *Chronicle*, p. 280.
31. *Inverness Courier*, 14 August 1844; *Stirling Observer*, 15 August 1844.
32. *Weekly News*, 23 October 1880.
33. Nixon, Pentland and Roberts, 'Material Culture', p. 35.
34. *Dumfries and Galloway Standard*, 8 April 1882.
35. *Weekly News*, 23 October 1880.
36. Dundee Central Library, Local History Department, Lamb Collection, Cat. No. 228 (32), *Proceedings at the Unveiling of the Burns Statue in Dundee* (1880); *Burns Centenary*, p. 31.
37. On 'New Paternalism' in industrial England see Joyce, *Work*, Chapter 4.
38. Ballantine, *Chronicle*, p. 397.
39. Patrick Joyce, *Visions of the People: Industrial England and the Question of Class, 1848–1914* (Cambridge: Cambridge University Press, 1991), pp. 27–55.
40. Joyce, *Visions*, pp. 51–2.
41. See Mark Nixon, '"Banner and Placard Poetry", The People's Voice: Scottish Popular Poetry, Song and the Franchise, 1832–1918' (http://thepeoplesvoice.glasgow.ac.uk), pp. 4–7.
42. Dick Institute, McKie Collection, Section XIII, Cuttings, 1868–1887, p. 81, 'Burns Demonstration at Kilmarnock, August 1886'.
43. *Courier & Argus*, 18 October 1880.
44. *Dumfries & Galloway Courier*, 28 March 1882.
45. Murray G. H. Pittock, *The Invention of Scotland: The Stuart Myth and the Scottish Identity, 1638 to the Present* (London and New York: Routledge, 1991), p. 79.
46. T. M. Devine, *Independence or Union: Scotland's Past and Scotland's Present* (London: Allen Lane, 2016), p. 89; Christopher A. Whatley, 'Contesting Memory and Public Places: Albert Square and Dundee's Pantheon of Heroes', in Christopher A. Whatley, Bob Harris and Louise Miskell (eds), *Victorian Dundee: Image and Realities* (Dundee: Dundee University Press, 2011), p. 190.
47. Davis, 'Robert Burns 1959 Centenary', p. 191.

48. Whatley, *Immortal Memory*, pp. 25–51.
49. *Illustrated London News*, 29 January 1859.
50. Ballantine, *Chronicle*, pp. 169–71.
51. *People's Journal*, 27 January 1877.
52. Ballantine, *Chronicle*, p. 218.
53. Whatley, *Immortal Memory*, p. 129.
54. Nixon, 'Banner and Placard Poetry', pp. 15–16; *Burns Centenary 21st July 1896*, p. 40; Nixon, Pentland and Roberts, 'Material Culture', p. 41.
55. Elspeth King, *The People's Palace and Glasgow Green* (Edinburgh: Richard Drew Publishing, 1985), pp. 19–41.
56. Ballantine, *Chronicle*, pp. 289–91.
57. *Burns Centenary*, p. 25.
58. Alex Tyrrell, 'The Earl of Eglinton, Scottish Conservativism, and the National Association for the Vindication of Scottish Rights', *Historical Journal* 53:1 (2010), pp. 87–107.
59. *Burns Centenary*, pp. 27, 29.
60. Dick Institute, McKie Collection, 'Burns Demonstration at Kilmarnock, August 1886'.
61. Dick Institute, McKie Collection, Section VIII, p. 28c, Andrew Park, *Festival to Honour the Memory of our National Poet, Robert Burns* (Glasgow, 1844), p. 39.
62. Ballantine, *Chronicle*, p. 324.
63. Ballantine, *Chronicle*, p. 129.
64. Ballantine, *Chronicle*, p. 246; *Dumfries & Galloway Courier*, 11 April 1882.
65. *The Witness*, 2 August 1844.
66. J. Gould (ed.), 'Robert Burns: Papers Relating to the Centenary etc., 1, 1859–1882', Mitchell Library, Glasgow, MS 52890, pp. 98–9, 107–8.
67. *Dumfries & Galloway Courier*, 28 March 1882.
68. *People's Journal*, 27 January 1877.
69. Park, *Festival*, pp. 8–17.
70. Davis, 'Robert Burns 1859 Centenary', pp. 189–91; Whatley, *Immortal Memory*, p. 48.
71. Joyce, *Visions*, pp. 27–31.
72. Ballantine, *Chronicle*, p. 214.
73. Ballantine, *Chronicle*, pp. 92–116.
74. *Courier & Argus*, 18 October 1880.

8

Robert Burns on the Twentieth-Century Stage

Rhona Brown

If Robert Burns was canonised as a Scottish secular saint in the nineteenth century, the profusion of Burns biographies in the early twentieth century placed sometimes sensational focus on his everyday life. In the 1930s, three major Burns biographies were published: Catherine Carswell's *The Life of Robert Burns* (1930), Franklin Bliss Snyder's *The Life of Robert Burns* (1932) and the translation into English of Hans Hecht's *Robert Burns: The Man and his Work* (1936). Simultaneously, fictional representations of Burns were in plentiful supply, with John A. Steuart's *The Immortal Lover: A Robert Burns Romance* (1929) alongside James Barke's later *Immortal Memory* novels, published between 1946 and 1954. The appetite for biographical and fictional representations of Burns could be extravagantly assuaged in the theatre, where Burns springs from the inert pages of books as a living being. For Leith Davis, late nineteenth- and early twentieth-century dramatic portrayals of Burns were a consequence of the 'truth-seeking' biographies of Allan Cunningham, John Gibson Lockhart, James Hogg and Thomas Carlyle; they were, Davis argues, 'a logical extension of a process that began long ago and that bases the "cultural memory" of the poet so firmly on narratives of his life'.[1] The three plays discussed in this chapter are indeed grounded on Burns's biography, but the poet's works loom large in their portrayals. For their playwrights, Burns's life is inextricable from his poems and songs; the portrayal of one is impossible without the other. In the plays, reference to and quotation from Burns's works constitute a metafictional dramatic device, providing a sub-narrative which unites the performers and audience through shared knowledge. The poems and songs as they are used in the plays reflect Burns's biography, but they also act as catalysts; as drivers which determine what happens next. The plays work as biographies come to life, but also as texts which appreciate that Burns's narrative is determined by his poems, songs and their reception.

Of the plays analysed here, two take Burns's entire life as their subject, while the third focuses on a significant relationship which occurred when the poet had achieved celebrity. H. Fletcher Lee's *Robert Burns: A Play in Three Acts* (1926) begins with the playwright's admission that, 'While the Play closely follows the life of Burns [. . .] there is some telescoping of events [. . .] to meet the requirements of drama, and to get the life into the scope of the Play.'[2] Lee emphasises that Burns's 'views, words, and even whole speeches are his own', but admits fictional additions, including the portrayal of Richard Brown, Burns's friend from Irvine, as the poet's cousin.[3] Tom Wright's *There Was a Man* (1965), although a very different play, takes a similar approach to Lee's, beginning with Burns's childhood reading and making liberal use of the poet's words. Robert Kemp's *The Other Dear Charmer*, first performed in 1951, centres on the relationship between Burns and Agnes Maclehose,[4] 'Clarinda'. Although Kemp utilises Burns's works, the playwright is emphatic in his 'Note to the Actors' that his is

> not 'a play about Robert Burns' [. . .] It is a play about a human being yielding to the mirage of a love for which she had not the capacity, and in the end finding only the parched sands where the mirage had soared. Its first subject is, therefore, Clarinda, and the importance of Burns in this play is only his importance to her.[5]

While Kemp emphasises Clarinda as his 'first subject', Burns's celebrity and personality drive the play's narrative: Clarinda is reactive, even if she is given vigorous voice. All three plays linger on Burns's relationships with women, and his 'womanising' becomes a central theme, albeit with varying levels of implied censure. While significant moments from Burns's biography are emphasised by all three playwrights, Burns's poems, songs and letters have equal, if not superior, power in their narratives. The poet's works create a silent dialogue between the actors and audience, enabling spectators to, as Kemp puts it, 'feel that the fourth wall of the room has been removed for their benefit, and should willingly submit to the illusion'.[6] All three plays are concerned with 'truth', but also in the creation of 'illusion'.

Although written forty years apart, Lee's *Robert Burns: A Play in Three Acts* and Wright's *There Was a Man* have much in common. Both take a three-Act, chronological approach, beginning with Burns's early life and ending with his death, thus 'telescoping' his thirty-seven years. If, thanks to its narrative style as a one-man show, Wright's depiction of Burns focuses more on the poet's inner monologue, mental health and the realities of eighteenth-century religious oppression, hard agricultural labour and emotional turmoil, Lee's and Wright's portrayals are united by the way in which they establish Burns's early character.

Both depict early familial influences on the poet alongside William Burnes's morally anxious attempts to curtail his son's irregularities.

In Lee's opening scene, Burns is at his father's farm in Ayrshire. The first voices we hear are those of Burns's mother and Betty Davidson, described as 'a favourite with the children',[7] thanks to her knowledge of traditional lore. The introductory description of Burns comes from his sister, Agnes: 'I'm no feared of your kelpies and witches, Betty! But (*whispering shrilly*) Rob is! He's aye keekin' round for them.'[8] Burns is immediately established as having instinctive links with a native Scottish literary tradition.

Wright's opening is different from and similar to Lee's. *There Was a Man* begins with a quotation from Burns's autobiographical letter to John Moore of 2 August 1787:[9] 'I have taken a whim to give you a history of myself. My name has made some little noise in this country. Perhaps a faithful account of what character of man I am and how I came by that character may amuse you.'[10] Rather than placing Burns as one among a cast of characters as Lee does, Wright presents an older poet looking back on his life. In Wright's depiction, Burns controls the narrative, going back further than Lee and recalling the poet's birth: '[W]hen my father got me, he got signs and wonders. Gales shuddered the coast of Ayrshire with their big bragging belly-laugh.'[11] The newborn Burns is carried 'through the roaring blackness'[12] by his father as the play's ironic foreshadowing comes into focus and meteorological violence sets the scene for Burns's passionate tale. Accordingly, Burns's father's early words address his son's instincts: 'If you desire to overcome the world, the flesh and the devil in yourself, you must overcome the irregular passions that jar and distract, and put them under.'[13] Burnes's early proclamations establish his role as moral guide, a portrayal shared by Wright and Lee.

Wright also stresses Burns's relationship with his mother and Betty Davidson:

> Such songs I learned from my mother, and from old Betty Davidson I learned stories. Old Betty! She knew every superstition that haunted the countryside, and believed them all. Sitting in darkness, old as cobwebs, her wheel spinning in the firelight, she would terrify herself and us with tales of Devils, Ghosts, Witches, Warlocks, Wraiths and Apparitions. As I huddled close to Gilbert in bed, the house whispered with Demons and Bogie Men.[14]

Echoing Lee's depiction, Wright portrays Burns as drawn instinctively to oral Scottish literature. This preference, as also seen in *The Other Dear Charmer*, has consequences for the way in which Burns makes literary, linguistic and even sexual choices, thus establishing the position that Burns was linguistically divided; that native Scottishness was his 'real' milieu and that his pretensions in English should be dismissed as unnatural. As argued below, Wright's portrayal echoes Kemp's in its insistence on Burns as 'authentic' Scots bard, thus edging these biographical-fictional works into politically-motivated literary criticism.

To emphasise that the war between 'natural' Scots and 'artificial' English was a lifelong one in Burns, Wright turns from the education Burns received from his mother and Davidson, to that administered by John Murdoch: 'From Mr Murdoch, the school teacher, and from his seven-tongued tawse, I learned to paraphrase, supply ellipsis, turn verse to prose, and substitute synonyms. But the book I liked best was "The Collected letters of Eminent writers of the reign of Queen Anne".'[15] While demonstrating Burns's linguistic education and attraction to neoclassical English literary models, Wright's depiction associates Burns's early reading with hard discipline and the 'tawse'. Although eliciting a delicious fear, Mrs Burnes's songs and Davidson's tales are Burns's 'natural' education; Murdoch's is administered by force. While focusing on a biographical 'moment', Wright makes the implicit statement that Burns's work is authentic only in Scots, and that English poetic models are an artificial imposition on his bardship. Thus, the depiction of Burns's character onstage is driven by the playwrights' readings of his works and their assumptions about his linguistic choices.

Lee's illustration of Burns's education makes similar declarations about the influences that mattered in his childhood. After Burns is established as unusually receptive to Davidson's tales, young Robert discusses his reading:

> *Burns*: Rob, bring me yon volume of Hervey's 'Meditations.' I'm not getting on with it as quick as I would like.
>
> *Rob* (*at the books*): Neither am I with Pope's 'Homer'... that's keeping me awake o' nights.[16]

As in Wright's portrayal, the poet's engagement with Augustan 'classics' is an uphill struggle. However, when Burns's 'elder brother in the muse', Robert Fergusson's Scots poetry is discussed, the tone shifts. Agnes says, 'There, Gilbert, is Fergusson's Poems to you. Rob'll no be wantin' them. He has them by heart.'[17] While Pope and Hervey keep Burns awake, Fergusson's poems are internalised effortlessly. Notwithstanding the fact that Lee has Burns discover Fergusson much earlier than facts allow (Burns is more likely to have read Fergusson's works at Irvine in the early 1780s than in his boyhood),[18] the Edinburgh poet's catalysing and horrifying example is a staple in all three plays. Wright has Burns find Fergusson in Irvine: 'His work was in the Scotch tongue and marched to old Scotch measures. I felt a strange kinship with him and a burning desire to carry on his work.'[19] In *The Other Dear Charmer*, Fergusson is an emblem of Burns's natural mode, albeit a problematic one in Enlightenment Edinburgh. Before Burns makes an appearance, Miss Nimmo states that he 'has not chosen the best English models such as Pope and Addison but [...] he has followed our own rude poets, like honest Allan Ramsay',[20] while Kemp's Burns connects 'the poor Rab Fergusson's' poems and Allan Ramsay's with his 'destiny' as 'a Scottish bard'.[21] All three playwrights show Burns in a linguistic battle between his natural Scots idiom and the artificialities of English, demonstrating the way in which the playwrights' linguistic and, by extension, political predilections influence his depiction.[22] As argued below, Kemp's preface grapples with similar divisions between popular and literary-critical responses to his work, demonstrating that these linguistic anxieties may belong to mid-twentieth-century Scotland more than Burns's eighteenth century.

Lee lingers longer than Wright in Burns's early adulthood, having Burns and Gilbert discussing their potential ruin and Gilbert lifting paper Burns 'has been scribbling on', to find three lines from 'Epistle to Davie, A Brother Poet' (1786): 'It's hardly in a body's power / To keep at times frae being sour / To see how things are shar'd.'[23] Lee then presents Richard Brown (fictionalised as Burns's cousin) in the guise of a tempter who introduces the naïve Burns to women and alcohol. After Burns's sincere declaration of innocent love for Nellie Kirkpatrick, Brown states, 'I'll learn ye mony a thing, I see,'[24] before giving Burns his first taste of spirits: 'Take a drink and see if that doesna cure your bashfulness.'[25] Lee's Brown introduces the young poet to sins of adulthood, making Brown a scapegoat for the most widely-mourned of Burns's faults: his relationships with women and alcohol. The poet's innocence is robbed by an older cousin who declares drink to be 'The finest thing in the world – except the lassies! (*winking evilly*)'.[26] Difficult questions about Burns's later conduct are evaded by this dramatic device, which rewrites the known relationship between Burns and Brown and opines that Burns's excesses in consumption come from outside himself; they were, like Pope's Homer, an unwelcome imposition on his 'true' self.

The poet's 'irregularities' could not, however, be avoided entirely, and Lee and Wright delineate Burns's uneasy relationship with the Presbyterian Church following Elizabeth Paton's pregnancy. Contextualising this moment with Burns's father's objections to his son attending a Dalrymple dancing school, Lee and Wright deal with the consequences of Burns's relationship with Paton in contrasting ways. In Lee's play, Rev. William Auld is a highly fictionalised concoction of benevolent patron and religious reprover. Auld enters announcing business with Burns, but before he does his religious duty, he comments on some verse he has found on the back of an account for farm produce. Burns says, 'sulkily and bashfully', 'It's not a sin, I suppose', to which Auld replies: 'A sin! Young man, if you are the author of these lines, let me tell you you've got *genius*. You could rise to great distinction'; 'that's one of the finest poems I've ever read'.[27] Only after he has delivered his warm opinion of Burns's poetry does Auld reveal his true business, that Burns must pay public penance for fornication with Paton. In Lee's depiction, one of the most vilified of Burns's 'unco guid'[28] becomes an early champion of his poetry, and the first to proclaim his genius. Burns declares to his mother: 'I've got gey hot blood – and passions wild and strong. I've never done real wrong till some months past – and now are come the consequences . . . Elizabeth Paton's had a bairn – and mine's the blame!'[29] In response, Burns rages weakly 'at thon Auld Licht ministers!' as he is '*prancing over to the window*'.[30] Notwithstanding Mrs Burnes's dismay at her son's failure in his duty, Lee's portrayal pardons Burns with the excuse of his 'hot' passions, ignited by tempter Richard Brown.

For Wright, Burns's affair with Paton is a consequence of his depression in Irvine when, he states: 'Misery and depression are never far from me. When they are nearest I fly solitude as if it were the devil and cling to company and noise for I could drown in loneliness.'[31] Consequently, and with his father's declining health, Burns 'stayed close to the farm – and close to the farm was Lizzie Paton. I buried my misery in her – and was horrified when it promised to bear fruit'.[32] Although refusing to shy from Burns's poor mental health, Wright's depiction washes away the poet's culpability. Lee and Wright allow Burns to blame external forces in the Paton affair, but they also have Burns's father deliver moral caution from his deathbed: in Lee, Burnes states, 'there's one among you for whom my heart is sairly troubled. I pray he may not fall',[33] while Wright's Burnes is 'afraid' for 'only one of you all'.[34] While Lee avoids details of Burns's penance, Wright has Auld condemn Burns as 'a miserable hell deserving sinner – a self confessed carnal, lecherous fornicating loon', while Burns recites 'Holy Willie's Prayer' and 'Address to the Unco Guid'.[35] Wright's depiction reveals Burns's disgrace as a source of inspiration; as a way to develop his poetic persona: Burns's works therefore exist in a synergetic relationship with his life, driving the dramatic narrative.

Lee and Wright move from Burns's shame and grief to unbridled conviviality in Poosie Nancie's tavern. In Lee's portrayal, Burns is already enjoying fame, recognised in Mauchline as a 'born poet' who recites 'To a Mountain Daisy' for the rapt drinkers.[36] Burns maintains humility as friends trumpet his success, with Richmond describing 'Gavin Hamilton and Mr Aiken takin' one of Rob's poems from his pouch, and reading it wi' the tears running down his cheeks'.[37] No sooner is this success shared, than '*The door on the left front opens, and Jean Armour enters . . . She is wrapped in a cloak, and in evident distress.*'[38] Without either uttering the words, Burns discovers that Jean is pregnant, and although aware of her father's anger, he states, 'Have no fear, lassie. I love you madly – and I'll stand by you,' before engaging her in an unofficial marriage: 'I, Robert Burns – acknowledge – that Jean Armour – is my lawful – wedded wife.'[39] Wright deals with this event in less sentimental terms, with Burns stating that he and Jean 'did the proper thing in the improper order – we started a family, then we got married, in secret, and in common-law'.[40] While Lee makes little mention of Mary Campbell, Burns's 'Highland Mary', Wright has Burns settling into 'widower's sorrow'[41] in Armour's subsequent enforced absence and finding another 'wife' in Campbell. As demonstrated below, Lee and Kemp credit Armour with a portion of Burns's success, whereas Wright states that it was Campbell who kept Burns in Scotland to try a career as a poet: 'Mary made it possible.'[42] In this account, it is not the phenomenal success of the 'Kilmarnock' edition that prevents Burns's emigration, but the love of the tragic muse that is Mary Campbell.

Lee and Wright now transfer Burns to Edinburgh, with Lee having Burns declare that 'I'll no have yon publisher, Creech, lookin' on me as a rustic . . . I'm not farmer, I'm poet here!',[43] contrasting with Wright's Burns, who has painful awareness of 'my ploughman's clothes, my ploughman's walk, my ploughman's hands',[44] before his reception proves that his 'clothes were no longer contemptible, they were the uniform of the ploughman poet!'[45] Lee depicts Burns fraternising with literati including Adam Ferguson and Monboddo, but his focus falls on Burns's relationship with two women who, thanks to Lee's 'telescoping', appear in the same drawing room: Maria Riddell and Nancy Maclehose. The latter gets Burns alone and asks him to 'Call me Clarinda. It's so poetic – and it's safer . . . And I like calling you Sylvander (*in a purring whisper*).'[46] In Lee's portrayal, Maclehose is a kittenish seductress who nonetheless keeps their relationship platonic; Burns learns 'to think more of your fame and welfare than of my own gratification. I've never loved like *that* before!'[47] While Maclehose is sexualised with her '*purring whisper*', Burns is educated in the ways of platonic love. Wright refuses to shy from the controversy of Burns's impregnation of May Cameron at this time, but emphasises that Maclehose 'set firm bounds to our friendship', sending the poet 'From friendship – to flirtation – to fever!'[48] As argued below, Kemp's nuanced exploration of Burns's relationship with Maclehose implies that their relationship moved beyond the platonic. For Lee, Maclehose is mere backdrop to Burns's 'Ae Fond Kiss', and the biography plays second fiddle to the poet's iconic works.

Both playwrights set their third Acts in Dumfries. Although they focus on different aspects of Burns's story, both employ a darkening tone in these final scenes, foreshadowing Burns's physical decline. Here, Lee highlights the poorly-understood fall-out between Burns and Walter and Maria Riddell, after Burns disgraced himself at their home. In Lee's portrayal, Burns is again absolved of responsibility, his behaviour portrayed as having been orchestrated by a jealous Walter Riddell, who says to Hyslop, 'You and I will see that Robert Burns gets his fill of drink – and we'll lead him on to destroy himself in Maria's eyes!'[49] Before his humiliation, Burns reveals his radical politics by drinking a toast to George Washington, to which the Supervisor threateningly responds: 'this is not the first time the day I've heard you – GOING AGEN THE GOVERNMENT!'[50] No more is said about Burns's radicalism in Lee's play, and his indiscretions at Riddell's home are played off-stage:

> *While the Curtain rises a buzz of voices, bursts of wild laughter, and the clatter of plates and glasses are heard off. Then the sound of scraping of chairs – of many footsteps – and the voices of women coming nearer. Then suddenly –* UPROAR:- *The noise of chairs overturned – shrieks – masculine maledictions – roars of rage – and some coarse laughter.*[51]

It is significant that Lee includes this biographical event, of which there has been much speculation: Hilton Brown states that 'all that can be said with any certainty is that Burns apparently drank too much at a dinner-party and misconducted himself in such a way as to give serious offence to his hostess'.[52] Whatever the reality, Burns is here framed and degraded by his social 'superiors'.

In Lee's final scene, Burns rejects life among the aristocracy for domestic contentment, extolling Armour as the driving force of his career: 'It's no only rhyme – it's reason! And never a man had better reason to prize his wife than I my Jean! . . . You've been the best o' life to me, lass!'[53] Burns is the faithful husband, finding his way to conventional morality in time for his premature death. He also reconciles with Riddell, who concedes that 'My husband admitted . . . that he himself was much to blame' for the poet's embarrassment.[54] Just as Lee absolves Burns of blame in his dealings with women, he is here given final forgiveness *by* women. Thanks to their reunion, Burns provides for his brother Gilbert by procuring a farm on Riddell's estate, and Armour and Riddell are by his side as he prepares for death. Burns believes he has 'failed sadly . . . Well, maybe, Jean, in a hundred years' time they'll think more of me than they do to-day!'[55] This ironic foreshadowing is followed by Burns's declaration that he does not fear death, quoting lines from 'It Was Upon a Lammas Night': 'I hae been blyth with comrades dear, / I hae been happy drinking, / I hae been happy getting gear, / I hae been happy thinking.'[56] Lee thus repurposes a song praising transitory earthly pleasures as Burns's 'My Way'; as his blithe rejection of guilt before death. Maria Riddell utters the play's last line: 'Whatever happens hereafter – YOU ARE ONE OF THE IMMORTALS!'[57] Lee's Burns, cleansed of sin, having made peace with his cherished women and provided a financial future for his beloved brother, is ready to face death and embrace personal and literary immortality.

Wright's ending is less sure of Burns's moral triumph than Lee's. After his 'relationship' with Maclehose ends, he receives word that Armour is destitute, having been thrown out of the family home after becoming pregnant by Burns.

At news of their twins' deaths, Wright's Burns accepts that 'I have dallied long enough with life',[58] forsaking the poet's life for marriage to Armour. His reflections on Armour contrast sharply with Lee's: 'My choice was not very romantic – it was as random as blind man's buff! – but Jean was destitute through my fault and there is no sporting with human misery.'[59] He now exchanges Edinburgh pretensions for Ellisland, where 'I live in a smokey old spence, sleep in a room where the wind and rain are sifted through holes in the walls.'[60] Wright conflates Burns's personal situation with international events, where 'horrid hypochondria'[61] coincides with his taking an excise position when 'The whole of Scotland is revolution, and so am I. Liberty, Equality, Fraternity, Fuller and more equal representation, and the end of degradation for the people.'[62] With these momentous events come upheaval within the poet, who opines that 'If we do not fall on our knees at the mention of William Pitt, we commit sedition.'[63] Capturing something of Scotland's political turmoil in the 1790s, Wright refers to the infamous incident at Dumfries Theatre when, faced with singing the national anthem, the audience called for the French revolutionary song, 'Ça ira'. In Wright's version Burns, the employee of the Crown, remains shrewdly silent: 'I am a placeman, however humble, and could not join in. I sat through the anthem with my hat on, and my arms folded. Perhaps a careful interpreter could read what my private sentiments are.'[64]

Wright's play ends in the domestic sphere, and its tone darkens as Burns's health deteriorates. Burns ruminates on his faults, stating that 'Drink has been the very devil to me,' but pardons himself by blaming 'private parties with hard-drinking gentlemen'[65] for over-indulgence. As in Lee, unnatural impositions on Burns – the events and company that came with fame – precipitate his collapse. The final lines address decline and regret, and Burns bemoans the deaths of Captain Riddell, his brother William and a daughter. With grief comes illness, and Wright's description of the poet being 'so feeble I need to be helped to my chair',[66] relies heavily on Burns's last letters.[67] At his conclusion, Wright is less certain of Burns's 'immortality' than Lee. Although Wright's Burns states that 'An honest man has nothing to fear,' the poet's final words are 'God will forgive us all.'[68] Reflecting Burns's egalitarianism, this levelling final speech implies that Burns needs to be forgiven, but so do we all.

While Lee and Wright present Burns's life in three Acts, Kemp's *The Other Dear Charmer* focuses on a moment – Burns's stay in Edinburgh following his first flush of fame – and a single relationship: that between Burns and Agnes Maclehose, the self-styled platonic lovers of the Age of Sensibility, Sylvander and Clarinda. While Lee and Wright portray what they see as a battle between Burns's 'natural' Scots idiom and English, Kemp reflects this division not only in his representation of Burns, but in his 'Note to the Actors'. From the start, Kemp sets up a differentiation between spectators: on one side, destructive drama critics and on the other, a 'wide generality of men and women', whom he wishes to 'charm' 'into our theatres'.[69] He states that he and his performers 'are not out to please the critics, nor are we out to please the highbrows'; indeed, the ordinary theatregoer 'should be our bodyguard when the intellectuals set out to bully us'.[70] Echoing Lee's and Wright's depictions of Burns battling fruitlessly against native nature to attain the literary manners of Pope, Kemp places these perceived divisions front and centre in his cast's minds. Drawing a line between intellectuals and popular audiences, Kemp perhaps demonstrates insecurity regarding the play's reception, as well as his preference for the 'natural' Burns. This preference comes into focus in *The Other Dear Charmer* when Burns is navigating Edinburgh's social scene and attempting a relationship with the socially 'superior' Maclehose. It also drives his depiction of Burns as more in tune with Ramsay and Fergusson than the sentimental poets that Maclehose admires.

Kemp is particularly interested in Burns's relationships with women, describing the poet as having 'merciless fertility. He won a prize with every coconut'.[71] Although the pregnant Jenny Clow appears in the play, Kemp's decision to focus on Burns's apparently platonic relationship with Maclehose allows him to scrutinise the poet's reputation as a womaniser. Lee and Wright show Burns attracted to a seductive Clarinda, but failing to 'win a prize'; Kemp's portrayal is more suggestive. In this spirit, and in response to 'those who cling stubbornly to the myth', Kemp promises 'a rationally consistent portrait'.[72]

Kemp may profess Clarinda as his subject, but the narrative is driven by Burns. At the start of the play, Maclehose is fashionable but vacuous, attracted by Burns's celebrity and hyper-aware of appearances in socially restrictive Edinburgh. When she meets Burns, there is undeniable attraction but also tension between them; in the end, she is changed, and Burns's mark is indelible. Kemp's opening scene establishes Maclehose's 'famous sensibility'[73] by showing her reacting empathetically to her lawyer uncle Lord Craig's tales of infanticide before expressing interest in Burns: Craig describes him as 'a libertine, a complete unblushing libertine'[74] while Miss Nimmo excuses his 'rudeness' by explaining that his literary models are Scottish rather than English. In early scenes, Maclehose sees herself as a potential moral and literary guide for Burns, wishing to be 'his mentor and by the light I hold aloft guide him to that correctness'[75] which, she implies, he lacks. As if to emphasise the impossibility of her task, Burns's first appearance in the play is of 'vitality and genius. He is in the midst of his Satanic period, which gives his charm a certain roguishness'.[76] From the start, Maclehose attempts to 'correct' his ways. When he describes his first poetic inspiration as 'a bonnie lass that bound the sheaves beside me in the harvest',[77] Maclehose opines that he is too humble: 'You have conquered the people of Scotland, Mr Burns. Go further, and you conquer England too! But that you'll never do without the correctness you despise.'[78] Just as Lee's Richard Brown scoffed at Burns's naïvely ardent declaration of poetic love for Nellie Kirkpatrick, so too does Maclehose deride the poet's first muse. Maclehose therefore represents the artificial 'correctness' soundly rejected in Lee's and Wright's portrayals of Burns. This linguistic antagonism acts as ironic foreshadowing, demonstrating the unsustainability of their relationship and Maclehose's failure to understand what Kemp depicts as Burns's authentic, and resolutely Scottish, genius.

Burns is unable, in Kemp's portrayal, to escape the censure of the Church, even in Edinburgh. The minister, also named Kemp, reminds Burns that they have an acquaintance in common – 'my old colleague and very dear friend, Mr Auld, the minister of Mauchline'[79] – and confirms that Burns's religious satires are in circulation. Here, as elsewhere, it is Burns's works that propel the narrative: Kemp has read 'The Holy Fair', describing it as containing 'some scandalous matter', and demonstrates that Edinburgh's oppression of Burns's nature will be heavier than ever: 'he may try these tricks in Ayrshire, but in Edinburgh . . .'[80]

Kemp now turns to Burns's private relationship with Maclehose. Encouraged by her letters as Clarinda, Burns wishes to drop the literary act and embrace reality: 'Oh, we have done with these Arcadian, china-figure names! I am no longer Sylvander, a cold thing of frozen postures! I am Robert . . . Robert Burns! . . . and you, you are not Clarinda. You are Nancie, my lovely, my adored – .'[81] When Maclehose reminds him that she is a married woman who offers only friendship, Burns beseeches her 'to enlighten me, for it is of a kind that no woman has offered me before'.[82] Kemp's poet is the fertile farmer, 'a good choice as life-imbuing paganism' in his sensitivity to 'the cycle of life'.[83] Maclehose, the city-dwelling gentlewoman, must educate the poet in platonic love, describing it as 'the pure essence of love . . . love, but with that left out which makes us common with the animals'.[84] Burns is both the butt of the joke and the rakish Scots bard familiar to the audience when he states, 'Ma'am, I find it hard to know what remains.'[85]

The tension between Burns's liberated naturalness and Maclehose's restriction is reflected when the narrative turns to Burns's works. When Burns gifts Maclehose with 'To Clarinda', 'Fair Empress of the Poet's Soul', the poet makes an admission that would not be out of place in Lee's and Wright's plays: 'I never strove more in any verse that I have written. It doesn't seem in any way stiff or formal to you? When I write in my own natural tongue the words come tumbling out, but faith, I wrote these lines as if I had the colic!' Clarinda responds with patronising patience: 'You must learn to make this your natural tongue, Sylvander.'[86] As per Lee and Wright, Kemp emphasises his view of the contrast between literary unaffectedness and affectation, and the playwright's linguistic-political assumptions about Burns's 'true' poetic self again drive the dramatic depiction. However, Kemp takes this implied division further, into Burns's sexual life. To emphasise his facility in Scots, Burns reads 'I'll Aye Ca' in by yon Toun' to Maclehose, who picks up on the text's praise of 'bonie Jean'. She responds with vicious but controlled jealousy: 'Jean? I suppose that's something you wrote for that Mauchline girl, Jean . . . Jean . . . oh, what's the creature's name, Jean Armour? So far as I understand, Mr Burns, she gave you very good reasons to "aye ca in by yon toun"!'[87] If literary Scots is associated with naturalness, so too is Armour; Maclehose is implicitly associated with a formality for which Burns must 'strive'. However, in this scene, which is based on Burns's correspondence with Maclehose,[88] the poet colludes with Maclehose's disdain for Jean:

> My Jean! She is not my Jean, and not fit to be named in the same breath with Clarinda. I am disgusted with her! I cannot endure her. Sometimes I have had the profanity to try to compare her with my Clarinda – 'twas setting the expiring glimmer of a farthing taper beside the cloudless glory of the meridian sun . . . There I found tasteless insipidity, vulgarity of soul and mercenary fawning, here . . . oh here, polished good sense, heaven-born genius, and the most generous, the most delicate, the most tender passion . . . I have done with her![89]

Later, he describes Armour as 'a dolt':[90] 'The memory of her sickens me.'[91] Kemp plays on the audience's knowledge of Burns's eventual marital fate with Armour, demonstrating that his pretensions to Maclehose's literary style are doomed to failure because they are a denial of his 'authentic' self. In this scene, Burns's works directly inform the way in which the scene plays out on stage, delivering a message to a well-informed audience.

Towards the end of Act 2, Kemp deals with Burns's legend.[92] Whereas Lee and Kemp maintain that Burns's relationship with Maclehose was platonic, Kemp suggests otherwise in his stage directions: '*Suddenly with his upstage arm, he catches her round the waist, and kisses her fiercely. She does not resist. The forgotten glasses spill backwards.*'[93] While Maclehose is consistently portrayed as the one woman Burns failed to conquer sexually, Kemp's directions imply that Maclehose was like all the others: that Burns won a 'prize' in the end. Notwithstanding the misogynistic implications of this depiction, Kemp demonstrates that Burns's irresistible naturalness won out; that his pretensions to sentimental artificiality were fleeting and fragile.

Kemp's third Act features the arrival of Jenny Clow, who calls at Maclehose's home asking for Burns's address to inform him of her pregnancy, thinking herself 'entitled to expect his help'.[94] Despite her shock, Maclehose is kind to

Clow, giving her some shillings and agreeing to relay the news. When the poet returns to Edinburgh, Maclehose and Burns have their final confrontation. She accuses him of dissolution: 'I verily believe shame has no meaning for you!'[95] Burns reminds her that their love was, 'except for the night before we parted',[96] platonic. He reveals that he has married Armour in the language of literary and social division:

> You're a married woman, and I'm a man of bedlam passions that I cannot master. You're a fine Edinburgh lady; I'm a tenant farmer who if he's to live must win a living from the soil. And never mock Jean Armour, I beseech you! Had I been able to make you lady of Ellisland, could you have risen in the dark to milk cows and make brose for the men? . . . Look at your small white fingers, and give me an honest answer![97]

Armour is here the right woman for Burns's authentic lifestyle, and although Maclehose maintains that 'I could have understood your mind, read to you, criticised your verses,'[98] Burns further justifies his choice as one of authentic 'fit':

> She sings sweetly . . . most sweetly. She can lilt over to me of an evening by the ingle the old airs I love . . . they pour out of her without a thought, as if they belonged to her and she to them. And as I sit and listen I know that I hear the life's breath of the nameless, forgotten poets that came before me . . . Yes Nancie, you preach to me of Doctor Blair and cold correctness, you have shown me our songs cribbed, cabined and confined by the latest German or Italian, but Jean . . . she is the fountain-head, the well, the pure upland spring where the Muses themselves would drink![99]

Even down to his choice of wife, Burns is the authentic Scot. Jean is a 'fountain-head' of song, a source akin to Mrs Burnes and Betty Davidson in his early days. In Kemp's portrayal, Burns chooses Armour's naturalness over Maclehose's 'cold correctness', literary/linguistic choices inform life choices, and the societal status quo is maintained: Burns remains in his preordained social sphere, and his Edinburgh pretensions are dismissed as empty social climbing.

Demonstrating the inextricability of Burns's life from his works, Kemp's denouement is driven by an iconic song. As a parting gift, Burns presents Maclehose with 'Ae Fond Kiss', which she promptly tears in half. Burns cries, 'When you rent that paper you rent a part of me! Then there is nothing left for me but to bid you farewell. Goodbye . . . Robert Burns will not trouble you . . . or Edinburgh . . . again.'[100] Although Maclehose soothes herself with cruelly envious thoughts about Armour, she is 'assiduously pasting'[101] the torn manuscript as the curtain falls. The play's final message is, therefore, that if Burns's actions are morally questionable, his works display immortal genius. Without the poems, songs and letters, the story of Burns is meaningless.

Lee's *Robert Burns*, Wright's *There Was a Man* and Kemp's *The Other Dear Charmer* offer meaningful insight into the reception of Burns in the early- to mid-twentieth century when, as Kemp states, Burns had 'become the central figure in a vague religion of kindness, tolerance and good-fellowship'.[102] In their engagement with that 'religion', the playwrights offer varying levels of criticism of the poet's moral irregularities while maintaining his literary genius and status as a Scottish national icon. However, all three playwrights imbue their portrayals of Burns with their shared assumptions regarding his 'naturalness' and 'authenticity'. In this, they both exalt and belittle the poet, demonstrating his unbridled, natural creativity in Scots, while bemoaning what they see as his conceited, doomed attempts at 'formal' English poetry and social climbing in Edinburgh. They prefer a 'heaven-taught ploughman'; a farmer-poet in a 'smokey spence' who has no need for education and the genteel ways of the drawing room. This preference extends into all aspects of their portrayal: Burns is not true to himself when he writes in English, just as he rebels against his nature when courting Maclehose. Burns, uninhibited in his physical and literary fertility, must nevertheless stick with his own kind: Mrs Burnes, Betty Davidson and Jean Armour. Those 'fountainheads' of the native Scottish tradition are, according to Lee, Wright and Kemp, Burns's real literary muses. In their portrayals, and in the words of Gerard Slevin, director of Wright's *There Was a Man*, the playwrights' 'original work is inextricably interwoven with that of Burns'.[103] The dramatic portrayals of Burns analysed here rely on the poet's works: his poems and songs drive the narrative, while references to his published letters give depth and authenticity to his voice. While Burns's works are central to Lee's, Wright's and Kemp's dramatic portrayals of Scotland's national bard, it is their readings of these works that have the most powerful effect on Burns's depiction on the twentieth-century stage.

Notes

1. Leith Davis, '"Rules of Art": The Life of Robert Burns on Page and Stage, 1800–1954', in Murray Pittock (ed.), *Robert Burns and Global Culture* (Lewisburg, PA: Bucknell University Press, 2011), p. 191.
2. H. Fletcher Lee, *Robert Burns: A Play in Three Acts* (London: Sands & Co., 1926), p. 8.
3. Lee, *Robert Burns*, p. 8.
4. A variety of spellings of this surname exist. For consistency between play-texts, this chapter uses the standard modern spelling.

5. Robert Kemp, *The Other Dear Charmer: A Comedy in Three Acts* (Glasgow: Brown, Son & Ferguson, 1985), p. 10.
6. Kemp, *The Other Dear Charmer*, p. 9.
7. Lee, *Robert Burns*, p. 10.
8. Lee, *Robert Burns*, p. 13.
9. Robert Burns to John Moore, 2 August 1787, in G. Ross Roy and J. De Lancey Ferguson (eds), *The Letters of Robert Burns*, 2 vols (Oxford: Clarendon, 1985), vol. 1, pp. 133–47.
10. Tom Wright, *There Was a Man*, p. 1. Wright's play was never published in book form, but the University of Glasgow's Scottish Theatre Archive holds two identical typed manuscripts, shelf-marked GB 247 STA Fd 6/3 and GB 247 STA Js 5/7. The page numbers given in references refer to the manuscript.
11. Wright, *There Was a Man*, p. 1.
12. Wright, *There Was a Man*, p. 1.
13. Wright, *There Was a Man*, p. 1.
14. Wright, *There Was a Man*, p. 2.
15. Wright, *There Was a Man*, p. 2.
16. Lee, *Robert Burns*, p. 15.
17. Lee, *Robert Burns*, p. 15.
18. In the letter to Moore of 2 August 1787, Burns describes encountering Fergusson's works in his 'twenty-third year' (Roy and Ferguson (eds), *Letters*, vol. 1, p. 142): the poet presumably refers to 1781–2, when he was in Irvine to learn flax dressing.
19. Wright, *There Was a Man*, p. 7.
20. Kemp, *The Other Dear Charmer*, p. 40.
21. Kemp, *The Other Dear Charmer*, p. 47.
22. This depiction reflects traditional critical readings that, in Susan Manning's words, 'assume a uniform distinction between the sterile competence in English and the "discovery" of a "natural" Scots idiom' (Susan Manning, 'Robert Fergusson and Eighteenth-Century Poetry', in Robert Crawford (ed.), *'Heaven-Taught Fergusson': Robert Burns's Favourite Scottish Poet* (East Linton: Tuckwell, 2003), p. 88.
23. Lee, *Robert Burns*, p. 28.
24. Lee, *Robert Burns*, p. 32.
25. Lee, *Robert Burns*, p. 34.
26. Lee, *Robert Burns*, p. 34.
27. Lee, *Robert Burns*, p. 41.
28. In a letter to Gavin Hamilton of December 1787, Burns describes Auld as 'that Boänerges of Gospel power' (Roy and Ferguson (eds), *Letters*, vol. 1, pp. 180–1).

29. Lee, *Robert Burns*, p. 43.
30. Lee, *Robert Burns*, p. 44.
31. Wright, *There Was a Man*, p. 6.
32. Wright, *There Was a Man*, p. 7.
33. Lee, *Robert Burns*, p. 47.
34. Wright, *There Was a Man*, p. 8.
35. Wright, *There Was a Man*, pp. 8–9.
36. Lee, *Robert Burns*, p. 53.
37. Lee, *Robert Burns*, p. 56.
38. Lee, *Robert Burns*, p. 57.
39. Lee, *Robert Burns*, p. 59.
40. Wright, *There Was a Man*, p. 11.
41. Wright, *There Was a Man*, p. 13.
42. Wright, *There Was a Man*, p. 13.
43. Lee, *Robert Burns*, p. 71.
44. Wright, *There Was a Man*, p. 14.
45. Wright, *There Was a Man*, p. 15.
46. Lee, *Robert Burns*, p. 100.
47. Lee, *Robert Burns*, p. 102.
48. Wright, *There Was a Man*, p. 20.
49. Lee, *Robert Burns*, p. 119.
50. Lee, *Robert Burns*, p. 124.
51. Lee, *Robert Burns*, p. 128.
52. Hilton Brown, *There Was a Lad: An Essay on Robert Burns* (London: Hamish Hamilton, 1949), p. 231.
53. Lee, *Robert Burns*, p. 137.
54. Lee, *Robert Burns*, p. 140.
55. Lee, *Robert Burns*, p. 143.
56. Lee, *Robert Burns*, p. 144.
57. Lee, *Robert Burns*, p. 144.
58. Wright, *There Was a Man*, p. 21.
59. Wright, *There Was a Man*, p. 22.
60. Wright, *There Was a Man*, p. 22.
61. Wright, *There Was a Man*, p. 23.
62. Wright, *There Was a Man*, p. 24.
63. Wright, *There Was a Man*, p. 28.
64. Wright, *There Was a Man*, p. 28.
65. Wright, *There Was a Man*, p. 30.
66. Wright, *There Was a Man*, p. 31.
67. See, for example, Burns to Alexander Cunningham, 7 July 1796 in Roy and Ferguson (eds), *Letters*, vol. 2, pp. 180–1.

68. Wright, *There Was a Man*, p. 34.
69. Kemp, *The Other Dear Charmer*, p. 7.
70. Kemp, *The Other Dear Charmer*, p. 7.
71. Kemp, *The Other Dear Charmer*, p. 17.
72. Kemp, *The Other Dear Charmer*, p. 21.
73. Kemp, *The Other Dear Charmer*, p. 29.
74. Kemp, *The Other Dear Charmer*, p. 32.
75. Kemp, *The Other Dear Charmer*, p. 40.
76. Kemp, *The Other Dear Charmer*, p. 41.
77. Kemp, *The Other Dear Charmer*, p. 44.
78. Kemp, *The Other Dear Charmer*, p. 46.
79. Kemp, *The Other Dear Charmer*, p. 49.
80. Kemp, *The Other Dear Charmer*, p. 50.
81. Kemp, *The Other Dear Charmer*, p. 54.
82. Kemp, *The Other Dear Charmer*, p. 54.
83. Kemp, *The Other Dear Charmer*, p. 23.
84. Kemp, *The Other Dear Charmer*, p. 55.
85. Kemp, *The Other Dear Charmer*, p. 55.
86. Kemp, *The Other Dear Charmer*, p. 67.
87. Kemp, *The Other Dear Charmer*, p. 67.
88. Kemp's source is the letter from Burns to Maclehose dated February 1788, in Roy and Ferguson (eds), vol. 1, pp. 243–4.
89. Kemp, *The Other Dear Charmer*, pp. 68–9.
90. Kemp, *The Other Dear Charmer*, p. 69.
91. Kemp, *The Other Dear Charmer*, p. 70.
92. See Kenneth Simpson, 'A Highly Textual Affair: The Sylvander-Clarinda Correspondence', *Studies in Scottish Literature* 35 (2007), pp. 258–93.
93. Kemp, *The Other Dear Charmer*, p. 76.
94. Kemp, *The Other Dear Charmer*, p. 87.
95. Kemp, *The Other Dear Charmer*, p. 92.
96. Kemp, *The Other Dear Charmer*, p. 92.
97. Kemp, *The Other Dear Charmer*, p. 95.
98. Kemp, *The Other Dear Charmer*, p. 95.
99. Kemp, *The Other Dear Charmer*, p. 96.
100. Kemp, *The Other Dear Charmer*, p. 97.
101. Kemp, *The Other Dear Charmer*, p. 101.
102. Kemp, *The Other Dear Charmer*, p. 20.
103. Gerard Slevin, Theatre Programme for *There Was a Man*, Dundee Repertory, 1967, p. 2.

9

Burns and Film

Alistair Braidwood

For many people Robert Burns and his work are indivisible, so it is important to consider how both have been treated in cinematic terms. Further, it is Burns's songs which have had the most enduring relationship with cinema, one which shows no sign of ending. At the current count, as I write this, the number of Robert Burns's song credits on the Internet Movie Database is 328, with the vast majority of entries for 'Auld Lang Syne'. As this is one of the best-known songs of all time it is only natural that it has been heard or sung multiple times in film and television, but there are other examples, including 'Green Grow the Rashes, O', 'Ae Fond Kiss', 'Flow Gently Sweet Afton', and 'My Love is Like a Red, Red, Rose'. The films range from 1925's *Auld Lang Syne* to a recent episode of the successful television series *The Crown* (2019) and just a few better known examples include Laurel and Hardy's *Sons of the Desert* (1933), *Mr Smith Goes to Washington* (1939), *Yankee Doodle Dandy* (1942), *Blackboard Jungle* (1955), *The Apartment* (1960), *The Prime of Miss Jean Brodie* (1969), *When Harry Met Sally* (1989), *Sunset Song* (2015) and *Wonder Woman* (2017).

However, beside the use of his songs, depictions of Robert Burns and his work on screen are more common than one may believe. I will examine five films that offer an insight into aspects of the relationship between Burns and cinema, and in turn how that relationship has influenced the way people have often viewed Burns and his legacy, both nationally and internationally, given that film is one of the most popular and, therefore, influential cultural media.

Auld Lang Syne (1937)

The first film to consider is a historical drama about the life and times of Burns directed by James A. FitzPatrick and starring Andrew Cruickshank, Christine Adrian and Marian Spencer. The film was what was known as a 'quota quickie'; low-cost British films made by American distributors in order to satisfy the quota requirements of the Cinematograph Films Act of 1927. The Act had introduced a requirement for British cinemas to show a quota of British films, for a duration of ten years, and was designed to prop up the struggling British film industry of the time. *Auld Lang Syne* was produced at Shepperton Studios in Surrey for distribution by Metro Golden Mayer, and, while it may have been produced to fill a quota, that does not mean it should be dismissed as a result.

The film opens with a rolling screen to set the scene, of the type that fans of the *Star Wars* films will be familiar with. Here it says,

> Surrounded by the proverbial repressions of an orthodox religion as well as poverty, ROBERT BURNS dared to sing his songs of wine and women, and the joy of living; and of all his immortal compositions none better reveals his unfailing spirit of friendship and brotherhood than 'Auld Lang Syne' the song which inspired this humble tribute to his memory.

I should point out the use of caps and the larger font are decisions taken by the director, but that opening immediately sets you up for a 'man against the world' story, and it is not going to be easy for Robert.

Aberdonian actor Cruickshank plays Burns. It was his first leading role, but he would go on to have a successful film career, the highlights of which are *The 39 Steps* (1959), *Kidnapped* (1960) and *El Cid* (1961), and then appear regularly on British television, perhaps most famously as Dr Cameron in the first televised iteration of *Dr Finlay's Casebook* (1962–71). Cruickshank plays Burns as 'hail-fellow-well-met', regularly quoting his own poetry to make his point, or to remind the audience who he is. Not that it is hard to work out. He easily stands out on screen against his oppressors who are almost all dressed in black, while Burns is introduced with light jacket and a rather flamboyant waistcoat, even when carrying out his duties at the farm.

Early on, he turns to his brother Gilbert, who has been setting him straight as to how most of the village of Tarbolton view him, and says, 'But Gill, the sweetest times I ever spent were spent among the lasses', directly quoting the opening line of one of his most famous poems. He then laughs, and says, 'And I havnae heard the lasses complain.' The film mainly consists of a series of well-known scenes in Burns's life, and the poetry that they are supposed to have inspired. So, we see him in church where he writes the most famous line in 'To a Louse',

> O wad some Power the giftie gie us
> To see oursels as ithers see us!

or considering his 'Address to the Unco Guid'. Later, as his poetry is denounced, lines from 'To a Mouse' appear on screen:

> The best laid schemes o' mice an' men
> Gang aft agley.

This is a device that director Fitzpatrick puts to good use (he will not be the last to do so), and it works both in introducing Burns's poetry to those unfamiliar with it, and pleasing those members of the audience who do know it. It also conveys the complex and serious sides of Burns that may have been indiscernible from Cruickshank's fairly one-dimensional portrayal. That seems to move from lusty and playful to angry and back again – repeat until fade.

The Romance of Robert Burns (1937)

Auld Lang Syne was not the only Burns biopic to be released in 1937. Indeed, it was not even the only one financed by the studios of Metro Golden Mayer. Directed by Crane Wilbur, *The Romance of Robert Burns* (1937) is a short film, with a running time of just over fifteen minutes, but it is one worth considering as it appears to have been made with an international audience in mind. The 'Farmer Poet' Robert Burns, after a bad romance, pens 'Auld Lang Syne' to much fanfare, eventually courting high society at the expense of a potential relationship with Jean Armour, a move he will come to regret. The film opens with 'Auld Lang Syne' (but of course), a still screen and these words, which once again set the tone:

> Is there a man or woman who has not sung the words of Auld Lang Syne? Let us walk the heather with the poet who penned this immortal ballad . . . Robert Burns of Scotland.

A bucolic scene is set to the strains of 'Flow Gently Sweet Afton' as a man sits and smokes as he fishes. There is some close harmony singing in the local hostelry and Burns himself is praised for writing 'such sweet words'. Meanwhile the bartender and some regulars mourn the loss of Burns's love 'Highland Mary' on his behalf, and seem to hatch a plot to matchmake between Burns and Jean Armour. The overly romantic style and look of the film will be familiar to anyone who has seen *Brigadoon* (1954) or its Irish equivalent, Walt Disney's *Darby O'Gill and the Little People* (1959), (starring Sean Connery who must have been considered to play Burns at some stage). More recent filmgoers could even draw parallels with these early pastoral scenes and those set in 'the Shire' in Peter Jackson's 'Middle Earth' movies, where the local hobbits live similar lives, and smoke similar pipes.

We then cut to Burns and Jean under a tree, where he is reciting 'To a Mouse'. It becomes clear that Burns is indifferent, or oblivious, to Jean's feelings, and he tells her he is off to Edinburgh the next day. Then we are told that 'Bobby Burns', as he is named on screen, 'soon becomes the favourite of the lords and ladies of Edinborouh [sic]'.

In Edinburgh Burns is wined and dined, and patronised by those lords and ladies. In a fascinating scene around the dinner table the poet is asked to perform, and there are overtones of *Pygmalion*, with these social high-fliers wanting to mould Burns into one of them, or ridicule him if they cannot. Burns teaches them a lesson by reciting first from 'To a Louse', and then 'A Man's a Man For a' That'. They, in turn, take the intended offence and a fist-fight (the choice of weapon of the working man, apparently) results, which our hero duly wins. Meanwhile, back home, Jean still pines for Bobby, but is now promised to another. Burns rushes to get home in time to halt proceedings (instructing the carriage driver to 'tak the low road' instead of the high road as it is quicker).

The Romance of Robert Burns is an interesting film. It is not great, or even very good, and nowhere near as thorough a telling as that 'contractual obligation' which was *Auld Lang Syne*, but it does give an insight into how Burns and his poetry were viewed at the time by an American director. It perhaps goes some way to explaining the popular view of him as almost another Caledonian myth, a legend similar to *Brigadoon* itself, one who is not just of another place, but another time and different level of reality. However, the fact it was made at all shows how popular his story and work remained. How many other poets would have a Hollywood-backed film made about them? I can only think of Sylvia Plath, Allen Ginsberg, Pablo Neruda and Emily Dickinson in recent years. No matter how much we may smirk at the accents, dialogue and characterisations, *The Romance of Robert Burns* still has his poetry and songs at its heart.

Coming Thro' the Rye (1947)

This is a more straightforward biopic of Robert Burns, one which is again punctuated by songs and poems. The film is one of only a handful directed by Walter C. Mycroft, a well-respected producer at Elstree Studios during the 1930s. This time the role of Burns is played by Terence Alexander (in his first film role), an actor best known for *The League of Gentlemen* (1960) and who would later find fame as Charlie Hungerford in BBC's *Bergerac* (1981–91). It also features a young Molly Weir who would become a regular on Scottish screens for many years. It opens with a dedication to: 'The Immortal Memory of Robert Burns'.

The famous Alexander Nasmyth portrait of Burns is shown at the beginning, and locations associated with Burns, either filmed or photographed, appear throughout. These lend the film a sense of realism and authority, and the feel of authenticity, that was clearly lacking in *The Romance of Robert Burns*. It is interesting to compare the two, there being only ten years between them. While *Coming Thro' the Rye* is more of a British and European film in style and tone, as opposed to the brash often-glib take of Hollywood of the time, they both refuse even to attempt to separate the man and his work. As well as the use of Burns's portrait there are also quotes on screen from other writers as if they wish to lend their support not only to Burns, but to the film itself:

The greatest peasant poet the world has ever seen.
Stephen Gwynn
The very first of the profoundly original British poets of the Romantic School.
G. K. Chesterton
Burns was the first poet who made common life classical.
H. C. Shelley
Deep in the heart of man, his power survives.
William Wordsworth
He was all heart and all man. And there's nothing, a least in a poor man's experience, either bitter or sweet, which can happen to him, but a line of Burns springs into his mouth and gives him courage and comfort if he needs it.
It is like a second Bible.
The Right Hon. J. M. Robertson, *Burns Chronicle 1928*

These are all strong and passionate appraisals of Burns, with the final one coming, somewhat ironically, close to blasphemy. All the while Burns's song 'Rantin' Rovin' Robin' plays over the opening credits, with lyrics that, to modern ears, have the feel of a self-referential, almost boastful song, toasting his own life and loves. It certainly sets up many of the themes that the film will touch upon.

Burns's life story then unfolds, with the strange directorial decision to have multiple narrators, perhaps to suggest that Burns belongs to all. However, it is a little distracting having so many different voices, often changing mid-sentence as if the film has been edited together from multiple others. The script throws up some lines that are striking; for instance claiming that Burns's father William had 'the Scottish peasants' almost grim passion for education', and that the family would 'trudge' to worship in Ayr each week – an interesting choice of words and imagery suggesting hardship and struggle. It is certainly a more gritty and realistic take on the Burns story than we have seen so far. There are scenes of

Burns writing some of the words as they are spoken in voiceover, inviting the audience to think that this is as close to Burns telling his own story as possible.

Coming Thro' the Rye is actually a very clear and direct telling of the Burns story, touching on every age of its subject's life, as well as all the stereotypes and attributes assigned to him, and once again backs everything up through Burns's own words. It is a fine introduction to the man and his work, and an examination of the influences and themes that are familiar to many. It is also a celebration of Burns's songs in particular, and it is not too much of a stretch to suggest an alternative title, *Burns: The Musical.*

The Ballad of Tam Lin (1970)

Largely composed from older versions of the supernatural ballad of the same name, Burns's version of 'Tam Lin' appeared for the first time in James Johnson's *Scots Musical Museum* in 1797. In it a young maiden summons the fairy, Tam Lin, who appears to her beside a well, often represented in the supernatural as the entrance to the underworld, and nothing good comes of it.

Burns's version of Tam Lin is undoubtedly the inspiration for *The Ballad of Tam Lin* [*aka The Devil's Widow*], notable as being the only film directed by the actor Roddy McDowall, and definitely of its time. It is an unsettling and unusual watch which can be viewed as either supernatural or psychological horror, at least initially. It certainly fed into many of the concerns of the time – the cult of youth, the occult, the dangers of drugs, and it warns against being seduced by the counterculture and dropping out of social norms. As with the supernatural ballad tradition, there is always a price to pay.

Imagine *The Wicker Man* meets Antonioni's *Blow Up*, with a hint of *Rosemary's Baby*, and you will have some idea of what to expect. The film stars a young, pre-*Lovejoy*, Ian McShane as Tom Lynn, a young man about town who finds himself in tow with a group who quickly look to resemble a cult. McShane would have been perfectly cast as Robert Burns around this time as he looks so similar to the previously mentioned Nasmyth portrait that I am tempted to suggest this was a major reason for his casting. With Cyril Cusack, Stephanie Beacham, Sinéad Cusack, Joanna Lumley, Jenny Hanley and Madeline Smith also appearing, this is just about the most typically 1970s UK cast list one can imagine.

But the main billing, and arguably the reason to watch the film even now, is the central performance from Ava Gardner as the mysterious Mrs Cazaret, an aging aristocrat, and possible witch, who still desires and demands the pleasures and playfulness of youth. She surrounds herself with a coterie of beautiful people, and she is wealthy enough, or powerful enough, to hold them in her thrall. Director McDowall effectively combines the fairy-tale origins of the film with a nightmarish and hallucinogenic tone that was an increasingly common response to the end of the Swinging Sixties. It is worth reflecting that the 'Manson Family' murders happened in 1969, and for some they marked the end of the 1960s as an ideal. Certainly, one can read a commentary on this in *The Ballad of Tam Lin.*

In some ways it reminds me of the 1974 film adaptation of Muriel Spark's *The Driver's Seat*, which also starred a Hollywood leading lady approaching the twilight of her acting years, Elizabeth Taylor. Both films dazzle with the colours, style, music and attitude of the time, but there is sadness and despair at the heart of both, and Taylor and Gardner are perfectly cast, and rarely better, in their respective roles.

Music is very important once more in *The Ballad of Tam Lin*, with a soundtrack by folk supergroup Pentangle, another aspect which helps firmly date the film. It makes sense, as Pentangle were steeped in the folk and ballad tradition, and would likely have been aware of Burns's 'Tam Lin' as well as his other songs. As the final credits roll the last two verses of their version are sung:

Out then spak the queen o' Fairies,
And an angry queen was she;
Shame betide her ill-fard face,
And an ill death may she dee,
For she's ta-en awa the bonniest knight
In a' my companie.

'But had I kend, Tam Lin,' she says,
'What now this night I see,
I wad hae ta'en out thy twa grey een,
And put in twa een o' tree.[1]

It is a chilling ending to a genuinely tense film (now considered a lost horror classic). Many will have viewed it unaware of the original source, but rarely has a Scottish ballad been used in such an interesting and contemporary way.

Red Rose (2004)

I looked briefly at the difficult production of *Red Rose* in 'Missing Reels';[2] if you want to know more then I recommend that discussion. Directed by Robbie Moffat, this is a film which concentrates on Burns's later life in Dumfries when, as the film's press release stated, 'Robert Burns, national poet of Scotland, is reduced to poverty when his many social marital affairs catch up with him.' The film had only a small theatrical release, and the reception for it was decidedly mixed from the few who saw it. It was later given away free with *The Sun* newspaper to mark Burns Night in 2008. The film was clearly made on a low budget and quickly. At one point an Arnold Clark rental van can be seen through the window, as well as electric street lights, and there are similar continuity errors that suggest they had to shoot a scene then move onto the next without much care and attention. That is often the lot of low-budget films.

It is interesting to return to *Red Rose* over a decade after speaking to Robbie Moffat about it. At the time I said that singer, and former television Game Show co-host, Isla St Clair, was the most famous person involved, and to some she still will be. While some of her co-stars have continued to work in film and television, no one has yet made a star turn, and certainly never appeared regularly on prime-time BBC1 on a Saturday night.

Despite all its faults, *Red Rose* remains the most recent successful attempt to bring Burns to the big screen and the fact it was made at all is some sort of triumph. Director Moffat was under no illusion that his film was going to win any awards but, as is often the case with Burns related projects, passion for the man and his work drives people on against all odds.

In recent years Burns has remained a television phenomenon, celebrated once a year with undeniable gusto, but that 'one-night only' approach does seem to lessen any impact for the rest of the year. On the most recent Burns Night (25 January 2020) the BBC had a full night's programming, long having moved away from one-man performances from the likes of John Cairney and Christopher Tait, and *The White Heather Club* approach where the songs were simply performed and played with little comment.[3] Today the coverage is more wide-reaching and imaginative, and often academic- and research-driven, which gives a more interesting overview of the man, his work and his importance to the nation's culture.

Robert Burns's relationship with cinema continues to be fleeting and the question remains whether there will ever be a biopic to give cinema a memorable, and potentially definitive, 'Robert Burns'. There are still rumours about a film in the pipeline, although as time goes on the potential casting surely has to move on from Gerard Butler who has been long-linked to a project known as *Burns: The Movie* (also reported by some sources as *Burns: The Elemental Might*), as has director Vadim Jean, best known for *Leon the Pig Farmer* (1992) and *One More Kiss* (1999). According to those rumours, actor James Cosmo was set to produce, with a script from Scottish novelist Alan Sharp, and Hollywood actor Julia Stiles at one point pencilled in to play Jean Armour,[4] but the last firm updates on this were in 2009–10 and there has been very little heard since. However, that is not the most unusual rumour of recent times.

In 2012 *The List* ran a story by Jen Bowden claiming that the Robert Burns Birthplace Museum were in talks about receiving a copy of songs co-written with Michael Jackson that were based on Burns's poems.[5] Apparently Jackson's friend and music producer David Gest visited the museum in Ayrshire as part of a programme being filmed for BBC Alba. He told them that he and Jackson had planned a musical based on the Ayrshire poet's life and had arranged some of his works into songs before recording them with friends. This conversation was confirmed with the then director of the Museum, Nat Edwards:

> We had a chat and thought it would be great if we could play them at the museum and he offered to look them out and provide copies so we could do that. We would very much be looking forward to getting hold of these recordings and if possible for us to produce some sort of CD that could help raise money for the museum. That would be fantastic. They'd be a way of getting other audiences interested in Burns and illustrating his international, enduring artistic legacy.[6]

Gest claimed that Jackson (who died in 2009) had been a huge fan of Burns's poetry and had been keen to be involved in the project that saw the Scot's work turned into show tunes, and also claimed that Jackson's 1983 hit 'Thriller' was inspired by Burns' poem 'Tam o' Shanter'. In conversation with BBC Alba, Gest claimed he was himself a Burns fan and had staged a show called *Red Red Rose* which was all about the bard's life starring the then little-known John Barrowman, who would go on to be time-travelling hero Captain Jack Harkness in *Doctor Who* spin-off *Torchwood*. If the rumours are to be believed (and the whole story seems barely credible), the proposed Jackson/Gest musical was to have been produced by *Psycho* actor Anthony Perkins and directed by the Hollywood musical legend Gene Kelly (*Singin' in the Rain*, *American in Paris*, *On the Town*). Just how close this incredible undertaking was to any sort of reality remains unclear.

Burns's influence on filmmakers, however, looks set to carry on despite the lack of a successful contemporary biopic, or perhaps even in part because of it. His songs continue to be sung on screen, and his poetry still inspires. Two recent examples of this are *TAM* (2017), a modern take on 'Tam o' Shanter' and *HAGGIS* (2020) both written and directed by Victoria Brown. Starring Martin Docherty in the title role, and *Still Game*'s Gavin Mitchell as 'Johnny Soutar', *TAM* is set in modern-day Glasgow, and follows the hallucinogenic journey of Tam as he descends into a visceral underworld of wild parties, violence and illicit highs, where he encounters demons, the Devil himself and the bewitching Cutty Sark. It is a thoroughly contemporary telling with updated characters, settings, music and song, but the themes, places and people would be recognisable to anyone who had read the original. Similarly, *HAGGIS* uses the inspiration of 'Address to a Haggis' not just to celebrate the dish itself, but the importance of bringing friends and family together. In the Highlands of Scotland Jimmy and Isobel MacNeep are planning a family reunion for Burns Night 2020, eager to brag about their latest award for their outstanding haggis recipe. However, their grown-up children have their own problems to deal with, all forcing them to find their own way of marking the evening, exploring their relationships with each other, Scottish culture and the national dish itself.

Victoria Brown's interpretations, while contemporary in every aspect, remain faithful to the originals in terms of attitude and intention, and here she explains the reasons for using Burns's work as an inspiration, and her thoughts on why he remains relevant today.[7]

Why did you choose to work on something related to Robert Burns?
VB: Originally it was the narrative story of the poem of 'Tam o' Shanter' which appealed to me, rather than seeking something by Burns, per se. As I began adapting the poem it made me realise how perfectly (and timelessly) constructed his works are, giving me a fresh appreciation. I have since revisited several poems by Burns, which each have a strikingly unique 'voice', addressing completely different aspects of Scottish identity.

Do you feel that Burns remains relevant to a modern-day audience?
VB: Burns speaks directly to the everyday man (or woman) on the street, about themes and subjects to which we can all relate. Although the language has become less accessible as the Scots tongue has evolved over the years, the domestic hopes, dreams, trials, challenges and joys of life remain the same – and are completely identifiable.

Has Burns and his work always been important to you?
VB: Not at all. I (like many other Scots) hated learning Burns at school – not even attempting to read his work again until my twenties. Rediscovering Burns on my own has been a wonderful journey, and I feel his work is now a big part of my own journey and creative identity.

Is the life of Robert Burns of interest to you, or only the work itself?
VB: I think a background to any artist helps appreciate their work so much more – I love how 'rock and roll' Burns' life was, and how controversial many of his works were at time of publication. This is precisely the reason that my personal aim has been to bring Burns out of the stuffy arena of middle-class Burns suppers, and bland schoolrooms – and more at the forefront of a younger, more rebellious audience.

The films discussed in this chapter, excluding *The Ballad of Tam Lin,* all tell the same basic story about the life, work and legend of Robert Burns, and for some that may be enough. However, with the exception of *Red Rose*, those biopics were made fifty to eighty years ago. It may be time for a serious attempt to bring Burns back to the big screen.

Notes

1. The word 'tree' often refers simply to wood in the ballad tradition – 'Tree *n., v.*'. *Dictionary of the Scots Language*, 2004. Scottish Language Dictionaries Ltd – dsl.ac.uk/entry/snd/tree [accessed 23 July 2020].
2. Alistair Braidwood, 'Missing Reels: An Investigation into Robert Burns' Absence from Cinema in the Second Half of the Twentieth Century', in Johnny Rodger and Gerard Carruthers (eds), *Fickle Man: Robert Burns in the 21st Century* (Dingwall: Sandstone Press, 2009), pp. 80–7.
3. *The White Heather Club* was a BBC TV Scottish variety show that ran on and off from 1958 to 1968.
4. MovieWeb – movieweb.com/julia-stiles-joins-the-cast-of-burns 2 November 2004 [accessed 25 May 2020).
5. *The List* magazine, article by Jen Bowden, 16 January 2012: list.co.uk/article/39909-michael-jackson-project-based-on-poems-of-robert-burns/
6. Former director of the The Robert Burns' Birthplace Museum, Nat Edwards, speaking to *The List* magazine, 16 January 2012: list.co.uk/article/39909-michael-jackson-project-based-on-poems-of-robert-burns/
7. Email, 21 May 2020.

10

Orchestral Manoeuvres: Burns on the Concert Platform, 1879–1959

Kirsteen McCue

While much recent work has highlighted the importance of Burns and his songs, little, if any, scholarship has focused on Burns in other musical genres.[1] When he wrote his pivotal *History of Music in Scotland* in 1947,[2] Henry George Farmer surveyed the nineteenth century as one full of collections of indigenous Scottish songs and tunes noting that 'the mighty influence of Burns' was uncontested, and had, indeed, given 'the melodies of the past [...] such a halo that the popular entertainment demanded the *auld sangs*'.[3] Bemoaning the Scots' lack of musical imagination, Farmer's history also paints a detailed picture of the energy of the later Victorian period, when Scottish musical life blossomed, on both amateur and professional platforms. Here, it appears, 'the mighty influence of Burns' was also prevalent. This chapter discusses the appearance of Burns within orchestral repertoire from 1879 until the bicentenary of the poet's birth in 1959. It aims to show why composers chose Burns and his work as musical inspiration and how these new orchestral pieces revisited and represented Burns to the concert-going public across the British Isles and beyond.

It was Edinburgh-born Alexander Campbell Mackenzie (1847–1935) who was the first major figure to use Burns as a stimulant for orchestral composition. Spending his early years in Edinburgh, Mackenzie was trained in Germany and returned to Scotland for only a short time, before working in Italy and then stepping into the role of principal of the Royal Academy of Music in London.[4] He presided over the RAM from 1887 until 1924. Furthermore, he acted as chief conductor for the Philharmonic Society concerts from 1892 to 1899 and was president of the International Musical Society between 1908 and 1912. His role as British Institutional Musician has not always sat comfortably with his fellow Scots.[5] Yet in his own lifetime Mackenzie received numerous honorary degrees – three from Scottish universities – was knighted in 1895 and appointed KCVO in 1922. These accolades aside, his niece, the writer Rebecca West, noted that he remained 'disappointed because he never was recognized as a composer'.[6]

As Duncan Barker's pivotal work has shown,[7] Mackenzie's impressive output included a number of large scale compositions with Scotland as their focus: *Three Scenes in the Scottish Highlands* for piano (1878); a Scottish opera, *Columba* (1882–3); *The Pibroch Suite* (1889) and *Highland Ballad* (1891); and incidental music inspired by Scottish writers – Scott's *Ravenswood* (1890) after *The Bride of Lammermoor* and *Marmion* (1891) and J. M. Barrie's *The Little Minister* (1897). Other later works included his *Ancient Scots Tunes* (1915). In addition to reissuing his father's National Dance tune albums,[8] Mackenzie contributed to J. Muir Wood's revised edition of George Farquhar Graham's *The Popular Songs of Scotland* published by Bayley & Ferguson in 1884 (revised 1891).[9] While few of these were settings of Burns songs,[10] such creative work clearly demonstrates Mackenzie's interest in Scotland's indigenous music; he would also lecture on 'The Traditional and National in Music' in 1895 for the Royal Institution (9, 15 and 23 February).[11]

If Burns did not feature strongly in his song arrangements, then he certainly did loom large across Mackenzie's orchestral works. Mackenzie knew and admired Franz Liszt (1811–1886), producing a monograph of the celebrity musician in 1922. Here he explained that Liszt had been deeply influenced by the gipsy music of his native Hungary which he wished, wrote Mackenzie, to hand down 'in an artistic form, as a national treasure'.[12] Starting their life as ebullient pieces for solo piano, Liszt's 'Hungarian Rhapsodies' inspired Mackenzie to develop the genre orchestrally, the first British composer so to do.[13] As John Rink has traced, by the eighteenth century the form of the literary rhapsody (the term had Greek literary roots) had become associated with music, and the piano repertoire of the nineteenth century often included the rhapsody as a piece of entertaining *Hausmusik*. But it was Liszt's work that anticipated the later use of the genre, establishing it also as a 'large-scale nationalistic "epic" for orchestra'.[14]

Arguably it was the concept of the national epic that Mackenzie was aiming for in his four orchestral rhapsodies, the first three of which pay direct homage to Robert Burns: the *Rhapsodie Ecossaise*, Op. 21 (1879), *Burns: Second Scotch Rhapsody*, Op. 24 (1880) and *Tam o' Shanter: Third Scottish Rhapsodie*, Op. 74 (1911).[15] One might imagine that Mackenzie would have come across Burns growing up in Edinburgh in the mid-nineteenth century, as he was a young boy when the Scots celebrated Burns's centenary in 1859, yet, while he refers to several key cultural figures, he makes almost no reference at all to Burns in his autobiographical memoir *A Musician's Narrative* (1927).[16] His first *Rhapsodie Ecossaise* appeared at the same time as the new expanded edition of *The Works of Robert Burns* in six volumes edited by William Scott Douglas, which featured many letters and other writings of Burns for the first time.[17] But Mackenzie's work was written at the behest of the German conductor August Manns, who suggested that he feature the Scots tunes he knew so well and that, in addition to the influence of Liszt, he also look to Johan Svendsen's *Norwegian Rhapsodies* as a model.[18] Mackenzie created a three-movement work, each based on a known Scottish tune: 'Muirland Willie' and 'Braw, Braw Lads' for the first two movements and the tune for Burns's autobiographical song 'There Was a Lad was Born in Kyle' as its finale. The support of Manns (1825–1907), who was working in Scotland, but was also, with George Grove (1820–1900), running the Crystal Palace Saturday concerts in London, proved highly significant to Mackenzie and the public reception of his orchestral work.[19]

The *Rhapsodie Ecossaise* was first performed at the Edinburgh Choral Union concert on 5 January 1880.[20] The *Musical Times* review stated that the piece had a 'marked effect on the audience'.[21] Indeed, as Barker also recounts, it was this work that later signalled for Farmer a vision of a 'National School' of music in Scotland which, established by Mackenzie, was then taken forward by the next generation of Scottish composers including Hamish MacCunn (1868–1916), Learmont Drysdale (1866–1909) and John Blackwood McEwen (1868–1948).[22] Yet, in a letter tipped in to the manuscript of the score, Mackenzie confessed to his friend A. C. Barry that he had taken liberties ('dotted notes where there are none') with the tunes and that, moreover, he considered his *Rhapsodie Ecossaise*, in all honesty, 'too slight to bear much talking about'.[23]

Personal reservations aside, and undoubtedly recognising the potency of Burns as national icon, Mackenzie did not delay in creating *Burns: Second Scotch Rhapsody*, Op. 24.[24] Written while he was in Florence, he dedicated the work to his neighbour, Madame J. Hillebrand, a friend of both Liszt and Wagner, and of the conductor Hans von Bülow, who would in turn become a close colleague of Mackenzie.[25] Again in the second *Rhapsody* there were three movements, this time all based on melodies associated with Burns: the ebullient (one might even say bombastic) opening movement is based on 'Scots! Wha Hae wi' Wallace Bled', or 'Robert Bruce's Address to his Troops at Bannockburn', and Mackenzie gives it the marking 'Molto maestoso e risoluto' (very majestic and resolute); the middle movement, which follows without a break, is more gentle and based on 'She's Fair and Fause that Causes my Smart' marked 'Andante, dolente' (at walking pace, sad); and the final movement uses the melody for 'The Cardin' o't' and is a happy dance marked 'Vivace' (lively).[26] Nodding more clearly to the literary foundations of the eighteenth-century rhapsody, Burns's texts also appear. The manuscript copy of the Burns Rhapsody shows that Mackenzie wrote an extract from each of the selected Burns texts at the beginning of each movement and these were retained when the piece was published by Neumeyer & Co. in both London and Leipzig. While Mackenzie is really experimenting and playing with the melodic content here, he clearly also nods to Burns's texts in terms of the mood he creates for each of his movements. 'Scots Wha Hae', penned by Burns in the early 1790s to the rousing march 'Hey Tutti Taiti', was as much about contemporary revolutionary wars as it was about the Bannockburn of its title. But by 1880 it had become something of an anthem employed for umpteen different political purposes across the century from Peterloo in 1819 to the 1884 Representation of the People Act, and it was thus associated with songs about nineteenth-century Britain – including John Mayne's 'English, Scots and Irishmen' – and not just the wars of Scottish independence.[27] There is little subtlety in Mackenzie's handling of this tune and it makes a powerful short opening movement to the rhapsody. 'She's Fair and Fause' provided a beautiful slow air (the tune was also known by the title 'The Lads of Leith').[28] Scored richly for wind and strings, this movement has a breathy and elegiac quality about it. Some editors believe that Burns wrote the song in 1789 for his close friend Alexander Cunningham, after having read of the wedding of Ann Stewart, to whom Cunningham had previously been engaged.[29] The choice for the finale was clearly based on the qualities of the tune 'The Cardin' o't' with its text beginning 'I coft a stane o' haslock woo', but it is a song not conclusively proven to be Burns's at all.[30]

While Barker lists the première of the work as having taken place in Glasgow in January 1881, it appears that Mackenzie's Burns Rhapsody was first performed in December 1880, once again under the baton of August Manns. Farmer's copy of the *Prospectus of the Seventh Series of Choral and Orchestral Concerts in St Andrew's Hall* includes details of the 'Fourth Concert' held on Tuesday, 28 December 1880, showing that Mackenzie's 'Rhapsody Ecossaise No 2 – "Burns"' appeared at the end of the first half of a concert featuring Cherubini's 'Overture to "Anacréon"', Mozart's 'Symphony in E flat (K.543)', the 'Scena and Aria, "Ah perfido"' by Beethoven, and a selection of the music from Schubert's 'Rosamunde'. Part 2 was given over entirely to Wagner and included his overture to *Tannhäuser* and various scenes from his operas, notably Walther's Prize song from *Die Meistersinger*, followed by the final piece, 'Der Walküren Ritt' or 'Ride of the Valkyries'. Farmer's *History* recounts that the Edinburgh and Glasgow Choral Union concerts, which led directly to the formation of the Scottish Orchestra in 1894 (later the SNO and RSNO), ensured that the quality of Scotland's concert life was as impressive as anywhere in the British Isles, excepting London and Manchester.[31] The Glasgow concert programmes, with detailed notes for each work, were clearly designed to give Scottish audiences a chance to hear and to learn about substantial works within the European concert repertoire.[32]

The Burns Rhapsody was heard in Wiesbaden in February 1881 and scheduled at Crystal Palace by Manns the following month, and by all accounts it was warmly welcomed by audiences.[33] Mackenzie later recounted Liszt being heartily cheered by playing through the recently published arrangement for four hands and two pianos.[34] But, this anecdote notwithstanding, he generally appears to have played down its success. Several years later he wrote to the classics scholar, Scots song historian and Burns biographer John Stuart Blackie, confessing that he was worried about paying lip service, or becoming a 'mere mannerist' musically speaking.[35] Indeed, this discomfort might be suggested by the inconsistency of titles across manuscripts, printed scores and printed programme titles for all three of his rhapsodies, which move between 'Ecossaise', 'Scotch' and 'Scottish'. Mackenzie clearly struggled to walk the line between being regarded as a serious composer, bearing the marks of his continental European training and aspiration, while continuing to make 'a little contribution to Scotch music'. He wished to turn his hand to the 'popular' (he refers here to some of his song arrangements) while, at the same time, delivering his 'more elaborate work'.[36] The programming of the Burns Rhapsody as the only native work in a concert of Cherubini, Mozart, Schubert, Beethoven and, notably, Wagner, might well have contributed to Mackenzie's feelings that his Scottish works were not worthy of attention. But such programming nevertheless illustrates that the figure of Burns, and notably the melodies associated with his songs, sat side-by-side with the best of the European concert repertoire for British audiences at this time.

Appearing much later, in 1911, Mackenzie's *Third Scottish Rhapsodie – Tam o' Shanter* is perhaps more successful as a piece of European concert music. *Tam* is not the medley of tunes that we find in either of the first two Scottish rhapsodies, but rather it aims to reflect the narrative of Burns's famous poem: here the notion of literary and orchestral epic is to the fore. As he recounts in his 1889 letter to Blackie, between his Burns Rhapsody in 1880 and turning his hand to *Tam*, Mackenzie had also set Burns's much-loved poem 'The Cotter's Saturday Night', for chorus and orchestra, thus suggesting a deeper interest in Burns.[37] This new orchestral rhapsody was created to be premièred at the London Congress of the International Musical Society where Mackenzie was clearly making a statement about the global reach of his national bard.[38] For *Tam* Mackenzie chose Allan Masterton's fine-fitting tune 'Willie Brew'd a Peck o' Maut' as the opening theme of the piece, highlighting the drunken Tam and Souter Johnny at the start of the poem. He deftly weaves snippets of the tune across the rhapsody, cleverly using the opening phrase of the chorus, to which the words 'We are na fou, we're nae that fou' are normally underlaid, to protest Tam's apparent innocence. While the other melodic content here is created rather than quoted, Mackenzie plays around with whole tones all the way through the piece. Moreover, he had initially written in a part for bagpipes, though this is scored out in the manuscript of the work, and if this had come to pass then it would have been decades in advance of the orchestral use of the Highland bagpipe.[39] Overall this score is much more original and atmospheric than its rhapsodic predecessors, marking a significant development in Mackenzie's compositional skill and style across the intervening period. Mackenzie might also have been inspired in this choice of Burns text by one of his younger musical compatriots. The privately printed *History of the Glasgow Society of Musicians 1884–1944* recounts that in 1889–90 'Learmont Drysdale, of Edinburgh, won the £30 award in the Society's Prize Competition, the judges being Sir Frederick Cowen and Sir A. C. Mackenzie'. The work was Drysdale's concert overture based on Burns's 'Tam o'Shanter',[40] which received its première in Glasgow under the direction of Manns in January 1891. Drysdale included a prefatory text taken directly from Burns's poem with the title 'The Hour Approaches, Tam Maun Ride'.[41]

Moira Harris has suggested that Drysdale, who was still only a student at Mackenzie's RAM at the time, had wanted to call his piece a 'symphonic poem', but was advised that the structure of the work sat more comfortably as an overture or 'tone picture'. Harris's analysis shows that Drysdale adhered to sonata form and she carefully reveals that he was, in fact, following Burns's poem in its entirety.[42] Overall for the listener, though, this is much more of an impressionistic piece than Mackenzie's *Tam* a decade later and there is no direct quotation of any obviously Scots tunes, real or imagined. The overture opens with the atmospheric orchestral striking of a clock, and Drysdale does whip up a wild chromatic ride through a stormy night. Although he evocatively portrays the sound of Maggie's movement, the love theme – for Tam and Nanie – is the most notable passage of the work, even nodding to the greatest love theme in all composed music, namely Wagner's famous 'Liebestod' from his opera *Tristan und Isolde*. Like most of his contemporaries Drysdale greatly admired Wagner's work, so this should come as little surprise.[43] Harris's research reveals that *Tam* was programmed regularly and often broadcast from the 1920s through to the 1940s, even though it has now been silent for many decades. It is highly likely, however, that it would have been heard by Malcolm Arnold (1921–2006), whose *Tam o' Shanter Overture*, Op. 51 (1955) has retained its place in the orchestral repertoire and taken the work of Burns to a broader range of listeners than any of his predecessors. Notably for both Drysdale and Arnold there is little reliance on Farmer's 'auld sangs'. Instead, both composers create a new kind of musical translation of Burns's poetry.

Arnold's choice of Burns was not, as Piers Burton-Page explains, 'a flash-in-the-pan'; he claims that Arnold was well acquainted from his youth in Northampton with John Gibson Lockhart's famous 1828 *Life of Robert Burns* and his study of Walter Scott.[44] Furthermore Burton-Page believes that Arnold's *Tam* was, along with his *Scottish Dances*, Op. 59 (1957), a duo of 'Scottish inspired masterpieces'. He notes that the *Dances* even incorporated a Burns-related tune that Arnold had used back in 1949 for a BBC Light Music film *The Beautiful County of Ayr*.[45]

Arnold was a student at the Royal College of Music and because of a lack of orchestral players across World War Two, he was often found playing trumpet in professional London orchestras, notably the London Philharmonic, which premièred many of his compositions, including *Tam*. He engaged in a broad range of composition from high-end symphonies (nine in total) to numerous film scores and popular pieces for amateur musicians and even for domestic equipment (in tow with musical caricaturist Gerald Hoffnung). It is true that many of his labelled 'occasional pieces' have 'outlasted their immediate purpose'[46] and his homage to Burns is perhaps the finest example.

To date, critical biographies give little space to the work, but all of them agree on its brilliance. Hugo Cole explains that Arnold was able to 'write illustrative music in which inhibitions could legitimately be cast aside', commenting that 'the headlong ride of the hero [Tam] is illustrated in boisterous, disruptive music'[47] while noting, at the same time, that Arnold was also able to incorporate the smallest details 'in the most concise and economical terms'.[48] Thus we have in this overture the gloriously drunken bassoons of Tam and his drinking buddy Souter Johnny, and the stormy ride through the countryside in flashing lightening and rumbling thunder; we also experience the wild skirling of the Deil's pipes and the dancing of the witches and warlocks – literally capturing the mirth and fun growing 'fast and furious'. Even the galloping of Maggie, encouraged by Tam's percussive whipping, is 'boisterous' and 'disruptive'.[49] But alongside this the textual subtlety of Burns's poem is illustrated by nuanced musical details: the eerie opening with its high pitch preluding the supernatural events to come; the moment when Tam 'croons o'er some auld Scotch sonnet'; the point when he shouts out 'Weel done Cutty Sark!'; and the rising bubbles, just after Maggie loses her tail, as the dream disperses and leads to Burns's 'moralitas', which Arnold quotes in full in his score. Indeed, he adds the relevant moments from Burns's text at key points in his manuscript, demonstrating that he was sticking closely to Burns's original.

If critics regard the work as a party-piece, albeit an impressive one, the press and public loved it. Arnold's personal books of news cuttings illustrate just how popular it was and how often the work was programmed after the success of its première.[50] The first cutting Arnold pasted in from the *Daily Mail* confirms that the earliest performance of the overture was at the BBC Proms in the Albert Hall on 16 August 1955, with the London Philharmonic and with the composer conducting. It 'fairly swept the Prommers along with it', as it 'gallops like Burns's original' perhaps even outrunning 'the wild tale of the printed page'. The review in the London *Star* (17 August 1955) agreed whole-heartedly, printing the header 'Weel done Malcolm Arnold!' and, playing perhaps uncomfortably with stereotypes, it noted that Arnold should have 'cast aside his evening dress and worn the kilt and tam o'shanter', adding 'That would have been a master touch.' The review from *The Scotsman* (23 August 1955) described the première as a triumph and drew particular attention to the virtuosic part for trombone, which represents Tam throughout the piece (this is often used today as an orchestral audition piece for trombonists).[51] The *Glasgow Herald* (18 August 1955) states that Arnold had long thought of creating a piece based on 'Tam' and had initially come up with the idea some fourteen years earlier – a fact not yet supported with evidence. But overall the Arnold 'News Cuttings' reveal that the work continued to be scheduled beyond that first performance (often as the first piece in programmes featuring other major new work by Arnold).[52] An article from *Music and Musicians* for April 1957 concluded that 'Since it was first heard at the 1955 Proms, less than two years ago, it has been played a total of 51 times,' with performances in Britain, Australia, New Zealand and in Paris, Brussels and elsewhere. For any work of new music this is seriously impressive.

The dedicatee of Arnold's work is also worthy of note. Michael Diack (1869–1947), director of Paterson's Music Publishers in Glasgow and London was referred to as Arnold's publisher in one of the first reviews of *Tam* and the first miniature orchestral score of the piece was published by the firm to coincide with the première of the work.[53] Arnold was clearly dedicating the work to Diack, *in memoriam*, and while no specific evidence has yet been located,[54] Diack may well have inspired Arnold's choice of subject. He was well-versed in Scottish music, as arranger (J. Michael Diack) of a considerable number of Scots songs for *The Scottish Orpheus*, and he also produced a range of vocal training books. He was superintendent of Music for Glasgow Schools and a founder member of the Royal Scottish Country Dance Society. And in 1923 he founded Beltona Records, which specialised in recordings of Scottish music.[55] Coincidentally, Paterson's published A. C. Mackenzie's arrangement of Burns's song, 'The Chevalier's Lament' for voice and piano. A copy housed in the RAM advertises, on its back page, several Scots song publications alongside J. Michael Diack's 'Vocal Exercises'. It is thus at least conceivable that Diack could have been Arnold's conduit to Mackenzie's earlier orchestral depiction of *Tam*, for there are some notable similarities in the drunken melodic duetting of Tam and Souter Johnny.[56]

It might seem strange that Arnold chose to produce his Burns work in 1955 and not four years later when the bicentenary of poet's birth was the focus of many publications and events. In 1955 American composer Serge Hovey (1920–1988) had come across James Barke's edition of *The Works of Robert Burns* in a second-hand bookshop in New York and became, from that time, obsessed with Burns's songs and the melodies associated with them.[57] By the end of his life he would have arranged over 320 of the songs for voice and small ensemble, a range of which were made famous by folksinger Jean Redpath, discussed in Chapter 12 of this volume. But Hovey's creative obsession with Burns really started in 1959 with his *Burns Rhapsody: A Scottish-American Fantasy for Full Orchestra*, also featuring a four-part chorus and two vocal soloists (mezzo-soprano and baritone). Like Mackenzie's Burns Rhapsody, Hovey begins (in his 'Overture') by quoting from 'Hey Tutti Taiti', the tune for 'Scots Wha Hae'. But this opening movement, which sounds like a film score, is really something of a medley of tunes associated with Burns including 'Afton Water' and 'Low Down in the Broom', the more popular tune sung to 'O My Love is Like a Red, Red Rose' (not Burns's original choice). And there are, towards the end of this opening, a few snatches of 'A Man's a Man for a' That' which Hovey returns to for his 'Hymn', the final movement set for chorus and orchestra. The second movement is based on the song 'Fair Jenny', beginning 'Where are the joys I hae met in the morning', set for baritone and orchestra with spoken text included. The third movement ('Springtime in Ayrshire') is based on 'O Tibbie I Hae Seen the Day', performed poignantly by solo clarinet at the very start. A male-voice chorus then sings the song with a swing-band feel (sung by female chorus later in the movement). Indeed, both middle movements speak to Hovey's music-theatre background. Nicely contrasting with Tibbie's aloofness towards her young suitor, the solo fiddle then changes the mood entirely by playing 'Todlin' Hame', the tune for Burns's lesser-known love-song 'The Primrose' (beginning 'Dost ask me, why I send thee here'), expressing the 'doubts and fears that lovers feel'. The mezzo sings this, with one section *a cappella*, before she is joined by chorus to complete the movement. The fourth movement ('Rock and Reel') harks back to Mackenzie in being a medley of up-tempo fiddle tunes providing a brief musical interlude before the final 'Hymn' on 'A Man's a Man'.[58] As with Hovey's Burns song settings, his main focus here is on the melodic content. This transatlantic rhapsody, performed in Berlin in 1959, clearly looks back to Mackenzie's first two Scottish rhapsodies: each piece relies on tunes associated with Burns, and all were performed at home as well as beyond their obvious national boundaries.

Across the period reviewed here, Burns's unrivalled public reach must surely have been a lure for new composers who wanted their work to be heard by as wide an audience as possible. As Christopher Whatley's work has illustrated, the strength of attachment to Burns during the Victorian period was 'overwhelming' and ranged across all social classes.[59] As the nineteenth century progressed, the adoption of the orchestral rhapsody with its obviously nationalistic connotations fitted neatly with Burns's role as National Bard. Mackenzie's first two Scottish rhapsodies, whether he felt comfortable about them or not, were successful and championed a new national school of musical composition in Scotland, and, with Mackenzie's institutional standing, arguably across Britain too. In his later years Mackenzie experimented more, and the musical soundscapes created by Drysdale and Arnold present Burns in new ways. If the composers of this school of Scoto-British music, emerging from a long period of darkness, were seeking a national epic, then they most certainly found it in Burns's consummate work of narrative poetry, 'Tam o' Shanter. A Tale'.

But orchestral responses to Burns were as contradictory as Burns was himself. In 1959 young Scottish composer Iain Hamilton (1922–2000) was commissioned jointly by the Edinburgh Festival Society and the Robert Burns World Federation to compose an orchestral work to commemorate the bicentenary. Glasgow-born Hamilton, much admired in the sphere of contemporary music, worked with the Scottish National Orchestra under the baton of Scots conductor Alexander Gibson and created his *Sinfonia for Two Orchestras*.[60] Hugh Macdonald has recounted the scandal of the première at the Edinburgh Festival that summer: the press reported that the audience had been 'slightly stunned' and it was said that the Federation president requested that its percentage of the commission fee was paid back.[61] As the BBC presenter of a later broadcast performance noted, the piece received 'some criticism' for having failed to reflect Burns in any obvious way, but Hamilton was adamant that this was his tribute to the great poet, 'entirely in his own terms'.[62] The work is a complex, multi-layered, avant-garde dialogue between the two orchestral groups, in eleven short sections. Always one for controversy, the young Gibson, newly appointed that year as principal conductor of the SNO,[63] scheduled the work for the following winter season and made a recording a few years later, but the piece has not been heard for decades. Christopher Grier's 1966 sleeve note stated that the *Sinfonia* left the audience 'disconcerted' and disappointed that they had not heard a work they could 'take comfortably to their hearts', but Hamilton refused to create what Grier refers to as 'an instantly forgettable Scottish pastiche'.[64] Hamilton was interviewed many years after the première of *Sinfonia*. He recalled, with some satisfaction, the responses to his radical contemporary musical nod to Burns, proving that even if audiences preferred it, composers are not always held back by a predilection for the 'auld sangs'.[65]

Notes

1. See, for example, new editions of Burns's songs for the *Scots Musical Museum*, ed. Murray Pittock (Oxford: Oxford University Press, 2017); and *Robert Burns's Songs for George Thomson*, ed. Kirsteen McCue (Oxford: Oxford University Press, 2021), namely vols 2, 3 and 4 of the *Works of Robert Burns*, general editor Gerard Carruthers. See accompanying online resources at: 'Editing Robert Burns for the 21st Century': https://burnsc21.glasgow.ac.uk/ [accessed December 2019]. Also essays in Sharon Alker, Leith Davis and Holly Faith Nelson (eds), *Robert Burns and Transatlantic Culture* (Farnham: Ashgate, 2012); Gerard Carruthers (ed.), *The Edinburgh Companion to Robert Burns* (Edinburgh: Edinburgh University Press, 2009) and Murray Pittock (ed.), *The Edinburgh Companion to Scottish Romanticism* (Edinburgh: Edinburgh University Press, 2011).
2. Henry George Farmer, *A History of Music in Scotland* (London: Hinrichsen, 1947).
3. Farmer, *History of Music*, p. 355.
4. See *ODNB* entry for A. C. Mackenzie, by Carnegie Moir, rev. Rosemary Firman, 2004: https://doi.org/10.1093/ref:odnb/34749 [accessed November 2019].
5. John Purser has commented that Mackenzie 'allowed himself to become an establishment figure'. *See Scotland's Music: A History of the Traditional and Classical Music of Scotland from Earliest Times to the Present Day* (Edinburgh and London: Mainstream Publishing, 1992), p. 221.
6. Rebecca West, *Family Memories*, ed. Faith Evans (London: Virago, 1987/ London: Lime Tree, 1992), p. 23. Her memoir includes a chapter on her 'Uncle Alick'.
7. Duncan Barker, *The Music of Sir Alexander Campbell Mackenzie (1847–1935): A Critical Study* (unpublished PhD thesis, Durham, 1999), 2 vols.
8. Alexander Mackenzie was leader of the orchestra at the Theatre Royal in Edinburgh. His *National Dance Music of Scotland* was first published in Edinburgh in 1859 and reissued by his son A. C. Mackenzie in 1889.
9. Farquhar Graham's first three-volume *Songs of Scotland* appeared earlier in 1848–9 published by Wood & Co. in Edinburgh.
10. Barker, *Music of Sir Alexander Campbell Mackenzie*, vol. 2, p. 359.
11. The Royal Institution has details of these appearances, but no copies of the lectures in its archive.
12. A. C. Mackenzie, *Liszt* (London: Murdoch, Murdoch & Co., 1922), p. 14.
13. Barker believes that 'The rhapsodies and their musical arrangement prefigure the work of the English folk song school of composers such as Vaughan Williams, Sharp and Holst in the early twentieth century': Barker, *Music of Sir Alexander Campbell Mackenzie*, vol. 1, p. 212.

14. John Rink entry for 'Rhapsody' in Oxford Music Online: https://doi-org.ezproxy.lib.gla.ac.uk/10.1093/gmo/9781561592630.article.23313, 2001 [accessed January 2020].
15. These are the printed titles for all three works; however, Mackenzie's manuscript titles are not always the same. He wrote his *Canadian Rhapsody* in 1904, perhaps unsurprisingly, at the time of his tour to Canada. He also used 'Auld Lang Syne' as one of the melodies in his *Fantasia on Scotch Airs* of 1867 (RAM MS 1205).
16. Alexander Campbell Mackenzie, *A Musician's Narrative* (London: Cassell & Company, 1927).
17. Published in Edinburgh by William Paterson. See J. W. Egerer, *A Bibliography of Robert Burns* (Edinburgh and London: Oliver & Boyd, 1964), pp. 248–52.
18. Johan Svendsen (1840–1911), violinist, composer and conductor: Barker, *Music of Sir Alexander Campbell Mackenzie*, vol. 1, p. 217.
19. See *ODNB* entry on Manns by Keith Horner, 2001: https://doi-org.ezproxy.lib.gla.ac.uk/10.1093/gmo/9781561592630.article.17664 [accessed December 2019]. See also H. Saxe Wyndham, *August Manns and the Saturday Concerts: A Memoir and a Retrospect* (London and New York: The Walter Scott Publishing Co. Ltd., 1909). Sir George Grove established the famous Grove Dictionary of Music and Musicians, begun in 1879. He was also founding director of the new Royal College of Music from 1882.
20. Barker, *Music of Sir Alexander Campbell Mackenzie*, vol. 1, p. 217. Mackenzie cites several German performances: *Musician's Narrative*, p. 95.
21. *Musical Times*, 1 February 1880, p. 81: as quoted in Barker, *Music of Sir Alexander Campbell Mackenzie*, vol. 1, p. 218. For fuller discussion of the three Scottish Rhapsodies see Barker, *Music of Sir Alexander Campbell Mackenzie*, vol. 1, pp. 215–26.
22. Farmer, *History of Music*, p. 518.
23. RAM 046505: includes two tipped in letters to A. C. Barry from Mackenzie sent from 7 South Charlotte Street, Edinburgh, dated 2 May 1881 and 7 April 1889. A bound copy of scores for the *Rhapsody Ecossaise*, Op. 21 and *Burns Second Scotch Rhapsodie*, Op. 24 is also held at RAM: MS 1123 RB08/53/007.
24. The piece is also sometimes given as 'Rhapsodie Ecossaise (no. 2)', as noted in Robert A. Marr, *Music for the People: A Retrospect of the Glasgow International Exhibition, 1888 with an Account of the Rise of Choral Societies in Scotland* (Edinburgh and Glasgow: John Menzies, 1889). Marr includes a biographical account of Mackenzie at the close of the introduction, pp. 1–4.

25. Mackenzie, *Musician's Narrative*, p. 101. Mackenzie recounts that von Bülow was engaged as conductor of the Glasgow Choral Union concerts and so they spent a great deal of time together in 1877 (p. 91).
26. The BBC Scottish Symphony Orchestra with Martyn Brabbins recorded a disc of Mackenzie's orchestral music, featuring the Burns Rhapsody in 1994: Hyperion CD A66764.
27. See Gerard Carruthers, 'Responses to Peterloo in Scotland, 1819–1822', in Michael Demson and Regina Hewitt (eds), *Commemorating Peterloo: Violence, Resilience and Claim-Making during the Romantic Era* (Edinburgh: Edinburgh University Press, 2019), pp. 120–39; *The People's Voice: Scottish Political Poetry, Song, and the Franchise, 1832–1918* database and Michael Shaw's online essay 'Burns and the Suffragettes' at: https://thepeoplesvoice.glasgow.ac.uk [accessed December 2019]; and Oskar Cox Jensen on John Mayne's 'English Scots and Irishmen' on *Romantic National Song Network*: https://rnsn.glasgow.ac.uk/english-scots-and-irishmen/ [accessed November 2019].
28. 'The Lads of Leith' was the tune title as it appeared in Oswald's *Caledonian Pocket Companion*, which was most probably Burns's source for the tune.
29. See Pittock (ed.), *The Scots Musical Museum*, vol. 3, p. 147. The song is *SMM* 4: 398.
30. Pittock (ed.), *The Scots Musical Museum*, vol. 3, p. 165. The song is *SMM* 5: 437.
31. Farmer, *History of Music*, p. 481.
32. The Farmer Collection (University of Glasgow Special Collections) includes an impressive amount of musical ephemera from the period, including this specific programme. See also James A. Webster's *Letters of a Musical Critic: Short Critical Review of Music in Glasgow Season 1989–94* (Glasgow Morison Bros, 1894) for further details of the concert programmes.
33. Barker, *Music of Sir Alexander Campbell Mackenzie*, vol. 1, p. 219.
34. *Second Scotch Rhapsody (Burns) composed by A. C. Mackenzie Op. 24. Arranged for Two Pianofortes by G. Alibrandi* (London and New York: Novello, Ewer & Co., 1881). Mackenzie, *Musician's Narrative*, p. 126.
35. A. C. Mackenzie to John Stuart Blackie: NLS MS 2638, f.4. Blackie produced his own *Life of Robert Burns* in 1888 (London: Walter Scott) and dedicated his new book on Scottish song to Mackenzie in 1889 with 'sincere esteem': John Stuart Blackie, *Scottish Song: Its Wealth, Wisdom and Social Significance* (Edinburgh and London: Blackwood, 1889). Blackie also provided the introduction to Glasgow music publishers Bayley and Ferguson's *The Scottish Students' Song Book* in 1897.
36. A. C. Mackenzie to John Stuart Blackie: NLS MS 2638, f.4.
37. A. C. Mackenzie to John Stuart Blackie: NLS MS 2638, f.4. Mackenzie notes of 'the Cotter's Saturday Night', Op. 39: 'I have a greater love for

this piece than any other choral matter which I have set down. Time will show, whether this is true. Anyhow I am convinced that it is national music, idealised so far as in me lies.' The first performance of the work was by the Edinburgh Choral Union possibly on 16 December 1889. An arrangement for chorus and piano was later published by Novello, Ewer & Co. in London and New York.

38. First performance was on 20 May 1911 as part of the congress, then on 4 December at the Queen's Hall performed by the London Symphony Orchestra (Barker, *Music of Sir Alexander Campbell Mackenzie*, vol. 2, p. 316).
39. MS RAM 1127. The most famous twentieth-century orchestral work to feature the Highland pipes is Peter Maxwell Davis's *Orkney Wedding with Sunrise* (1985).
40. For further discussion see Moira A. Harris, 'The Life and Work of (George John) Learmont Drysdale (1866–1909)' (PhD thesis, University of Glasgow, 2006), 2 vols, vol. 1, p. 48. Harris notes that there was also an 'organ version' of 'Tam' which was 'arranged and performed by the Glasgow organist and teacher H. Sandiford Turner' (vol. 1, p. 84).
41. The section of the text quoted begins with 'That hour o' night's black arch the keystone' and ends with 'The deil had business on his hand'. It was published in 1919 by Stainer and Bell as part of its 'Carnegie Collection of British Music' which featured over fifty key works by some of the most famous British composers of the period including Holst, Vaughan Williams, Bridge, Stanford and Drysdale's Scottish contemporary John Blackwood McEwen.
42. Harris, 'Life and Work', vol. 1, pp. 250–8.
43. Harris, 'Life and Work', vol. 1, pp. 104–5.
44. Piers Burton-Page, *Philharmonic Concerto: The Life of Sir Malcolm Arnold* (London: Methuen, 1994), p. 56.
45. Burton-Page, *Philharmonic Concerto*, p. 56 and p. 75.
46. See Piers Burton Page, 'Malcolm Arnold', in *Oxford Music Online*: https://doi-org.ezproxy.lib.gla.ac.uk/10.1093/gmo/9781561592630.article.01303, January 2001 [accessed January 2020].
47. Hugo Cole, *Malcolm Arnold: An Introduction to his Music* (London: Faber & Faber, 1989), p. 87.
48. Cole, *Malcolm Arnold*, p. 88.
49. The skirling reels are reminiscent of the score Arnold then created for the 1960 film of James Kennaway's novel *Tunes of Glory* (1956).
50. See 'Malcolm Arnold News Cuttings, Book 2', long-term loan at Eton College Library. Arnold died in 2006 and at present a range of his materials is held at the Eton College Library. My warm thanks to Lucy Gwynn at Eton College who located the Arnold scrapbooks during my visit there.

Arnold often gave his manuscripts away as gifts. The fair copy manuscript of *Tam o' Shanter* with several of Arnold's performance marks is now held at the National Library of Scotland (MS. 21863).

51. Paul R. W. Jackson, *The Life and Music of Sir Malcolm Arnold – The Brilliant and the Dark* (Farnham: Ashgate, 2003), pp. 54–5. Jackson notes that the trombone solo is 'one of the most difficult and exhilarating solos for trombone in the repertoire which borders just on the right side of playable'.
52. For example, the *Tam o' Shanter Overture* was the first work at the première of Arnold's Horn Concerto in July 1957 at the Cheltenham Music Festival, with the Hallé Orchestra and horn player Dennis Brain.
53. The magazine *London Musical Events* for August 1955 includes a half-page advertisement for the printed score of the work.
54. I have not been able to find any extant manuscript correspondence relating to Arnold and Diack. There is some basic biographical information online for J. Michael Diack, though dates are not always consistent: see Bach Cantatas website: http://www.bach-cantatas.com/Lib/Diack-John.htm [accessed December 2019].
55. I am most grateful here to James Hunter, musician and former Head of Television, BBC Scotland for sharing details of Diack's biography and additional notes on related 'Tam o' Shanter' compositions with me: email correspondence 16 December 2019.
56. 'Tam' would not end here as the source of musical adaptations. Others included newly-composed iterations for brass band ('Tam o' Shanter's Ride' by Peter Wright); see performance by the Grimethorpe Colliery Band: https://www.youtube.com/watch?v=oa9CClTA1n0 [accessed January 2020]. See also 'A Choral Version of Tam o' Shanter and Songs by Robert Burns', Bearsden Burgh Choir, conductor Renton Thomson, narrator Bill McCue: Lismor Recordings, Glasgow, 1979.
57. See Patrick Scott, 'The Songs of Burns and the Serge Hovey Archive', in *Robert Burns Lives!*: https://www.electricscotland.com/familytree/frank/burns_lives142.htm [accessed December 2019]; see also Kirsteen McCue, '"Magnetic Attraction": The Transatlantic Songs of Robert Burns and Serge Hovey', in Alker, Davis and Nelson (eds), *Robert Burns and Transatlantic Culture*, pp. 233–46.
58. The USC archival recording is of a performance from Berlin in 1959 (perhaps the première) and the texts are sung in German, but there is little other information yet available about the work itself.
59. See Christopher Whatley, 'Robert Burns, Memorialisation and the "heart beatings" of Victorian Scotland', in Murray Pittock (ed.), *Robert Burns in Global Culture* (Lewisburg, PA: Bucknell University Press, 2011), pp. 204–28. See also Whatley's *Immortal Memory: Burns and the Scottish People* (Edinburgh: John Donald, 2016), as well as his chapter in this volume.

60. See Conrad Wilson, *Playing for Scotland: The History of the Scottish National Orchestra* (London: Harper Collins, 1993). Wilson's Appendix II lists the 1959 Hamilton commission from the SNO as 'Ecossaise'.
61. See Hugh Macdonald's review in 'Top 20 … Scottish Classical Music Events of All Time', *The Scotsman*, 27 March, 2007: https://www.scotsman.com/arts-and-culture/music/top-20-scottish-classical-music-events-of-all-time-1–692694 [accessed December 2019].
62. Archival recording of BBC SSO with Norman Delmar at the Bute Hall in the University of Glasgow now held at the Scottish Music Centre: www.scottishmusiccentre.com [accessed November 2019]: cb35199 from radio (BBC SSO/Susskind; 28 Feb 1977). Thanks to Alasdair Pettinger for his assistance.
63. See Wilson, *Playing for Scotland*, pp. 74–94.
64. EMI ALP 2279, 1966. A copy is housed now at the Scottish Music Centre.
65. The interview with Iain Hamilton was made in the late 1990s for the BBC Radio Scotland music programme *The Score*.

11

Enactments and Representations of the National Bard: Burns and the Folk Context

Katherine Campbell

This chapter will explore the performance of Burns's songs in folk tradition, where memory, variation and choice can all play a role in what people sing. It will draw primarily on two major collections for evidence: *The Greig-Duncan Folk Song Collection*, made in the early years of the twentieth century in Aberdeenshire, and the Tobar an Dualchais website, an online resource of audio archival recordings, including those from the School of Scottish Studies Archives, which date mainly from the 1950s onwards. Although both of these sources date from the twentieth century, it has to be remembered that singers were often drawing on what had been handed down to them orally, thus we have in some cases a window to the past. Inevitably, coverage has to be selective in a chapter of this length.

The Folk Context

Burns frequently drew on songs he knew in Scottish tradition to create new material, as has been demonstrated on a song-by-song basis in the major editions of Burns's songs by Dick, Kinsley and Low, and in the work by Pittock on the *Scots Musical Museum* (*SMM*).[1] A song that illustrates something of his technique is 'Last May a Braw Wooer', which is based on an earlier folk song entitled 'The Queen o' the Lothians' (*SMM* 522), the opening verse of which runs:

> The Queen o' the Lothians cam cruisin' to Fife
> Fal de ral, lal de ral, lairo,
> To see gin a wooer wad tak her for life,[2]
> Sing hey, fal lal de ral, lal de ral, lal de ral,
> Hey, fal lal de ral, lairo.

In a letter dated May 1795, Burns makes reference to the tune as being one of promise, and mentions that his music editor, Stephen Clarke, is in agreement:

> 'The Lothian Lassie', I also inclose: the song is well known, but was never in notes before. – The first part is the old tune. – It is a great favorite of mine, & here I have the honor of being of the same opinion with STANDARD CLARKE. – I think it would make a fine Andante ballad. – [3]

The tune has a lively and catchy feel. Instead of the elaborate refrain, Burns simply repeats the end of each line. His first verse for 'Last May a Braw Wooer'[4] runs:

> Last May a braw wooer cam' down the lang glen,
> And sair wi' his love he did deave me;
> I said, there was naething I hated like men,
> The deuce gae wi' him to believe me, believe me
> The deuce gae wi' him to believe me.

'Last May a Braw Wooer' appeared in chapbooks and broadsides very soon after its publication, as Egerer notes,[5] and this was one way in which the songs of Burns were spread and eventually absorbed into the unwritten oral tradition – where people were singing from memory rather than relying on print.

The classic definition made by the International Folk Music Council in 1954 helps us to understand some of the hallmarks of the folk tradition as well as Burns's own contribution.

> Folk music is the product of a musical tradition that has evolved through the process of oral transmission. The factors that shape the tradition are: 1) continuity which links the present with the past; 2) variation which springs from the creative individual or the group; and 3) selection by the community, which determines the form or forms in which the music survives.
>
> The term can be applied to music that has been evolved from rudimentary beginnings by a community uninfluenced by popular and art music, and it can likewise be applied to music which has originated with an individual composer and has subsequently been absorbed into the unwritten living tradition of a community.
>
> The term does not cover composed popular music that has been taken over ready-made by a community and remains unchanged, for it is the re-fashioning and re-creation of the music by the community that gives it its folk character.[6]

It is in the specific context of music that 'has originated with an individual composer and has subsequently been absorbed into the unwritten living tradition of a community' that Burns's songs will be explored in this chapter.

Anne Dhu McLucas in her book *The Musical Ear* draws attention to the difference between instrumental and vocal music, and makes the important point that the tune is often of less importance than the text to singers:

> One of the primary distinctions to make is the difference between instrumental and vocal music in oral tradition. The use of an instrument versus the use of text introduces variables that make it necessary to consider certain aspects of these traditions separately. The externalization possible with the presence of an instrument brings in a kinesthetic [sic] and visual awareness that is not so present in vocal music. Besides relying on the ear and the memory, hand and finger movements on a fiddle, flute, or other instrument may be important ways of remembering certain tunes, for example. On the other hand, text also provides opportunities for and constraints upon memory that are not present in instrumental music. The text is often so important to singers that they pay no particular conscious attention to the tune. This can be both an advantage and disadvantage for the researcher. Since the changes in tunes in the case of vocal traditions are usually not consciously thought out, the unconscious process of the brain can be studied. On the other hand, singers will seldom be able to talk about their tunes or compare them to others, as instrumentalists often can.[7]

Text, tune and context will be explored in this chapter using specific songs as examples.

Burns's Songs in *The Greig-Duncan Collection*

The Greig-Duncan collection was made by two collectors: Gavin Greig, a school master at Whitehill outside New Deer, and James Bruce Duncan, a Free Church minister at Lynturk near Alford. The collection is of major cultural importance, containing as it does almost 2,000 separate songs, many in multiple variants. In addition, we are fortunate to have a good deal of context about the collectors' views on song and about the informants they collected from.

With regard to the songs of Burns, an important source is a newspaper column written by Greig entitled 'Folk Song of the North-East' which appeared in the *Buchan Observer* between 1907 and 1911. Greig used the column to share the collectors' views and their findings on folk song to date, as well as to encourage readers to send in further versions of songs or new material. In Ob. 9, Greig devoted an entire column to 'Burns and Folk-Song'.

The following text represents a summary of his main points:

> The songs of Burns have never been sung by the Scottish peasantry in general. The rustic, we admitted, knows his Burns. He admires the poet's songs, and likes on occasion to hear them rendered by those who *can* sing them. But they are hardly for him – as songs. *His* true minstrelsy is derived from other sources [. . .] [O]ne significant illustration of the peasant's attitude in this matter is that, while he will hardly himself sing the songs of Burns, he will sing *about* Burns *and* his songs, but it must be in lays that have got the folk-song hall-mark.[8]

Greig and Duncan categorised the songs of Burns – and those of other literary figures, for example, Lady Nairne, James Hogg, Walter Scott – as 'book-songs as distinct from folk-songs which hitherto have remained in the keeping of tradition'.[9] Greig noted that, in his era, piano accompaniments were often being employed for performance, and regarding the melodies he felt that 'the tunes of the books are not, in the main, the genuine melodies of the Scottish people'.[10] He also contended: 'Seldom indeed have we found a rustic singer who knew any book-song as he knew his native ditties – entirely by heart.'[11]

Although Greig and Duncan did not set out to collect material from this 'book-song' tradition, they were interested in manifestations of the songs of Burns within the folk tradition and in songs about Burns (as noted above). One song here was 'Burns and His Highland Mary' (GD 1249), a popular song which shows the folk response to the poet, that emerged out of the broadside and chapbook tradition.[12] Ford attests to its popularity in his book, *Vagabond Songs and Ballads*:

> No song touching the life of Robert Burns and his idealised Highland Mary – not any one of the poet's own, perhaps – has found more favour with the country people of Scotland than this rhapsody of unknown authorship, which has been widely circulated in broad sheet form. Ballad-hawkers, indeed, still find it a 'catch' at country markets and fairs.[13]

The first three verses (of fourteen) as collected from Mrs Margaret Gillespie are shown below.[14]

> 'Burns and his Highland Mary' [. . .]
> 1. In green Caledonia there ne'er were twa lovers
> Sae enraptured and happy in each other's arms
> As Burns the sweet bard an his dear highland Mary
> Sae fondly and sweetly he sang o her charms.

2. It was a May day when the flowers o the forest
Were blooming in wildness sae lovely and fair
When twa loves meet in a grove o green bowers
That grew on the banks o the clear winding Ayr.

3. And oh to them baith twas a meeting so tender
As this was the last for a while they could hae
In love's purest rapture they tasted together
Till the red setting sun show'd the close o the day.[15]

Mrs Margaret Gillespie (1841–1913), the sister of James Bruce Duncan, was a major contributor to the collection. She provides an interesting case study of the sorts of Burns songs that a female singer had in her repertoire in the second half of the nineteenth century and of the ways in which the songs of Burns were actually being sung within the oral tradition. One of her songs was 'The Weary Pun, The Weary Pun' (GD 1867). Mrs Gillespie had the chorus and first verse only of the song, as follows:

The weary pun the weary pun, the weary pun o' tow,
An' I think my wife will end my life before she spin her tow O.
I bocht my wife a stane o' lint as good as ere did grow O,
An' a' that she has made o' it is a puir pun o' tow O.

The Burns version is found in the *Scots Musical Museum* (1792, no. 350), where there are four verses in all plus chorus. The part that corresponds to Gillespie runs as follows.

'The Weary Pund' (Dick, no. 215)
Chorus
The weary pund, the weary pund,
The weary pund o' tow!
I think my wife will end her life,
Before she spin her tow.

I bought my wife a stane o' lint
As gude as e'er did grow,
And a' that she has made o' that
Is ae poor pund o' tow.

The two openings are very similar – the main differences are the 'O' that Mrs Gillespie adds at the end of lines 2 and 4 and the wording 'my life' instead of 'her life' in line 2. What is significant is that the tunes are completely different. Mrs Gillespie uses 'The Cogie', which she gives elsewhere in the collection, set to the song of that title (GD 1872). It is likely here that the original tune – if it was known – was simply substituted with something with which the family was already familiar.

'The Weary Pun' was a song that Mrs Gillespie learned from her father.[16] His name was William Duncan and he was 'born in 1814 and learned many of his songs from his stepmother, Mrs Duncan of Craigculter, and her mother, Jean Strachan, who was believed to be in her eighties when her daughter married John Duncan in 1821'.[17] William Duncan worked as a millwright near New Deer.[18] Although we cannot say for certain, there is the potential for this song to have been in the family for a long time – perhaps even dating back to the time of Burns himself.

The song 'We're A' Dry wi' the Drinkin' o't' (GD 1871), highlights the complexity that could occur as a result of the reworkings of folk tradition. Its Burns equivalent is 'My Love, She's but a Lassie Yet', which appeared in the *Scots Musical Museum* (1790, no. 225).

> 'My Love She's But a Lassie Yet' (Dick, no. 182)
> 1. My love, she's but a lassie yet,
> My love, she's but a lassie yet;
> We'll let her stand a year or twa,
> She'll no be hauf sae saucy yet;
> I rue the day I sought her, O!
> I rue the day I sought her, O!
> Wha gets her needs na say he's woo'd,
> But he may say he's bought her, O!
>
> 2. Come draw a drap o' the best o't yet,
> Come draw a drap o' the best o't yet;
> Gae seek for pleasure whar ye will,
> But here I never miss'd it yet.
> We're a' dry wi' drinkin o't,
> We're a' dry wi' drinkin o't;
> The minister kiss'd the fiddler's wife –
> He could na preach for thinkin o't.

Mrs Gillespie's version runs as follows.

> 'We're A' Dry wi' Drinking' o't (GD 1871)
> 1. We're a' dry wi' the drinkin' o't,
> We're a' dry wi' the drinkin' o't,
> The minister kissed the fiddler's wife,
> And couldna get preached for the thinking o't.

2. We'll draw a drap of the best o't yet,
We'll draw a drap of the best o't yet,
Gae seek for ever where ye will,
For joy I never missed it yet.

3. My love she's but a lassie yet,
My love she's but a lassie yet,
I'll let her stand a year or twa,
And she'll nae be half sae saucy yet.

4. I rue the day I socht her, O,
I rue the day I socht her O,
Who gets her needna say he's woo'd,
But he may say he's bocht her, O.

James Bruce Duncan regarded these verses 'as falling into two pairs', and he states that the tune of both is 'the air of "Green Grow the Rashes" see Lyric Gems 2.27'.[19] Verses 1–2 were 'heard from father and others', and the last two were 'heard from mother'.[20] Mrs Gillespie's verses reveal a reversal of those by Burns, with her verses 3 and 4 having equivalence with Burns's verse 1, and her verses 2 and 1 corresponding to Burns's verse 2. Once again, the tune is different from that given in the *SMM*.

Other Burns songs from Mrs Gillespie include (GD 521) 'My Heart's in the Highlands' which was 'From Mrs Duncan, Craigculter, William Smith (Gamrie) and others',[21] where the melody is different from that given in the *SMM* (no. 259), and for which Duncan notes similarities[22] with his sister's tune for 'The Waukin' o' the Claes' (GD 1492B). 'My Heart's in the Highlands' (GD 521), sung by Mrs Margaret Gillespie (verse 1 of 4) runs:

My heart's in the highlands my heart is nae here
My heart's in the highlands a-chasing the deer
Chasing the wild deer and following the roe
My heart's in the highlands where ever I go.

The Duncan family clearly loved singing and they may well have had a number of Burns's songs in their repertoire but James Duncan would not normally have included them in his collection unless he felt that there was some overlap with folk song. In the case of one song, however, his manuscripts contain the Burns version, a broadside version and an amalgamation of the two. This is Burns's 'Farewell, Ye Dungeons Dark and Strong' that appeared in the *Scots Musical Museum* (1788, no. 114):

'Farewell, Ye Dungeons Dark and Strong' (Dick, no. 311)
1. Farewell, ye dungeons dark and strong,
The wretch's destinie!
McPherson's time will not be long
On yonder gallows-tree.

Chorus
Sae rantingly, sae wantonly,
Sae dauntingly gaed he,
He play'd a spring, and danc'd it round
Below the gallows tree.

2. O, what is death but parting breath!
On many a bloody plain
I've dared his face, and in this place
I scorn him yet again!

3. Untie these bands from off my hands,
And bring to me my sword,
And there's no a man in all Scotland
But I'll brave him at a word.

4. I've liv'd a life of sturt and strife;
I die by treacherie:
It burns my heart I must depart,
And not avengèd be.

5. Now farewell light, thou sunshine bright,
And all beneath the sky!
May coward shame distain his name,
The wretch that dare not die!

The song with these words with only a few slight differences, such as 'gie' for 'bring' (3.1) and 'be on' for 'distain' (5.3), appears in a manuscript source from George F. Duncan. George had been an enthusiast for song from boyhood and had written down songs from the singing of their parents in 1885. This one was 'from father' and James notes dismissively: 'This is simply Burns's form.'[23] He would not have found it relevant to collect it himself and there would not have been a record of it but for George's more open and unselective collecting. James himself collected two forms from Mrs Gillespie's singing. One (version A) consists of four eight-line stanzas of the broadside song (which James Duncan calls 'the older words') with the chorus much as in Burns. The other (version B) is an interesting hybrid form. Mrs Gillespie's verses 1–4 plus chorus match Burns's lyrics closely, with 'prisons' being substituted for 'dungeons' in line 1, and 'Take off' being substituted for 'Untie' in verse 3. There are then a further five verses which are not found in Burns. At the very end, Burns's verse 5 appears as Gillespie's verse 10. The additional verses are:

5. He's taen his fiddle in his hand,
An broke it o'er a stone
Said There's nene on earth shall play on thee
When I am deed an gone.

6. Farewell my friends and comrades a'
Farewell my wife an bairns
There's nae repentance in my breast
For the fiddle's in my arms.

7. The laird of Grant that highland saunt
His might and majesty
He pled the cause o Peter Brown
An lets Macpherson dee.

8. But Braco Duff in rage enough
He first laid hands on me
And if that death would not prevent
Avenged would I be.

9. As for my life I do not care
If justice would take place
And bring my fellow plunderers
Unto the same disgrace.

Other traditional versions are also amalgamations which arguably got the best of both worlds (see Roud, no. 2160 'MacPherson's Lament/Farewell' for other instances). Burns took the song out of its historical context and offers a generalised defiance. More of the bitterness caused by the actual event, when the Traveller, James MacPherson, was hanged at Banff in 1700, is retained in Gillespie. Further detail of the story is given in broadside versions such as, for example, the earliest known version, dated 1700, to be found in 'The Word on the Street', National Library of Scotland (NLS) online,[24] and the one published by Herd[25] of which the final eight verses are quoted here:

As for my life, I do not care,
If justice would take place,
And bring my fellow plunderers
Unto this same disgrace.

For Peter Brown, that notour loon,
Escap'd, and was made free;
O! curse upon this fate of mine,
To hang upon a tree.

Both law and justice buried are,
And fraud and guile succeed,
The guilty pass unpunished,
If money interceed.

The Laird of Grant, that Highland saint,
His mighty majestie,
He pleads the cause of Peter Brown,
And lets Macpherson die.

The dest'ny of my life contriv'd
By those whom I oblig'd,
Rewarded me much ill for good,
And left me no refuge.

For Braco Duff, in rage enough,
He first laid hands on me;
And if that death would not prevent,
Avenged wou'd I be.

As for my life, it is but short,
When I shall be no more;
To part with life I am content,
As any heretofore.

Therefore, good people all, take heed?
This warning take by me,
According to the lives you lead,
Rewarded you shall be.

The Gillespie form, which has three of these verses in a different order, has omitted much of the moralising. The allusions to MacPherson's enemies in Gillespie are too brief for full comprehension but it should be remembered that songs could be, and often were, accompanied by explanatory comments which formed part of the performance. The striking and memorable image of the breaking of the fiddle[26] was known to Gillespie in two forms. James notes: 'Mrs Gillespie gave the following stanza at an earlier date as coming just before No. 5':[27]

He took his fiddle in his hand,
And three times roun' went he,
There wad neen o' them his fiddle tak,
And he brak her owre his knee.

The fine Burns form of the chorus is given. It had been developed from the form given at the end of the earliest broadside:[28]

Than wontonly and rantingly
I am resolv'd to die
And with undaunted Courage I
shall mount this fatall Tree.

Here it is the Burns chorus, retained in tradition, that emphasises the role of the fiddle.

Sae rantingly, sae wantonly,
Sae dauntingly gaed he,
He play'd a spring, and danc'd it round
Below the gallows-tree.

Burns's Songs: Archival Recordings

Moving forward to the mid-twentieth century, the Tobar an Dualchais/Kist o Riches website, based on recordings held in the School of Scottish Studies Archives (SA) and elsewhere, provides a rich repository of information on Burns, through performances dating mainly from the 1950s onwards. As noted in the introduction, though, the performance of such songs can take us much further back in time in terms of performance practice, by virtue of the 'carrying stream' of tradition.

Amongst these is 'Westlin Winds', which provides an interesting case study regarding tune choice. Burns's original tune was 'I Had a Horse, I had Nae Mair'; he subsequently suggested the use of 'Port Gordon' for the song in the *Museum*, but the song was in the end set to 'When the King Comes o'er the Water' (wrongly entitled 'Come Kiss wi' Me, Come Clap wi' Me' there), and then to 'Ally Croaker' in George Thomson's collection.[29] The song, originally called 'Song, Composed in August'('Kilmarnock' Edition, 1786)[30] opens:

> Now westlin winds, and slaught'ring guns
> Bring Autumn's pleasant weather;
> And the moorcock springs, on whirring wings,
> Amang the blooming heather:
> Now waving grain, wide o'er the plain,
> Delights the weary Farmer;
> And the moon shines bright, when I rove at night,
> To muse upon my Charmer.

Three versions of 'Westlin Winds', all performed in a very expressive way, appear on Tobar an Dualchais. The recordings were made in the 1950s – two are from Jock Cameron (1906–1971) from Cowdenbeath in Fife,[31] recorded six years apart (SA1953.262.A3 and SA 1959.017), and one is from an unknown male contributor (SA1955.157) recorded at St Boswells. Jock Cameron's first verse (Transcription of 'Westlin Winds' sung by Jock Cameron, SA1953.262.A3) runs:

> Ye Westlin winds, and slaughtering guns,
> Brings Autumn's pleasant weather
> The moorcock springs on whirring wings
> Amangst the bloomin heather.
> Now waving grain, wide o'er the plain
> Delights the weary farmer,
> And the moon shines bright, as I rove by night,
> To muse upon my charmer.

Cameron sings five verses of the song which he learned from his grandmother who was from the west of Fife. Whereas Cameron's text is reasonably close to Burns's original, the singing of the anonymous man differs substantially – this text is presented alongside Burns's full text below.

Comparison of Westlin Winds, anon. contributor, with Burns's text

Tobar an Dualchais – anonymous male contributor, SA1955.157	Burns's original text – 'Kilmarnock' edition (1786)
1. Noo Westlin Winds, and slaughterin guns Brings aftimes pleasant weather, Where the moorcock springs with werblin wings In amang thon bloomin heather. Now the partridge loves thy full, full field The plover loves the mountain, The woodcock hants on lonely glen As the heron's chiel(?) the fountain.	1. Now westlin winds, and slaught'ring guns Bring Autumn's pleasant weather; And the moorcock springs, on whirring wings, Amang the blooming heather: Now waving grain, wide o'er the plain, Delights the weary Farmer; And the moon shines bright, when I rove at night, To muse upon my Charmer.
	2. The Partridge loves the fruitful fells; The Plover loves the mountains; The Woodcock haunts the lonely dells; The soaring Her'n the fountains: Thro' lofty groves, the Cushat roves, The path of man to shun it; The hazel bush o'erhangs the Thrush, The spreading thorn the Linnet.
	3. Thus ev'ry kind their pleasure find, The savage and the tender; Some social join, and leagues combine; Some solitary wander: Avaunt, away! the cruel sway, Tyrannic man's dominion; The Sportsman's joy, the murd'ring cry, The flutt'ring, gory pinion!
2. Now it's Peggy dear, thy evening's clear, Flies high thon screamin swallows, The skies a-blue, and fields in view, The fading green and yellow. Now I gently walk, I will love and talk, While the silent moon shines clearly, I will clasp my arms and fondly place And swear I'd love ye dearly.	4. But PEGGY dear, the ev'ning's clear, Thick flies the skimming swallow; The sky is blue, the fields in view, All fading-green and yellow: Come let us stray our gladsome way, And view the charms of Nature; The rustling corn, the fruited thorn, And ev'ry happy creature.
	5. We'll gently walk, and sweetly talk, Till the silent moon shine clearly; I'll grasp thy waist, and fondly prest, Swear how I love thee dearly: Not vernal show'rs to budding flow'rs, Not Autumn to the Farmer, So dear can be, as thou to me, My fair, my lovely charmer!

There are many textual differences here, including 'Autumn's pleasant weather' in verse 1 being replaced with 'aftimes pleasant weather'. But the main feature of this version is the compression of key ideas in Burns's text, which draws on the start rather than the end of verses, and which still provides a coherent though abridged story:

verse 1 = Burns's verse 1, lines 1–4, plus verse 2, lines 1–4
verse 2 = Burns's verse 4, lines 1–4, plus verse 5, lines 1–4

Neither tune from the male singers resembles any of the aforementioned airs from the historical collections. Taking this evidence into account, it does not appear as though there was any one fixed tune associated with 'Westlin Winds' either in print or oral tradition. It is worth pointing out too that the tunes sung in the archival recordings both work very well for the song – this is evidently a set of words which lends itself well to a variety of melodies.

Tobar an Dualchais includes recordings of the songs of Burns being sung by members of the Travelling community. These include Jeannie Robertson (1908–1975) of Aberdeen, discussed by Porter and Gower,[32] whose mother sang a number of Burns's songs. Jeannie sings a version of 'Though Cruel Fate' (SA1962.26.B4) set to her 'own tune'. She sings the song slowly and meaningfully, and recalls that she found the verses 'in an old, old book of Burns'. Burns's song appears in the *Scots Musical Museum* (no. 118), under the title, 'The Northern Lass'. It is short, with just one verse, and Jeannie's text is shown alongside it below.

'Tho' Cruel Fate' – Dick, no. 62	**'Though Cruel Fate' – Jeannie Robertson transcription of recording, SA1959.008.B5**
Tho' cruel fate should bid us part Far as the pole and line, Her dear idea round my heart Should tenderly entwine. Tho' mountains rise, and deserts howl, And oceans roar between; Yet dearer than my deathless soul, I still would love my Jean.	Though cruel fate should us part, As far as the pole and line; Her dear ideas around my heart Would tenderly entwine. Tho' mountains frown, and deserts howl, And oceans roar between; Yet, dearer to my deathless soul, I still would love my Jean.

Even in this one verse there are textual differences:

Line 1 – 'bid' is omitted
Line 2 – 'As' is added at the first word
Line 3 – 'around' for 'round'
Line 4 – 'Would' for 'Should'

Line 5 – 'frown' for 'rise'
Line 7 – 'to' for 'than'

Dick notes that Burns's original tune was 'She Rose and Let Me In'[33] but that Johnson had already used this, so it was printed instead in *SMM* with the tune 'The Northern Lass'. This is another Burns song then for which the tune has not remained stable. Jeannie's tune is a simple one which fits the words very well. She also used a different tune from the one commonly known for 'Flow Gently Sweet Afton' (SA1962.025), which she performs very slowly, in a stately fashion. She sings six verses in all. She recalled singing the well-known melody whilst at school.

Betsy Whyte (1919–1988) of Montrose, also a member of the Travelling community, had a number of Burns songs in her repertoire. She performs fragments of 'Bonnie Wee Thing', 'Mary Morrison' and 'Flow Gently Sweet Afton', which were all sung by her father (SA1975.100). She also performs a full version of 'Ca the Yowes' (SA1979.128) in which those assembled join in on the chorus, and at other points where they know the words, including her husband, Bryce, who begins the song.[34] 'Ca the Yowes' is clearly a song which many people had in their memory, in whole or in part, and this performance illustrates the role that Burns's songs can play in a communal setting ('Auld Lang Syne' being the most famous example). The song text is closest to that found in the *Scots Musical Museum* – another version was later sent by Burns to Thomson for publication in *A Select Collection of Original Scotish Airs*.

'Ca the Yowes', Betsy Whyte text, transcribed from SA1979.128	**'Ca' the Ewes', Burns text, *SMM*, no. 265**
[*Ca them whaur the burnie rowes* *My bonnie dearie.*]	*Ca' the ewes to the knowes* *Ca' them whare the heather grows,* *Ca' them whare the burnie rowes,* *My bonnie dearie.* 1. As I gaed down the water-side, There I met my shepherd-lad, He row'd me sweetly in his plaid, An he ca'd me his dearie. Cho. *Ca' the ewes &c.*
1. Will ye came doon the water side Tae see the waves sae sweetly glide Beneath the hazels spreading wide My bonnie dearie.	2. Will ye gang down the water-side And see the waves sae sweetly glide Beneath the hazels spreading wide, The moon it shines fu' clearly.

Chorus *Ca the yowes tae the knowes* *Ca them whaur the heather growes* *Ca them whaur the burnie rowes* *My bonnie dearie.*	Cho. *Ca' the ewes &c.* 3. I was bred up at nae sic school, My shepherd lad, to play the fool, And a' the day to sit in dool, And nae body to see me: Cho. *Ca' the ewes &c.*
2. I'll gie ye goons and ribbons meet Cauf slippers for yer feet And in a faulding we will meet If ye will be my dearie. Chorus	4. Ye sall get gowns and ribbons meet Cauf-leather shoon upon your feet, And in my arms ye'se lie and sleep, And ye sall be my dearie. Cho. *Ca' the ewes &c.*
3. Tho I be true ye tell tae me Still I'll hae my shepherd lad Tae rowe me sweetly in his plaid And ca me his dearie. Chorus	5. If ye'll but stand to what ye've said, I'se gang wi' you, my shepherd lad, And ye may rowe me in your plaid, And I sall be your dearie. Cho. *Ca' the ewes &c.*
4. For I was bred at nae sic school My shepherd lad tae play the fool And aa tae lang tae sit in dool Wi naebody tae cheer me Chorus	6. While waters wimple to the sea; While day blinks in the lift sae hie; Till clay-cauld death sall blin' my e'e, Ye sall be my dearie, Cho. *Ca' the ewes &c.*

Immediately following the song she states: 'Everybody kens [knows] the last verse.' This is a slightly shorter version of the Burns song, and one of the textual differences is that verse 4 in Burns's version comes earlier in Betsy's version, in verse 2. The use of 'And in a faulding we will meet' is significant. The word 'faulding' is not present in the *SMM* version, but it is found in Thomson, where line 1.3 runs, 'Then a faulding let us gang', i.e. penning the ewes for milking. It appears that Burns's first text has been conflated with part of his second in the performance.

Conclusion

This chapter has shown that Burns's songs could sometimes vary substantially from their original format in performance as a result of the reworkings of the folk tradition. Burns's verses could be amalgamated with those of other songs, certain of his verses/lines could be absented due to either forgetting or deliberate omission, his lyrics could be reshaped, and the story could be compressed. All of these features are hallmarks of the folk process in general where variation is a key characteristic.

Of perhaps greater significance is the fact that the tune desired by Burns was evidently quite often not used once the song entered the oral tradition. This could be due to a variety of factors, including the singer's personal preference, that the words had appeared in a source with no tune, that the printed tune could only be read by someone with the ability to read music, or the fact that the tune was unfamiliar to the listener, and so another familiar tune was selected instead. Another possibility is that a simpler tune was substituted for something more complex – and this would certainly be understandable in cases where the range of the tune presented a challenge (e.g. instrumental tunes from fiddle tradition). Singer Jo Miller notes: 'Singers who have tried a few Burns songs will quickly discover they can be technically challenging, with their wide ranges and large intervals.'[35] She suggests that some tunes can be adapted, however, to maintain the 'character while reducing the high register hazards'.[36] In general, though, archival evidence seems to support the practice of finding another tune rather than adapting one that is more difficult to sing.

Although Burns normally set out to write a song with a particular tune in mind, and often with the mission of preserving Scottish melodies through his song writing, the examples in this chapter show that the oral tradition did not always honour his tune choice in the way that he would probably have hoped for.

Notes

1. James C. Dick, *The Songs of Robert Burns* (London: Henry Frowde, 1903); James Kinsley (ed.), *The Poems and Songs of Robert Burns*, 3 vols (Oxford: Clarendon Press, 1968); Donald A. Low (ed.), *The Songs of Robert Burns* (London: Routledge, 1993); Murray Pittock, *The Oxford Edition of the Works of Robert Burns*, vols 2–3: *The Scots Musical Museum*, Part One, Introduction and Text; Part Two, Notes and Appendices (Oxford: Oxford University Press, 2018). See also the study by Mary Ellen Brown, *Burns and Tradition* (Urbana: University of Illinois Press, 1984).
2. See *Dictionary of the Scots Language*, www.dsl.ac.uk, for the meanings of Scots words.
3. G. Ross Roy, *The Letters of Robert Burns*, 2 vols (Oxford: Clarendon Press, 1985), Letter 670.
4. George Thomson (1793–1841), *A Select Collection of Original Scottish Airs for the Voice*, 6 vols (London: J. Preston and Edinburgh: George Thomson, 1799), no. 52.
5. Joel W. Egerer, *A Bibliography of Robert Burns* (Edinburgh: Oliver and Boyd, 1964), pp. 64–5.
6. Cited in Philip V. Bohlman, *The Study of Folk Music in the Modern World* (Bloomington: Indiana University Press, 1988), p. xiii.

7. Anne Dhu McLucas, *The Musical Ear: Oral Tradition in the USA* (Farnham: Ashgate, 2010), p. 7.
8. Patrick Shuldham-Shaw, Emily B. Lyle et al. (eds), *The Greig-Duncan Folk Song Collection*, 8 vols (Aberdeen and Edinburgh: Mercat Press for the University of Aberdeen in association with the School of Scottish Studies, University of Edinburgh, 1981–2002), GD vol. 6, p. 586.
9. *Buchan Observer* (1907–11), Gavin Greig's column 'Folk Song of the North-East' in this newspaper; reprinted in *Folk-Song in Buchan and Folk-Song in the North-East by Gavin Greig*, with a foreword by Kenneth S. Goldstein and Arthur Argo (Hatboro, PA: Folklore Associates, 1963), Ob. 9, p. 1.
10. *Folk-Song in Buchan*, Ob. 9, p. 2.
11. *Folk-Song in Buchan*, Ob. 9, p. 1.
12. The Roud index (Roud, no. 820) provides evidence of multiple copies being printed in broadside form (see https://www.vwml.org/search?q=last may a braw wooer&is=1 [accessed 17 September 2019]).
13. Robert Ford, *Vagabond Songs and Ballads of Scotland* (Paisley: Alexander Gardner, 1899), p. 126.
14. GD 1249A. Her tune is a variant of 'Flowers of the Forest'.
15. Songs about Burns continue to form an important strand in Scottish culture, e.g. 'Jean Armour's Song' written by Sheila Douglas, which can be heard on Tobar an Dualchais, and 'The Star o' Rabbie Burns'. See also Paul Maloney's chapter in this volume.
16. Shuldham-Shaw et al., *Greig-Duncan Collection*, 2002: vol. 8, p. 414.
17. Elaine Petrie, 'Mrs Margaret Gillespie', in Shuldham-Shaw et al., *Greig-Duncan Collection*, 2002: vol. 8, pp. 559–64; p. 559.
18. Petrie, 'Mrs Margaret Gillespie', p. 560.
19. See John Cameron, *Lyric Gems of Scotland: A Collection of Scottish Songs*, first and second series (London: John Blockley, n.d), vol. 2, p. 27.
20. Shuldham-Shaw et al., *Greig-Duncan Collection*, 2002: vol. 8, p. 415.
21. Shuldham-Shaw et al., *Greig-Duncan Collection*, 1987: vol. 3, p. 655.
22. Shuldham-Shaw et al., *Greig-Duncan Collection*, 1997: vol. 7, p. 538.
23. Appears at Dw 2: 167 as copied by James Duncan from the text written out by his younger brother George F. Duncan in MS 998/7/4/35. These are original manuscripts which underpin the published 'Greig-Duncan Folk Song Collection'. Dw refers to 'Folk-Song Words of the North-East' compiled by Duncan, 6 vols (shorthand). Shuldham-Shaw et al., *Greig-Duncan Collection*, 1987: vol. 3, p. 687.
24. https://digital.nls.uk/broadsides/view/?id=14482 [accessed 30 November 2019].
25. David Herd, *Ancient and Modern Scottish Songs*, 2 vols (Edinburgh: printed by John Wotherspoon, for James Dickson and Charles Elliot, 1776), vol. 1, pp. 99–101.

26. Pittock, *Works of Robert Burns*, vol. 3, pp. 33–5.
27. Shuldham-Shaw et al., *Greig-Duncan Collection*, 1987: vol. 3, p. 687.
28. See note 25.
29. Katherine Campbell and Emily Lyle, *Robert Burns and the Discovery and Re-Creation of Scottish Song* (Glasgow: Musica Scotica, forthcoming), see Chapter 10.
30. Robert Burns, *Poems, Chiefly in the Scottish Dialect* (Kilmarnock: John Wilson, 1786), pp. 224–6.
31. http://www.tobarandualchais.co.uk/en/searchperson?id=9 [accessed 30 November 2019].
32. James Porter and Herschel Gower, *Jeannie Robertson: Emergent Singer, Transformative Voice* (East Linton: Tuckwell Press, 1995).
33. Dick, *Songs of Robert Burns*, p. 373.
34. 'Ca the Ewes' was also recorded by George Inglis Fraser (1889–1965) of Strichen in Aberdeenshire (http://tobarandualchais.co.uk/en/fullrecord/60520 [accessed 20 November 2019]). He had a number of Burns songs in his repertoire, including 'A Man's a Man', 'The Deil's Awa', 'The Silver Tassie' and 'Open the Door to Me, Oh'. He sings all the songs unaccompanied in a style which illustrates his north-east dialect.
35. Jo Miller, 'Burns's Songs: A Singer's View', in Kenneth Simpson (ed.), *Burns Now* (Edinburgh: Canongate Academic Press, 1994), p. 194.
36. Miller, 'Burns's Songs', p. 200.

12

'Frae my ain countrie': Robert Burns in the Archive of Jean Redpath

Moira Hansen

In March 1961, twenty-three-year-old Jean Redpath (1937–2014) moved from her native Scotland to the USA. Although she started in San Francisco, she would quickly find herself in Greenwich Village, New York and at the heart of the folk music revival that would sweep America. To this, she would bring her own repertoire of Scottish folk songs, sung in her clear and expressive mezzo-soprano with little or no instrumental accompaniment. Increasingly integral to this body of work were the songs of Robert Burns.

Redpath would spend the rest of her life living and working between the USA and Scotland, continuing to add to the range of Scottish traditional song she recorded and performed, including that of Burns, through her own research and teaching on both sides of the Atlantic. Following her death in 2014, her extensive archives were given to the Centre for Robert Burns Studies at the University of Glasgow and the Irvin Department of Rare Books and Special Collections at the University of South Carolina.

Drawing on the content of those archives, this chapter will explore Jean Redpath's place within the folk music tradition and her relationship with the bard – the breadth and depth of her work – to better understand the nuance of his songs, the various contexts within which she recorded those songs, including a project conceived with Serge Hovey to record Burns's entire catalogue, and the impact of her career on the placement of Burns as a central figure in both national and international folk song traditions.

Jean Redpath and the Folk Tradition

Jean Redpath was a Fife girl, born in Edinburgh on 28 April 1937 but brought up in the town of Leven, the second child and only daughter of James (Jim) and Isabella (Bluebell) Redpath. From the earliest age, music was a presence in her life, with many musicians in her family, particularly within her own home. Her father played the hammer dulcimer and sang. Redpath felt she inherited from him her own voice, her sense of rhythm and her initial shyness as a performer.[1] This is not, however, to detract from the influence of her mother. While not as strong a voice as her husband, Bluebell 'could hold a tune perfectly well and had an amazing repertoire of everything from kids' songs to old Scottish songs, classic ballads and bothy ballads, Victoriana and piano-stool music to whatever came off the radio in those days [. . .] if she heard anything, it stayed with her'.[2] From her mother, Redpath took this power of memory, giving her the capacity for the equally expansive body of songs she would draw on throughout her own career. Despite encouragement from various quarters that '[y]e should dae something wi' that lassie's voice', Redpath's formal vocal teaching consisted of a single lesson at the age of sixteen, when she was deterred by the teacher presenting her with sheet music for one of those Scottish songs typically sung in a stiff and artificial manner which sounded nothing like the spoken Scots she was used to, the way in which she thought such songs should be sung.[3] Consequently, Redpath never learned to read music, instead learning new material by ear, arguing that if 'I hear a song that I admire, it's the most natural thing in the world for me to listen, study, memorise and begin performing it [. . .] That's simply the way it has been done with Scottish folk music for hundreds of years.'[4]

At nineteen, Redpath took up a place at the University of Edinburgh studying English language, although she would later switch to medieval studies. In her second year, she attended a talk by Hamish Henderson from the university's School of Scottish Studies on the Scottish oral tradition and song culture. This proved a pivotal moment in Redpath's life, introducing her to the idea of traditional songs being a legitimate field of study, to Hamish Henderson as someone who would repeatedly open new connections for her, and to the university's folk song society. With friends from the society, she would form her first group – The Night Hawks – initially singing at ceilidhs in friends' houses, then in local bars for payment in beer.[5] Redpath became increasingly disillusioned with university life; the timely arrival of an invitation from an American friend to sing at her wedding in California changed the direction of her life.

After moving to the United States, Redpath initially lived with her friend's parents and made a living through a series of hourly-paid jobs, as well the occasional singing gig. Her professional break appears to have come when she was invited by an agent to perform in Philadelphia, Hamish Henderson having made the agent aware of her. The Philadelphia gigs would never happen, the agent having disappeared without paying previous performers or making any actual bookings for Redpath. At a loss for what to do next, she accepted a lift to New York City where she was introduced to Miki Isaacson who owned an apartment inhabited by a constantly shifting body of folk singers in need of a place to stay while they sought their own big breaks. Redpath become one of the residents of Isaacson's apartment, regularly participating in impromptu jam sessions with her flatmates, including Bob Dylan and Rambling Jack Elliot, and musicians such as the Greenbriar Boys who used it as rehearsal space.[6] Within six weeks of arriving in the city, Redpath would perform at Gerde's Folk City in Greenwich Village, marking her first paid performance in New York and beginning her establishment as a key figure in the 1960s folk revival.[7] Robert Shelton of *The New York Times*, in his hugely positive review of the performance, would particularly comment on the breadth of Redpath's repertoire of 'some 250 songs, enough to keep a ceilidh going for hours', before listing a range of song type reminiscent of Redpath's own description of her mother's repertoire – classic and bothy ballads, mouth music, drinking and love songs, children's songs and 'songs of Robbie Burns'.[8]

Shelton's description of Redpath's body of material illustrates her attitude towards traditional song and to Burns's place within it. By the mid-1970s, she had recorded seven albums. Burns is certainly present within those albums but he does not dominate, instead taking his place as a part of the landscape of traditional Scottish song.[9] There are other songs, often the lyricist unknown, which were equally deserving of a place within her performance sets. In interview and during performances, she would emphasis her unwillingness to take requests from the audience, arguing it would narrow rather than broaden her repertoire, that she'd 'be singing "Danny Boy" and selections from "Brigadoon" [when] we have other songs to offer', songs offering a more positive representation of Scotland and its people.[10]

For Redpath, the folk tradition was still very much a living entity, one in which she was 'simply one more singer in a long line of female singers who have kept the traditional ballads alive'.[11] She was transmitting the songs, the messages, the emotions and the voices of the past to her modern audience. While her early performances saw her draw on the phrasings and arrangements of others, maturity and experience taught her to put her own mark on the songs, to add her own life story to her delivery. This was, however, always with an awareness of the weight of history behind her, the knowledge that those historic voices 'lived on, buried somewhere, in their songs', that music 'provides continuity, some kind of anchor line; contact with, not necessarily a way of life, but with the culture and values of another time'.[12] Thus, for Redpath, she had a responsibility to ensure that what was transmitted was not narrowed by public popularity to that handful of best-known or most-loved songs but that, as far as possible, the whole was preserved and transmitted. Consequently, her performances would often include requests to the audience for any additional verses or variants of songs about which she might not be aware. Songs would be introduced with some background about where she had learned the song herself or the song's origins or variations in melody found in different areas of Scotland and their relation to American country and folk music.[13] To facilitate this aspect of her performances, as well as writing liner notes for her albums, Redpath would undertake her own research, fascinated by the whole of Scottish song culture and preserving the stories it told. The breadth of her repertoire necessitated an equally broad-ranging research, something mirrored by the wide variety found in the archive of books, recordings and personal research materials spread across her US and Scottish homes.

The Jean Redpath Archives

During the course of her life, Redpath was the recipient of several awards and honours including honorary degrees from the universities of Stirling and St Andrews and an MBE in the 1995 Queen's Birthday Honours list. In 2009, when Scotland celebrated both its Year of Homecoming and the 250th anniversary of the birth of Robert Burns, Redpath was awarded the honorary degree of Doctor of Music by the University of Glasgow, in recognition of her services to Scottish music and particularly the songs and music of Robert Burns. Alongside her, receiving his own honorary degree of Doctor of Letters was G. Ross Roy, Professor of English and Comparative Literature at the University of South Carolina, in recognition of his contributions to Robert Burns scholarship. Strong research connections already existed between the University of Glasgow, home of the Centre for Robert Burns Studies (CRBS), and the University of South Carolina (USC), home of one of the largest collections of Burns-related materials outside Scotland, much of it amassed by G. Ross Roy. In 2014, these connections were further cemented on Redpath's death on 21 August. In her will, Redpath bequeathed much of the material relating to her professional life from her Scottish and US homes to CRBS and USC respectively. The cataloguing of these materials at both sites shows the contents of the two collections to be quite different from each other, yet entirely complementary and reflective of Redpath, her career and her life within the folk music tradition.

The USC archive predominantly consists of paper materials relating to Redpath's professional engagements – performance contracts, running orders of songs to be performed, reviews and media coverage of performances, handwritten accounts of trips. There are letters and notes from various individuals providing her with information about various songs – different settings, additional verses or variants, new material – talking to the success of those requests she made of her audiences to assist in further broadening her repertoire. There is also substantial material relating to the recording project with Serge Hovey, as well as to plans for a *Jean Redpath Songbook* which has never made it to fruition.[14]

In contrast, the Scottish archive bequeathed to CRBS is more reflective of Redpath's work around and beyond her performances, arguably more reflective of her as an individual, combining the personal and professional – her wide-ranging and somewhat eclectic interests, as well as her personal research around many aspects of song culture and significant individuals within it. While Redpath spent a notable period of the year in Scotland, the differing contents of this archive also likely reflects the simple fact that this type of material is more widely available in Scotland. The collection of books, pamphlets, vinyl, cassettes, CDs, videotapes and DVDs runs to more than 1,500 items. As might be expected, a large proportion of these relate to folk and ballad traditions through the centuries, particularly in Scotland but also in England, Ireland and North America. However, there are also substantial materials on protest song, children's lullabies and playground songs, choral and classical music. There are video and audio recordings of Redpath's own performances and media appearances, and dozens of cassettes containing only melody lines for songs – as previously mentioned, her inability to read music necessitated learning by ear and these cassettes are what Redpath would use to learn new material for performance or recording, often while in the car travelling from engagement to engagement. There are considerable papers relating to her research on Caroline Oliphant, Jacobite song, preparations for teaching at traditional song summer schools at the University of Stirling, and for various television programmes recorded for different broadcasters. Many of the books have evidently been bought second-hand from various bookshops local to her Fife home, volumes which speak to her interest in the broad historical and contemporary contexts of traditional song culture.[15] Across the USC- and CRBS-held archives, it is evident that, for Redpath, traditional song was both a professional and personal passion.

Among all this, there is Robert Burns. Volumes of the different editions of his songs and poems, including a complete set of George Thomson's *Select Collection of Scottish Airs*, sit alongside various commercial recordings from the likes of Ewan MacColl and Peggy Seeger. Copies of her own Burns recordings show the final results of the hours spent listening to those cassettes of melody lines. Handwritten and photocopied pages show Redpath undertaking her own research around the background of the songs and the songwriter. Exploring Redpath's archives across both sites allows for a unique insight into her attitude towards Burns, his songs and their performance, and song culture more widely. Such exploration makes it possible to understand the scope of her own influence on positioning Burns as a key figure in Scottish traditional song culture. Therefore, to the Burns-related aspects of Redpath's collections, and especially her own performances of the bard, the focus of this chapter now turns.

Jean Redpath Performing Burns

As previously mentioned, among the items in the USC-held Redpath Archive are papers relating to a proposed *Jean Redpath Songbook*, a project which never made it to completion.[16] The pages include a suggested list of 127 songs to be included, each having a checklist recording that the text of the lyrics, the relevant score, glosses, notes and anecdotes for each song had been identified. The list also identifies which of Redpath's recordings would act as the musical source for each track and the format it was available in. Of these 127 songs, sixteen of them are Burns. All but two of these Burns tracks were to be drawn from Redpath's recordings which emerged from her projects with Serge Hovey in the United States and Donald Low in Scotland.[17]

The relatively small proportion of Burns's songs which Redpath planned to include in this publication is an obvious indicator of where she saw Burns within her performance repertoire – he is certainly a presence but by no means a dominant component – a position which appears not to have changed over the thirty-odd years of her professional career as a performer. The songs of Burns are part of the landscape of Scottish song culture but he does not define it or encapsulate it completely.

Yet, in looking across the body of Redpath's commercial recordings, Burns is, by far, the most frequently featured songwriter.[18] Seven albums with Hovey and four with Low produced a total of 178 tracks, and almost all of her solo artist recordings featured at least one song by Burns.[19] This, coupled with Redpath's own commentary, makes clear that, although she does not see him as the entirety of Scottish song culture, she regarded him highly as a writer, collector and editor of songs, and for his ability to give voice to those traditionally silenced by history. By dint of the vast body of Burns recordings within her work, whether she wanted it or not, she became an unofficial ambassador for the bard and his work in preserving and continuing Scottish folk song tradition.

Redpath emphasised how '[Burns] could come up with poetry bordering on the heroic, then write something so immediate, so tender, so emotional, and frequently expressed from the woman's point of view – something you don't find many late-nineteenth [sic] century writers doing. You don't find many of them doing it yet,' something which 'frequently fascinated' her.[20]

More importantly for Redpath, however, is Burns's status as 'one of the first dedicated, educated, discriminating collectors of traditional songs. With his own songs he was trying to preserve a whole national music. He didn't ever make up a tune, they were all traditional.' Burns's secret lay in his ability to recognise 'the strength of existing songs'; he 'had the perception and ear to collect, which of course, he is not given much credit for'.[21] This lack of credit received by Burns for his role as collector and preserver of song was an ongoing issue for Redpath, having regularly railed against the perception of Burns as nothing but a poet, typically commenting 'Robert Burns believed he would be remembered most of all for his songs [. . .] It infuriates me when Burns songs are presented as poetry. He wrote twice as many songs as poems.'[22] Recognising Burns as a songwriter and collector is also to acknowledge the purpose of these activities, Redpath arguing that she did not consider that 'his primary aim was to produce a song that was immediately singable so much as to preserve what was already there, to keep traditional music intact'.[23]

A fascination with keeping intact the music which Burns had collected had also driven more than twenty years of research by American composer and arranger Serge Hovey. During this time, Hovey undertook to identify and reunite with the lyrics the original tunes Burns had selected for those songs he had written or edited, predominantly for James Johnson or George Thomson. This resulted in *The Robert Burns Song Book*, lyrics and musical arrangements for 324 songs, with accompanying notes emerging from Hovey's extensive personal research.[24]

Through Hovey's connection with Hamish Henderson, the same Edinburgh scholar-collector who had encouraged the young Redpath in her interests in traditional music, Hovey and Redpath would be introduced in 1972. With Hovey's scores for small musical ensembles and Redpath's vocal interpretations, the pair would record a total of seven albums of these new arrangements of Burns's songs.[25] Redpath's involvement with this project in developing her understanding of Burns's role in preserving Scottish song culture appears to have promoted her own desire to emphasise the importance in performing his music to preserve his own contributions.[26] She was, for example, 'appalled' to see a documentary which used both 'Auld Lang Syne' and 'A Red, Red Rose' but neither played to the melody that Burns indicated should be used, asserting that 'if somebody is going to make a documentary of the sort that is going to be seen by a wide audience then the facts ought to be checked'.[27] Consequently, having an artist of Redpath's calibre sing the songs of Burns to the tunes assigned by Burns, and a wider range of songs than was generally seen in performance, enhanced their standing within the traditional song community, leading to further and wider performance by other artists.[28]

By her own acknowledgement, the making of the Hovey albums was not 'part of my recording career that I remember with any real pleasure or satisfaction'.[29] This arose from the recording of the tracks in layers, initially Redpath with piano accompaniment, with Hovey adding strings and wind sections in later sessions. Not being able to hear the whole arrangement at the time of recording her own vocal left Redpath with 'no opportunity to connect with and react to the other instruments', having to imagine where they would take over from her in musical breaks, particularly in Hovey's 'tendency to wait for three bars before the delivery of the punch line in the song', something she felt went 'against every instinct'.[30] While this process did result in a completed album, there are songs on the Hovey albums she never sang again.

Following Hovey's death in 1989, and emerging from her work on traditional song summer schools at the University of Stirling in the 1980s, Redpath would collaborate with a very different partner for her next major Burns project. This time, Donald Low, Professor of English Studies at Stirling and respected Burns scholar, would provide the stimulus. In a work which parallels, but was independent of, the work of Hovey, Low had produced a scholarly edition of the words and music of Burns's songs, with extensive notes on each.[31] To accompany this, Redpath recorded a series of four albums.[32] Unlike the Hovey project, this was never intended to be a completist recording of all the songs, but simply a selection of what might be considered representative of the breadth of style and material that Burns contributed to the Scottish song tradition, focusing particularly on the songs included in James Johnson's *Scots Musical Museum*. Consequently, by her own admission '[m]y final choice of songs for the cassettes were purely personal and somewhat arbitrary in that I was guided by melody as much as anything else'.[33] This connection with the music, the link between the emotion and the melody, is central to Redpath's approach to Burns's songs (and her wider repertoire). In contrast to the Hovey albums, those recorded with Low and as a solo artist, as well as her live performances, are far simpler in both arrangement and in approaches to recording, 'knowing full well that I am going to sing the material either unaccompanied or with only guitar in performance'.[34] This comes in part from her belief that 'an unaccompanied song is the ideal outlet for very strong emotion [. . .] some of these settings that Burns came up with raises the goosebumps right up the back of my legs. Marvellous stuff'.[35] The Low albums, for example, were recorded in a small church in the Trossachs, because it had good acoustics, and in Low's own living room.[36] Recording her own albums was similarly relaxed; she tried out arrangements to see how they felt and rerecorded as necessary.[37] The Low project and her own recordings are, however, united in intention with the Hovey project to 'get the hell away from this poorly printed, high-color picture postcard version of the hard-drinking elbow-in-the-ribs womanizer Scot. Robert Burns was an incredibly talented, deep-thinking, well-rounded, hard-working, hard playing product of his time'.[38]

The interplay – the similarities and differences – between these three key aspects of Redpath's work with Burns's songs – the Hovey arrangements, the Low recordings and her own interpretations – are perhaps best appreciated in looking at the presentation of the same song across each of these contexts. This is not as immediately easy as it might seem. Redpath's extensive repertoire of songs coupled with her attempts not to repeatedly record the same material, and the broad remits of both the Hovey and Low recording projects, means that fewer than two dozen songs can be found in all three bodies of work.

One such song is 'A Red, Red Rose'. As well as being one of the few tracks that appears in both the Hovey and Low projects, and in Redpath's own commercial recordings, it is the only such track which also appeared on the list for inclusion in *The Jean Redpath Song Book*. The Hovey arrangement is relatively simple instrumentally, Redpath accompanied by piano and cello as she sings the melody known as 'Major Graham', the tune indicated by Burns.[39] Redpath's vocal is simple and straightforward, the only real ornamentation being a long 7-second sustain on the final 'love'.[40]

Likewise, the Low recording is sung to 'Major Graham', although this time Redpath sings unaccompanied.[41] Apart from accompaniment, the most notable difference between this and the Hovey recording is the track length. Allowing time for the instrumental intro and outro on the Hovey track, Redpath sings for around one-and-a-half minutes. In contrast, the Low track runs just over two minutes in length, the entirety of which is Redpath's vocal; that long sustain in the Hovey track is nearly half the length in the Low, and Redpath manages more than a quick intake of breath between phrases. Combined, this gives the Low track an appreciably slower tempo which, for the listener, enhances the melancholic longing of the lyrics, the sorrow of the narrative voice being separated from their love.

Perhaps the closest Redpath ever came to her *Jean Redpath Song Book* is her album entitled *By Request*. Released in 2004, it consists of twenty-five tracks of songs she knew would have been the most frequently requested had she allowed such a thing. 'Red, Red Rose' is included on the album as the Low arrangement.[42] Likewise, she indicates in her notes for the *Jean Redpath Song Book* that it is the Low arrangement that should be used there. The contrast in the Hovey and Low recordings seems, in part, to be down to the fact that Hovey had already scored his arrangement by the time he was introduced to Redpath, so there was an element of singing what the composer wanted. In contrast, she had more creative input for the Low recording, resulting in her recording a track which better reflects her own personal sense of the 'right' presentation of the song, a presentation which is more akin to that intended by Burns in terms of the pacing and phrasing and, therefore, the message and emotion conveyed by the combination of melody and lyric. In doing so, she works to ensure that Burns's contribution to song culture is preserved.

The same can be said of another lyric usually sung with a mismatched melody: 'Auld Lang Syne'. It is best known sung to the melody printed by George Thomson in his *Select Collection of Scottish Airs* in 1799. This, however, was a melody selected by Thomson, whereas Burns had indicated the melody as published by James Johnson in his *Scots Musical Museum*. It is the melody published by Johnson that Redpath sings in both the Hovey and Low recordings. Whereas the first volume of Hovey recordings was driven by what Hovey had already scored, 'Auld Lang Syne' did not appear until the second volume, by which point Redpath likely had more creative input. Consequently, the Hovey arrangement of 'Auld Lang Syne' is simply Redpath's vocal, unaccompanied by any instrumental arrangement.[43] Thus, as with 'Red, Red Rose', it is Redpath's voice alone that does the work of conveying the message and emotion of Burns's lyric. Although similar to the popular tune, the melody indicated by Burns has a more melancholic tone, adding to the sense of longing for days gone by and friendships lost that the song recollects. For Redpath, the closing notes of the song, which fall in pitch rather than rise as with the popular tune, create a sense of 'unfinished business' more apt to the subject matter.[44] That sense that Redpath had more involvement in arranging the song, and thus that it represents something closer to that 'right' presentation, is made more certain when turning to the Low recording.[45] Again, Redpath sings unaccompanied but, in contrast to the 'Red, Red Rose' recordings, both the Hovey and Low tracks are near identical in length, pointing to Redpath performing in a manner she feels comfortable and natural, and fitting with the sentiment of the song. Again, there is little vocal ornamentation, Redpath allowing the simplicity of the melody in combination with the lyric to do the work. This cuts to the core of her attitude to traditional music and its performance – '[a]s a performer you have to have a belief that what you are doing is worth listening to [. . .] that the songs you are singing have something to say'.[46] Nevertheless, Redpath recognises what she calls '[t]he whole spectre of, basically, people want[ing] to hear what is familiar', that 'they don't want to know what the original was'.[47] She recounts performing 'Auld Lang Syne' to Burns's chosen melody at an event and being physically removed from the microphone by an audience member with the admonition that 'that's the wrang tune'.[48] And so, she would still perform 'Auld Lang Syne' to the popular tune but ensure that Burns's legacy was maintained by singing his lyrics, not substitutes such as 'my dear' for 'my Jo' or insertions of 'days of' before 'auld lang syne', and emphasise the Scots words and pronunciations.[49] For Redpath, even though the tune might not be what Burns intended, she was determined that the lyric remain so, protecting and preserving not just Burns's contribution in the form of his words but the inherent Scottishness of them, and their contribution to the wider character of traditional Scottish song culture.

Jean Redpath's Legacy

In no small part due to her extensive coverage of Burns's output, those 250 songs in Redpath's repertoire that Robert Shelton identified in 1961 grew to more than a thousand by the time of her death. She never stopped gathering and learning new material, and she never stopped seeking to move Burns away from 'the poorly printed, high-color picture postcard version' of popular culture.

In a similar manner, in Neat's documentary, *The Tree of Liberty*, Hamish Henderson asks 'How is it possible to rescue this poor, painted, cosmeticized cadaver of a dead poet from the ghastly mess which he is laid in? Can it be done?'[50] Fortunately, his answer was a positive one and that 'the key is the song' with the combination of Serge Hovey and Jean Redpath resulting in 'Burns the songwriter en route for liberation'.[51]

For Redpath, however, it seems not to have been the liberation of Burns the songwriter that was her priority but the liberation of the songs themselves. She was emphatic that he received the credit he was due, the recognition that he was more than just a poet, but equally, if not more, emphatic that it was *what* was written rather than who wrote it that mattered. In the same way that Burns did not consider many of the songs attributed to him as 'his' but as things he collected to ensure their preservation and protection, Redpath never considered herself a 'Burnsian' but simply a singer of traditional Scottish songs which happened to include those written and collected by Burns. The narrowing of public understanding of the extent of Burns's contribution to the field almost gives a sense of Redpath's vast array of Burns recordings being a re-collecting of those songs, seeking to preserve and protect 'a treasure of beautiful traditional song [that] was hidden and scrambled and needed to be brought back to life' in the same way Burns first did more than two centuries previously.[52]

Redpath's work with Hovey and Low, and her own recordings and performances popularised Burns's songs and opened the door for the many subsequent 'Best of' recordings available from a diverse range of artists. In traditional music performances, Burns has moved from being barely heard to a standard feature. Consequently, Redpath was, and arguably remains, at the forefront of the preservation of Burns as a songwriter but also of his and his songs' place within the great tradition of Scottish folk music and song culture.

Acknowledgements

Moira Hansen would like to acknowledge the support of the Shaw Summer Scholarship which funded the cataloguing of the Centre for Robert Burns Studies' Jean Redpath Archive, and Professor Kirsteen McCue's guidance during the work. She would also like to acknowledge the support of

Elizabeth Sudduth (director of the Irvin Department of Rare Books and Special Collections) and Jessica Dowd Crouch (archivist, Irvin Department of Rare Books and Special Collections) in providing access to the University of South Carolina's Jean Redpath Archive, and the support of the W. Roy Ormiston Visiting Scholar fund in making the trip possible. Other than those taken from Redpath and Brownrigg, and from Keith, all references in this chapter are drawn from materials within the Jean Redpath archives in Glasgow, Scotland and Columbia, South Carolina.

Notes

1. Jean Redpath and Mark Brownrigg, *Giving Voice to Traditional Song: Jean Redpath's Autobiography, as told to Mark Brownrigg* (Columbia: University of South Carolina, 2018), p. 12.
2. Redpath and Brownrigg, *Giving Voice*, p. 12.
3. Redpath and Brownrigg, *Giving Voice*, p. 14.
4. Pete Heywood, 'Jean Redpath, 28 April 1937 – 21 August 2014', *The Living Tradition*, Issue 104 (Dec. 2014/Jan. 2015), p. 11.
5. Redpath and Brownrigg, *Giving Voice*, p. 23; The *Oxford English Dictionary* defines 'ceilidh' as 'In Scotland and Ireland: (a) an evening visit, a friendly social call; (b) a session of traditional music, storytelling, or dancing', a far less formal affair than modern organised events which are advertised under the same banner.
6. Dylan's music shows a strong Scottish folk influence, recognised in 2004 by the University of St Andrews when it conferred on Dylan an honorary degree of Doctor of Music, and in 2008 by Dylan himself when he identified Burns's song 'A Red, Red Rose' as the lyric which had had the most impact on his life. Pete Heywood, in his obituary of Redpath (see note 4) commented that '[t]here is little doubt Jean had a significant influence on that aspect of Dylan's music' (p. 10).
7. Although Redpath would later comment this folk revival reached 'enormous fad proportions [...] it really was a fad, it had nothing to do with a folk revival after a certain stage'. (Interview with Jean Redpath, date unknown, cassette labelled 'Jean Redpath at Edinburgh and Abroad', CRBS Jean Redpath Archive).
8. Robert Shelton, review of Redpath performance in *The New York Times* (16 November 1961), cited in Thomas Keith, 'Jean Redpath, The Accidental Burnsian', *Burns Chronicle*, 2017, p. 73.
9. Of the ninety-five songs across the seven albums, ten were written or collected by Burns.

10. Roger Catlin, 'Redpath stresses broad repertoire', *The Hartford Courant*, 8 June 1987, n.p.; Archie Mackenzie, 'People We Meet: Jean Redpath', *Scottish World* (Winter 1993), p. 72.
11. Redpath and Brownrigg, *Giving Voice*, p. 78.
12. Redpath and Brownrigg, *Giving Voice*, p. 79; Jean Redpath, 'The Question: Why is Folk Music So Popular in New England?', *New England Folk Almanac* 4:3 (1994), p. 3.
13. Catlin, 'Redpath stresses broad repertoire'.
14. Further details of the University of South Carolina's Jean Redpath Archive, including finding aid are available at https://sc.edu/about/offices_and_divisions/university_libraries/browse/irvin_dept_special_collections/collections/jean_redpath_archive.php
15. Further details of the Centre for Robert Burns Studies' Jean Redpath Archive, including finding aid are available at https://www.gla.ac.uk/schools/critical/research/researchcentresandnetworks/robertburnsstudies/ourresearch/jeanredpatharchive/
16. Notes for *The Jean Redpath Song Book*, USC Jean Redpath Archive, Box 3.
17. The two tracks not drawn from these recordings were 'Hallowe'en', to be taken from her album *Leaving the Land* (Philo PH1131; 1990), and 'Rantin' Dog the Daddie o't', to come from *My Ain Countrie* (Folk-Legacy Records FSS-49; 1973). 'Hallowe'en' does not appear in either the Hovey or Low recordings, while 'Rantin' Dog the Daddie o't' appears in the Low recordings but as part of a medley with other tracks.
18. Complete details of Redpath's commercial recordings, including track listings, can be found as an appendix to Redpath and Brownrigg, *Giving Voice*, pp. 195–214.
19. Impressively, across the 178 tracks recorded in the Hovey and Low projects, 156 different songs are represented. Those songs which do appear in both projects' recordings often feature in different arrangements. This very much reflects Redpath's desire not to repeatedly record the same material (Redpath, 'Synopsis of Recordings' (n.d.), USC Jean Redpath Archive, Box 2).
20. David Scott Skipper, 'Jean Redpath Staples: Burns and Traditional Music', *The Scottish-American* (Jan.-Feb. 1989) (Part One: p. 3) and (Mar.-Apr. 1989) (Part Two: p. 3).
21. Skipper, 'Jean Redpath Staples', Part Two, p. 3.
22. Skipper, 'Jean Redpath Staples', Part Two, p. 3.
23. Scott Alarik, 'Redpath is kept busy by a Scottish poet', *The Boston Globe*, 21 January 1988, p. 85.
24. Esther Hovey, 'The Genesis of Serge Hovey's *The Robert Burns Song Book*', *Burns Chronicle* (1999), p. 141; following Hovey's death, his wife and son

prepared parts of his research, some 155 songs published in two volumes of *The Robert Burns Songbook*, 2 vols (Fenton, MO: Mel Bay Publications, 1999 and 2001).

25. The project was estimated to run ultimately to twenty to twenty-four albums, covering all 324 songs of Burns. The pace of recording was restricted, as is often the case, by the availability of time on the part of Redpath and financial support for the inherent costs; it was also affected by the ongoing functional deterioration of Hovey as a result of amyotrophic lateral sclerosis (ALS, also known as Lou Gehrig's disease). Neat's documentary, *The Tree of Liberty* (1988; Everallin Limited) demonstrates how Hovey and Redpath worked with the support of Hovey's wife and son to keep the project going despite this adversity. By the time of Hovey's death in 1989, six albums had been recorded while a seventh, which had been scored, was recorded in 1990. The seven albums are now available on four CDs from Philo Records (Vols 1 and 2: PH1187; Vols 3 and 4: PH1188; Vols 5 and 6: PH1189; Vol 7: PH1126).
26. Keith, 'Jean Redpath, The Accidental Burnsian', p. 75.
27. Jean Redpath and unknown interviewer, 'Transcript of an Interview Recorded on 31 October and 2 November 1986', 22pp. (p. 21), USC Jean Redpath Archive, Box 4.
28. Keith, 'Jean Redpath, The Accidental Burnsian', p. 76.
29. Redpath and Brownrigg, *Giving Voice*, p. 105.
30. Redpath and Brownrigg, *Giving Voice*, p. 105.
31. Donald Low, *The Songs of Robert Burns* (London: Routledge, 1993).
32. Originally released as four albums on cassette, the Low recordings are now available as three CDs from Jean Redpath Records (Vol. 1: JR-103; Vol. 2: JR-104; Vol. 3: JR-105).
33. Jean Redpath, 'Synopsis of Recordings' (n.d.), USC Jean Redpath Archive, Box 2.
34. Redpath, 'Transcript of an Interview', p. 10.
35. Neat, *The Tree of Liberty*, 1988.
36. Redpath and Brownrigg, *Giving Voice*, p. 134.
37. Redpath and Brownrigg, *Giving Voice*, p. 104.
38. Alarik, 'Redpath is kept busy', 1988.
39. The song is now probably better known sung to the tune 'Low Down on the Broom'.
40. Jean Redpath, 'A Red, Red Rose', *The Songs of Robert Burns: Vols 1&2*, Track 12 (Philo: PH 1887, 1996).
41. Jean Redpath, 'A Red, Red Rose', *Songs of Robert Burns: Vol. 3*, Track 1 (Jean Redpath Records: JR-105, 1997).

42. In keeping with her attitude throughout her career, despite the proportion of Burns material in her recordings, *By Request* shows him only as a piece within a wider landscape of Scottish traditional music.
43. Jean Redpath, 'Auld Lang Syne', *The Songs of Robert Burns: Vols 1&2*, Track 21 (Philo: PH 1887, 1996).
44. Interview with Jean Redpath, date unknown, cassette labelled 'Jean Redpath at Edinburgh and Abroad', CRBS Jean Redpath Archive.
45. Jean Redpath, 'Auld Lang Syne', *Songs of Robert Burns: Vol. 3*, Track 20 (Jean Redpath Records: JR-105, 1997)
46. Heywood obituary, p. 11.
47. Interview with Jean Redpath (n.d.), cassette labelled 'Jean Redpath at Edinburgh and Abroad', CRBS Jean Redpath Archive.
48. Mackenzie, 'People We Meet'. In another interview, Redpath continued this anecdote by recounting how she soldiered on singing to Burns's melody despite everyone else singing the popular tune (Interview with Jean Redpath (n.d.), cassette recording, Radio Clyde, CRBS Jean Redpath Archive).
49. Jean Redpath, 'The World of Robert Burns: Sanders Theatre, Cambridge, 20 January 1995', cassette recording, 2 cassettes, CRBS Jean Redpath Archive; despite her many years in the US, Jean never lost her Fife accent.
50. Neat, *The Tree of Liberty*, 1988.
51. Neat, *The Tree of Liberty*, 1988.
52. Skipper, 'Jean Redpath Staples', Part One, p. 3.

13

Performing the Work of Robert Burns

Sheena Wellington

What an amazing, enriching and perpetually challenging gift to a singer are the songs of Robert Burns! To fully explore this cornucopia of romance, sorrow, joy, philosophy, satire and bawdry would take several lifetimes. Only having one at my disposal, it has been an immense privilege to spend a fair amount of it in the enjoyable task of singing them, to usually appreciative audiences everywhere from Lerwick to Coldstream, Los Angeles to Cairo. The worldwide love for our National Bard's songs and poems is immense and it is not just from Scots, the diaspora and those of Scots descent.

I have been singing the works of Burns since I was a small child and some seventy-odd years on I still love the songs I learned in childhood – 'Coming thro' the Rye', 'O A' the Airts', 'Bonny Wee Thing', 'Afton Water' and so many more. I still, too, enjoy learning yet another Burns song. There are a lot of them, you know!

It is always a delight when the audience knows the songs and even more so when you can introduce them to a song that they have never heard. So many people are not aware of the breadth and depth of his repertoire and I like that I am continuing a strong family tradition.

My father possessed a fine tenor voice and was much in demand for local concerts, private functions, smokers (whatever they were!) and, of course, Burns Suppers. In those far-off days, virtually all Burns Suppers were strictly men-only and reputed to be wild, raucous, bawdy affairs.

That this was true I found out at my first official Burns Supper. It was 1959, the year of the bi-centenary of Robert's birth. At the invitation of the High Heid Yin of the masonic lodge of which my father was a member, the school-girl Sheena sang a couple of songs at this prestigious event. Naturally, I was only allowed into the sacred place to sing and spent the rest of the time in the kitchen where the ladies made a great fuss of me and I got to finish the trifle. As

I sang my first song, 'Ye Banks and Braes', I did see, out the corner of my eye, an eminent legal personage lose contact with his chair and slide gracefully under the table. Sadly, I missed the highlight of the evening when a distinguished local politician was sick all over the other top table guests. I am tempted to say things haven't changed as not too long ago I was at an event in Glasgow where there was dancing on the tables and tartan boxer short clad bottoms were flashed! You can't take accountants anywhere.

Having absorbed Burns songs almost by osmosis in my youth and then had them taught to me at school in the twee, hands-below-the-bosom, clipped-consonants and tortured-vowel manner that was the norm in the 1950s and 1960s, I early came to realise the charm of the songs of Burns is so strong that they can rise above the manner in which they were sung.

I am very fortunate that among my friends and colleagues are many of the great Burns experts of our day and from them I have learned so much. Heart-felt thanks are due to them for their willing, and amazingly patient, assistance across the years with lyrics, tunes, background and all the general interesting titbits of information. They have allowed me to understand more about the genius whose work I try to interpret in as authentic a form as possible, and have helped me in presenting his songs in an interesting and accessible manner.

Virtually without exception, the songs of Robert Burns can bypass the head and go directly to the heart, and while it is the heart that draws you to the song, using the head to understand its meaning, its context, what motivated Burns to write it, matters. It's the meld of the singer's love and understanding of the song which makes the bond with the hearer. It need not be explicit, just there.

Of course, Robert can also produce a zinger that goes straight to the funny bone, and these are a joy to sing. Many of them being numbered among the *Merry Muses*, you have to have a care for who is in the audience before you sing them but that, too, can be a revelation. Once you have, as it were, loosened the stays, your listeners, particularly of an older generation, will not only enjoy your songs but will have some of their own to share! There is also, let us be honest, the odd occasion when the lyrics go immediately to 'What in the name of Hairy Mary's canary was he thinking about?' But after all, only mediocrity is always at its best!

Is it the words or is it the tunes or is it a tantalising amalgam of the two? Burns had an amazing knowledge of tunes, not all of them Scottish, and it is obvious both from his own letters and the fact that he often used the same tune for several lyrics that he loved and understood them.

Almost always the tune that he chose for his lyrics is the one that suits it best. 'Low Down in the Broom' is a lovely air, but put the words of 'My Love is Like a Red, Red Rose' to the correct set of Niel Gow's 'Major Graham of

Inchbrakie' and magic happens. It not only fits the poet's words to perfection but its beauty, enhanced by its very brevity, is sublime.

Of course, this opinion is not shared by everyone. When I first started singing the original tune, having learned it from the work of Jean Redpath and Serge Hovey, the reaction was often an indignant 'That's the wrong tune!' An explanation of the history usually evoked a harrumph and 'Ye should sing the tune abdie kens.' I gave up trying to point out that at one time all tunes were new to our ears and just went on singing the Gow, though I sometimes sing the other just for a change.

To be fair, I do have some sympathy with the 'sing the familiar' viewpoint. I know and sometimes sing 'Ae Fond Kiss' to the poet's intended 'Rory Dall's Port' and it is beautiful. My heart, however, cherishes the version I had from my father and, whenever I sing it, I hear his voice ringing down through the decades. It was years before I learned from the Burns scholar Kirsteen McCue, one of my favourite singers, that the melody is 'Mo run an diugh mar an dé thu' ('My Love Today as Heretofore') and is in the Simon Fraser Collection. If I am pushed, I will admit that it does not follow the bard's intention to differentiate between the first four and second four lines of each stanza. Actually, it could be argued that, if the words were not so heartbreakingly eloquent and the tune did not flow so melodically, we could have had a monotonous drone – but they are, it does and we haven't.

The 'wrong tune' business, however, did provoke one of my favourite reviews of all time. I had answered a frantic SOS call from the secretary of the Women's Guild in a neighbouring village to fill in when their intended speaker's van had broken down on the M9. I never did find out if the members were disappointed to hear me rather than the expected talk on 'The Bird Life of Patagonia' but the minister's wife was graciousness itself. 'That Gow tune was charming, absolutely charming,' said she, patting my hand in an encouraging manner as we sat enjoying the usual tea and home-made scone, 'and, of course, the more usual melody does need a proper singer'. That's one of the things I really love about being Scottish – getting above yourself is never an option.

One of the other things that I like about being Scottish is that so many of my fellow countrymen are willing to air their opinion on the life, loves and work of Robert Burns. Some, naturally, do so with a deep passion and knowledge and they are a pleasure to meet. Others might only know one and a bit of his songs, two lines of his poetry and the juiciest of the rumours, but they are more than ready to get into a lively discussion in support of what they believe and that can be fun, too. I have also defended Rab from accusations of an affair with Queen Victoria, who was born twenty-three years after his death and of having been 'too cowardly to fight at Culloden', which happened thirteen years before he was born.

The more scurrilous charges I tend not to engage with, but I did once spend the interval between 'The Selkirk Grace' and coffee listening to a very involved explanation of the process of extracting poison from linseed. My companion's thesis was that the 'Kilmarnock' edition being a roaring success, the bard now had options. He was still pining for his true love Jean, he did not relish the thought of the journey to the West Indies, or being committed to a pregnant Highland Mary, so he used the skills learned as a flax-dresser to solve his dilemma by poisoning her. I was really looking forward to seeing if this was going to be in his speech, but it turned out that he was the non-speechifying spouse of the lady who was to give the 'Reply to the Toast to the Lassies'. She was very good.

People have become indignant when I have declined to agree that Burns's best song was 'Annie Laurie', 'The Bluebells of Scotland' or, even, 'The Star o' Rabbie Burns'. The gentleman who insisted that 'The Laird of Cockpen' must have been the work of Robert Burns rather than Lady Nairne, because a woman would not have been capable of such humour and style, was very lucky not to have found himself face down in his cranachan. And don't get me started on 'Land o' the Leal'!

But there are, too, moments of pure delight. I had gone to Singapore for the weekend – as you do – to sing at a Burns Supper and was seated next to an anthropologist from, if I remember correctly, Dorset, a real and informed enthusiast. One of my songs was 'The Slave's Lament' and I mentioned Serge Hovey's comment that the tune was very similar to the sixteenth-century East European Ashkenazi melody for 'Rachel's Lamentation for her Children', though none of my Jewish friends have been able to shed any light on that. My friend knew more. 'It's actually much older, Spanish Sephardic, around twelfth/thirteenth century,' he said, 'and it's sung in North Africa but to a different rhythm.' I could see a logical line there and noted down the details but, sadly, not his name and as I have been quoting him for years I do feel guilty.

Some years later, during the Smithsonian Folk Life Festival in Washington, I sang it at an informal evening sing-around. The Mali musicians present joined in, singers humming along and koras being plucked. When I finished one of their fine griot singers sang a lyric to the same tune with a staccato but attractive rhythm. I was very excited, hoping this was the ancient African original and that I might learn phonetically at least a verse. It turned out to be Robert Burns's words translated into Wollof, though she and the others did know the song from further north which had the same melody. I thought she said the translation had been made by the great Ali Farka Touré but, as her English was only slightly better than my French and there is never a multi-linguist in the room when you need one, that is open to doubt.

I have sung and taught the songs of Robert Burns in schools, churches, marquees, concert halls, community centres, art galleries, supermarket car parks, museums, Highland Games fields, five-star hotels, cruise ships, Captain Scott's *Discovery*, the oldest British built ship afloat HMS *Unicorn*, 250 feet up on a scaffolding stage surrounded by fireworks in Nanning in China's Guangxi province. I have sung at the Brig o' Doon, the Globe, Burns Cottage and Ellisland and felt so close to him that I would not have been surprised to see Jean calling to him to stop rewriting that 'Tam o' Shanter' again for a minute and come and get his dinner. There have been so many memorable events, so much enjoyment, that choosing the very special times is hard.

A truly spine-tingling moment was in the Theatre Royal in Dumfries – and it wasn't even a Burns song. The Theatre Royal has a very special place in the Burns story and in November 2006, I had the privilege of taking part in David Purdie's 'Burns – Alive!' show in that historic venue. The concert itself was rich mixture of pictures, informed commentary and a chronological selection of well-loved and not-so-familiar lyrics from 'Song Composed in August' to 'Wert Thou in the Cauld Blast' performed to an appreciative and very savvy audience. Then I sang 'Ça ira'. The response was immediate and almost overwhelming. They joined in, I had to sing the chorus three times and the applause nearly took the roof off.

And the proudest occasion of them all? Well, that goes without saying! Thursday, 1 July 1999 in the Assembly Hall on Edinburgh's Mound at the official Opening of the Scottish Parliament. As someone who had wanted Home Rule for Scotland all my life, who campaigned in both devolution referendums and who eagerly looked forward to the new constitutional era, I was thrilled to be asked to take part. I even quite enjoyed the furore when the news of the chosen song was leaked and we had the Scottish Office in a panic, paparazzi leaping out from every corner and the usual suspects queueing up to chunter on about 'this republican insult to the Queen'. Of course, Her Majesty had been consulted and had warmly approved all of the programme, including 'Is There For Honest Poverty', long before I had been asked to sing, but that seemed to escape the over-excited commentators.

The day itself is, overall, a wonderful memory. The Inverness Gaelic Choir and the brass section of the Royal Scottish National Orchestra have my undying gratitude for keeping me reasonably calm beforehand. Usually I am nervous before I sing and then I am fine. On this occasion, I started to sing and realised, to my horror, that I was about to weep. Suddenly, the significance of the moment, the responsibility of getting it right and the knowledge that my parents would have been so proud of me and of Scotland had hit, and the tears came unbidden. All I could do was carry on, hope for the best and take a huge swallow on the last line of the second verse. I think I got away with it.

Notes on Contributors

Alistair Braidwood runs the Scottish cultural website Scots Whay Hae! and hosts the podcast of the same name. His PhD in Scottish Literature at Glasgow University examined Jean Paul Sartre's philosophy of literature and applied it to writers Iain Banks and James Kelman. He reviews for and contributes to various publications on Scottish literature and culture.

Ian Brown is Honorary Senior Research Fellow in Scottish Literature at Glasgow University and Professor Emeritus in Drama at Kingston University, London. Widely published on aspects of theatre, literature and cultural policy, he has edited a wide range of volumes. A playwright and poet, his most recent monograph is *Performing Scottishness: Enactment and National Identities* (2020).

Rhona Brown is Senior Lecturer in Eighteenth-Century Scottish Literature and the Periodical Press at the University of Glasgow. Author of *Robert Fergusson and the Scottish Periodical Press*, she is currently involved in two major, AHRC-funded textual editing projects: 'Editing Robert Burns for the 21st Century', where she is co-editor of Burns's letters, and 'The Edinburgh Allan Ramsay', where she is editor of Ramsay's poems and prose.

John Burnett retired as Curator in the Department of Scotland and Europe in the National Museum of Scotland. He is author of *Robert Burns and the Hellish Legion* (2009) and *Riot, Revelry and Rout: Sport in Lowland Scotland before 1860* (2000).

Katherine Campbell is a former Senior Lecturer in Ethnomusicology at the University of Edinburgh. With Emily Lyle she co-authored *Robert Burns and the Discovery and Re-Creation of Scottish Song* (Musica Scotica, forthcoming). A performer, singing and accompanying the songs of Burns, she brought out in 2019 the solo CD, 'Robert Burns: Tune Unknown'.

Gerard Carruthers FRSE is Francis Hutcheson Professor of Scottish Literature at the University of Glasgow, General Editor of the multi-volume *OUP* edition of Robert Burns's collected works and Principal Investigator of the related Arts and Humanities Research Council (AHRC) project, 'Editing Robert Burns for the 21st Century: Correspondence and Poetry'. He is Convenor of Burns Scotland partnership, the 'National Burns' collection involving national and local authority institutions Scotland-wide.

Tracy Cattell is a professional stage manager and freelance lecturer. Her PhD at the University of Warwick explored the history and development of UK stage management practice. Her research includes practical staging of Shakespeare, stage manager as director, and interpretation of prompt annotations. In 2017 she was inaugural winner of the Theatre and Performance Research Association Research Fellowship for early-career researchers.

Jim Davis is Professor of Theatre Studies at the University of Warwick. His major research interest is in nineteenth-century British theatre, on which he has published widely. He is author of *Comic Acting and Portraiture in Late-Georgian and Regency England* (2015) and joint author of *Reflecting the Audience: London Theatre-Going 1840–1880* (2001).

Moira Hansen recently completed her PhD in Scottish Literature at the University of Glasgow's Centre for Robert Burns Studies, exploring Burns's physical and mental health through his life and their impact on his creative activities and output. Her research interests lie within the medical humanities and intersections between literature, science and culture, focusing mainly on the long eighteenth century.

Paul Maloney is Research Fellow in the Faculty of Arts, Humanities and Social Sciences at Queen's University Belfast. Author of *Scotland and the Music Hall, 1850–1914* (2003) and *The Britannia Panopticon Music Hall and Cosmopolitan Entertainment Culture* (2016), he has written extensively on Scottish popular theatre and nineteenth-century entertainment culture.

Kirsteen McCue is Professor of Scottish Literature and Song Culture and Co-Director of the Centre for Robert Burns Studies at the University of Glasgow. She has published widely on Romantic song and is co-investigator on the AHRC project 'Editing Robert Burns for the 21st century: Prose and Songs', for which she has edited *Robert Burns's Songs for George Thomson* (*OUP*, forthcoming).

Adrienne Scullion is Pro-Vice-Chancellor for the Faculty of Arts, Humanities and Social Sciences at Queen's University Belfast. As well as her particular research interest in Scottish theatre and drama from the eighteenth century to the present, she has worked on theatre and drama for children and young people, eighteenth- and nineteenth-century women playwrights and cultural policy.

Sheena Wellington, one of modern Scotland's finest traditional singers and interpreters of Burns's songs, has toured worldwide. Patron of the Traditional Music and Song Association of Scotland, her recordings include *Kerelaw* (1986), *Clearsong* (1990) and *Strong Women* (1995), besides many compilation albums. Her rendition of 'A Man's A Man' at the 1999 opening of the Scottish Parliament is a signal performative moment in recent Scottish cultural history.

Christopher A. Whatley OBE, FRSE, FSA (Scot) is Professor of Scottish History at the University of Dundee and best-known for his work on eighteenth-century Scotland. This has included the Union of 1707, industrialisation, social relations, everyday life and popular culture – including Robert Burns memorialisation. His most recent relevant publication is *Immortal Memory: Burns and the Scottish People* (2016).

Ronnie Young is Lecturer in the Scottish Enlightenment for Scottish Literature at the University of Glasgow, where he also convenes online courses on Robert Burns. Currently co-editing a new edition of the poet's correspondence for *OUP* as part of the AHRC-funded 'Editing Robert Burns for the 21st Century' project, he is also preparing a chapter on the Kirk Satires for a forthcoming *Oxford Handbook to Robert Burns*.

Index

EU Authorised Representative:
Easy Access System Europe Mustamäe tee 50, 10621 Tallinn, Estonia
gpsr.requests@easproject.com

Printed and bound by CPI Group (UK) Ltd, Croydon, CR0 4YY
24/09/2025
01961607-0002